The Conversation of Art

Al Beckett

www.art-tales.org

ISBN 978-1-916722-41-5

One never finishes learning about art. There are always new things to discover. Great works of art seem to look different every time one stands before them. They seem to be as inexhaustible and unpredictable as real human beings.

Sir Ernst Hans Josef Gombrich, OM, CBE

This work is dedicated to Magnus and Cleo. Long may you enjoy a richer life through art.

Greetings to lovers of art

Thank you for opening 'The Conversation of Art'.

I do hope you'll find it enjoyable and rewarding, and that it enhances your appreciation and understanding of the picture in front of you, wherever you are.

It's a tale of the evolution, composition and creation of paintings in the western world, from the caves at Lascaux to the art of our modern times.

We will consider topics such as the role of colours and the gaze, avant-garde to establishment acceptability, provenance and display.

In order to achieve our aims you are invited to imagine that you are having a conversation with the author, the artists, and the picture in front of you.

This conversational technique also involves 'listening' to a number of featured artists. Their comments on their works are purely imaginary but are ones they quite possibly would have liked to share with you.

The works selected are familiar pieces from the world of paintings, and some particularly iconic works are referred to several times in view of their importance to illustrate and clarify salient aspects of art.

All the pictures in this book, except for a few of the more complex works, have been sketched by the author. Reproducing a work of art in your own way enhances the appreciation of each artist's skill and mastery of painting. Studying works with such intensity is a most rewarding experience. Perhaps explore and sketch works of art that particularly appeal to you. I recommend that you have a go yourself whatever your artistic skill.

This book has been written for the modern busy reader, using bite-sized chunks rather than lengthy expositions. The prose is straightforward and to the point. Complex explanations have been avoided.

Each section is deliberately concise to encourage page turning, yet with obvious stopping places so that you, the reader, can pause and pick up again to fit in with your schedule. I hope that your engagement and enrichment will be enhanced with that picture you see before you.

Enjoy our journey of exploration.

www.art-tales.org

Contents

The Conversation of Art

How do you feel when you wander into a gallery, a museum or a friend's house and see a picture on the wall that immediately captures your attention?

Millions of people visit galleries every year. Art is inviting, it's compelling, it removes us from the humdrum of ordinary life. We are drawn to experience something different, something deeper, something that can reach out to our emotions.

The visual image is all-powerful through its beauty, its ugliness, its drama. Can it work its power on us by delving into our thoughts, to identify with what is important to us or what we can let go? The way we allow our gaze to focus on an image, a whole picture (or a component within), a figure, an action, a gesture, or a story inside that picture, can influence how we want to be guided in life. This may be physically or particularly with our belief and value systems and from there, determine how we engage with the world.

A picture can be all-powerful if we indulge our gaze.

It can make us feel happy with a sense of well-being, conversely it can make us uncomfortable and ill at ease. We can be scandalised, reassured, shocked, or comforted.

We can reflect on what we see before us:

- Who created it, when and why?
- What is its historical context?
- What led to and influenced its creation?
- What did it achieve?
- Who paid for it?

Bear in mind that all works of art are products of their time and are influenced by the historical, cultural and social context within which they were created.

We can look at the work from different perspectives, how it was created, what paints, brushes and canvas the artist chose to use.

And what about the artist? Who were they? What compelled them to paint that subject matter in such a way? What is their history, their circumstances, beliefs, prejudices, motivations. Perhaps most importantly: what was their support; who sponsored them, and who paid them to produce what they did?

It's worth noting here that the majority of works covered in this book are by men. Regrettably this is perhaps the result of the historical misogyny of the art world until recent times (and, arguably, even now). Even of the 2,300 works held by London's National Gallery only 27 are by women. In 1989 an anonymous group of female artists calling themselves the Guerrilla Girls concentrated on New York's Metropolitan Museum of Art and counted the ratio of female to male works. Whilst less than 5% of the works were by those identifying as women, 85% of the nudes were female.

Such was/is the world of western art. The women featured in this book are not mere tokenism but a spirited attempt to redress the balance against the weight of historical dominance of the DWM (Dead White Male). And, of course, the distressing absence of cultural alternatives featuring in this story. Maybe that will change now that we are well into the period of Post Modernism and Internationalism.

With that in mind, the work in front of us could be about politics, a landscape, a portrait. It could be representational, impressionistic or abstract.

It can appear revolutionary or iconoclastic, conforming to historical social, religious and economic norms of its time. Or it may have challenged the status quo. Indeed, we might find it has a deeper resonance with us if we consider it through the 'period eye', that is: imagining we are looking at it through the eye of its contemporary viewer.

The work before us can provoke. It can stimulate our imagination. Or it can bore us.

We can debate it with others, and it can certainly provoke conversations, even with strangers.

That picture in front of us can help us to identify with our recognised social and religious values, it can be tribal, or it can dare us to reject such identifications and consider society's divisions and unifiers.

We enter the gallery and we can drift past what we see in front of us. Or we can pause, stand still and gaze, allowing ourselves to engage in conversation with that picture before us. By so doing it may deepen our experience and add a little enrichment and fulfilment to our life.

So, let's begin our dialogue with that picture.

How many times have you visited an art gallery and wished that you better understood the art and artist? Perhaps thinking of it as a stand-alone or within the context of its creation.

For many people the world of art is a mystery. There are many books, documentaries and podcasts on art, on artists, and on styles, movements, form and composition.

Having a conversation with a picture is a little like having a chat with a new acquaintance in a café; delving a little deeper to broaden your relationship further. It may encourage our critical thinking and to challenge us to think about different perspectives and situations.

The more you know about a picture the more you can appreciate it and the circumstances that created it and the context in which it was made. We might even understand ourselves a little more.

Art has been produced by humans. Humans with different experiences, living within particular historical events and with different technological and cultural opportunities to make art.

In looking at that very modern piece of conceptual art in that modern art gallery, it may be fulfilling to know where that artist drew their inspiration from, how and why they were so influenced.

Art intersects with literature, philosophy, politics and religion, economics and sociology and psychology. We can be enriched if, when we look at that picture, we also think about these intersections and how it can all impact on our personal values, beliefs and perspectives.

Above all, having a conversation with a picture can be a deeply personal one. In can invite introspection and evoke our emotions and reflections on our own life and circumstances.

Art is humanity's collective narrative, giving knowledge and inspiration, comfort, assurance and challenges. Art is not a by-product of social development, but one of the original elements that form a society.

So, let's take it all step by step and open up our conversation with that picture and its artist creator and start our dialogue by asking:

What are you all about? When were you painted and by whom?

What was your location? Indoors or outdoors, daytime or night?

Who or what stands out in the frame: the principal protagonists, the trees, river, animals, machines? Who or what is in the background and perhaps why?

How has the artist framed the work, to the fore or receding into the background? How have colours been used and can you tell what tools were used and how? What is the picture's size? How has the gallery placed it with other works?

What impact is that picture having on me and why?

You are having a personal encounter with the picture and the person who created it.

You, the artist and the work before you are having a conversation. Perhaps a conversation over centuries.

My first impressions in a gallery

Upon entering a gallery, you ask "what is it?"

Representation

The artist has painted the picture as a realistic representation of the subject matter.

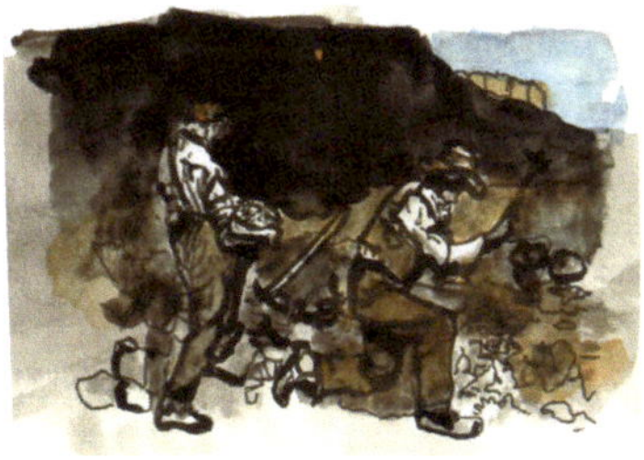

Gustav Courbet 1819-1877
***Stonebreakers* 1849**

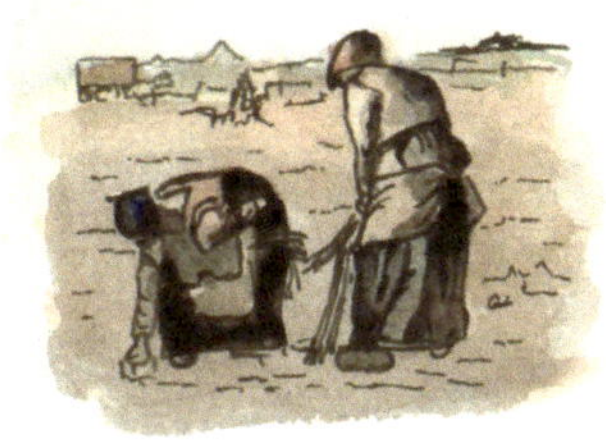

Jean-Francoise Millet 1814-1875
***The Gleaners* 1857**

Impression

Capturing the effects of light and colour in scenes from everyday life using loose brushwork with an emphasis on the momentary effects of atmosphere and movement.

The immediate effect or feeling that a piece of artwork evokes in the viewer encompassing an emotional response and an aesthetic transient experience.

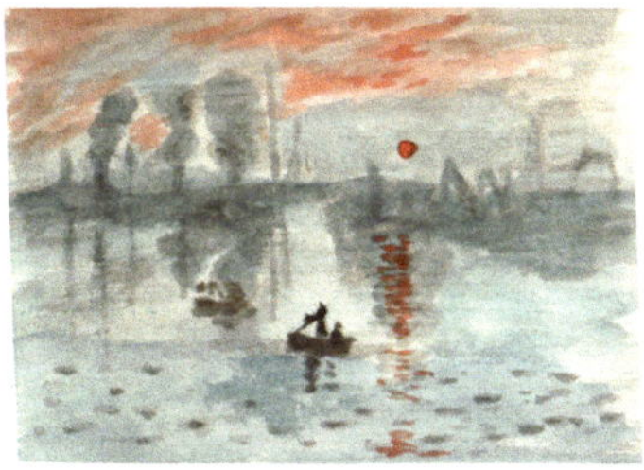

Claude Monet 1849-1926 *Sunrise* 1872

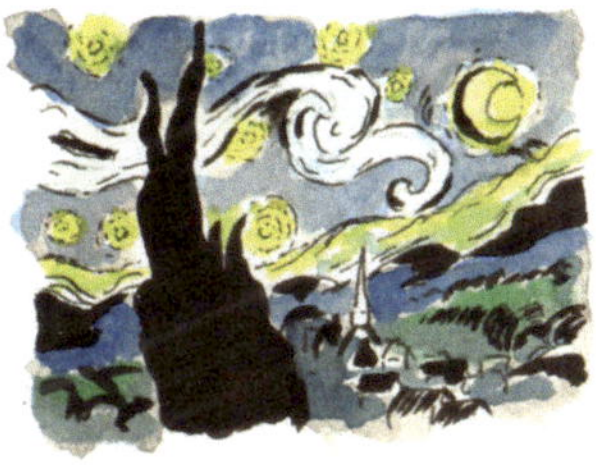

Vincent van Gogh 1853-1890 *The Starry Night* 1889

JMW Turner 1775-1851

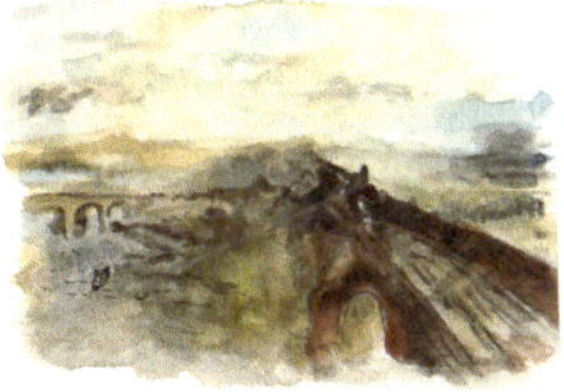

***Rain Steam and Speed The GWR* 1844**

Abstract

The picture is an abstraction from a real image. It does not display a physical or concrete existence. It does not attempt to represent or give an impression of external reality but works using colours, textures and shapes.

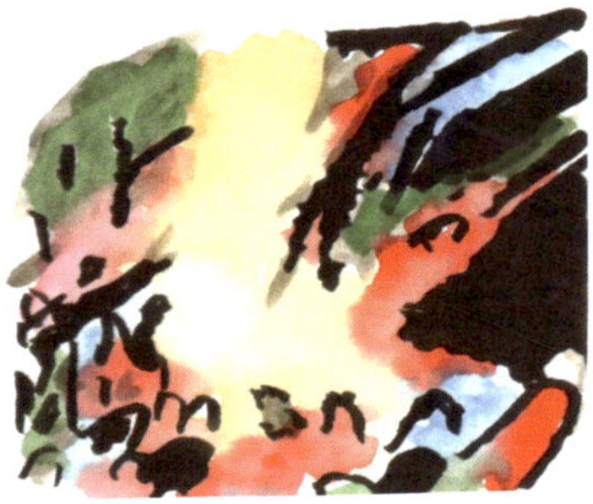

Wassily Kandinsky 1866-1944 demonstration of his *'abstract'* style

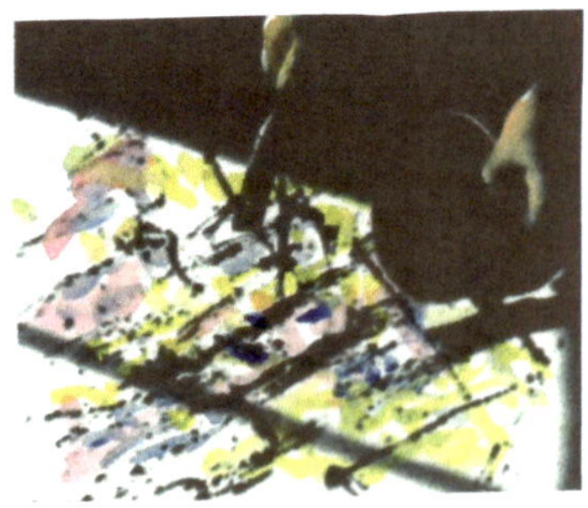

Jackson Pollock 1912-1956 demonstration of his *'drip painting'* style

What is the picture about? What is its subject matter, its 'genre'?

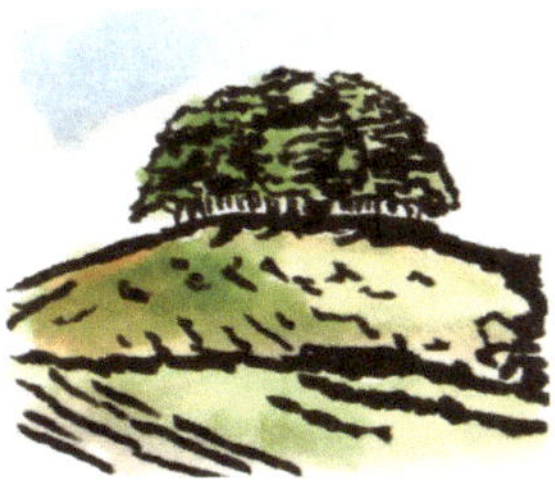

Is it a landscape?

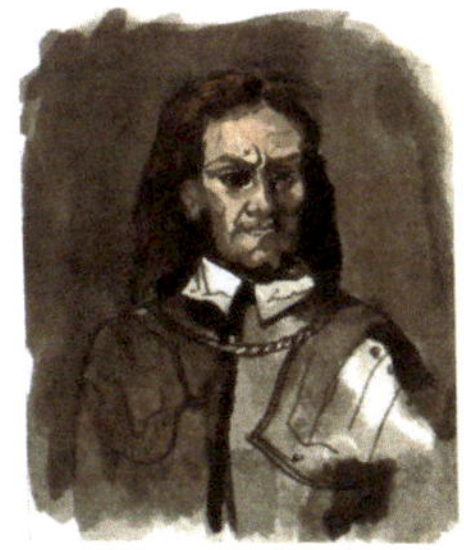

Is it historical?

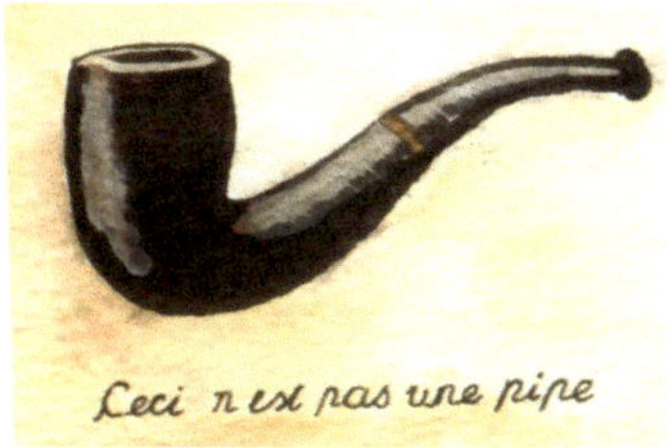

Is it a still life?

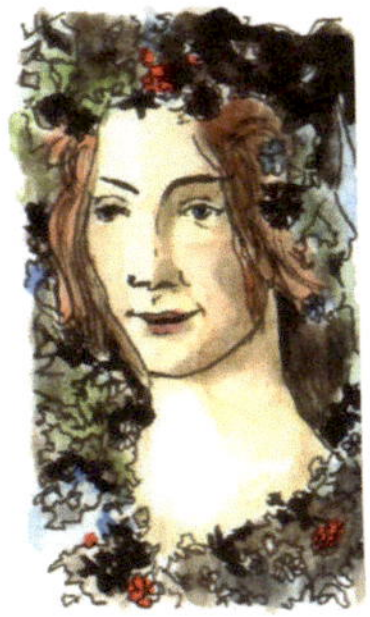

Is it a portrait?

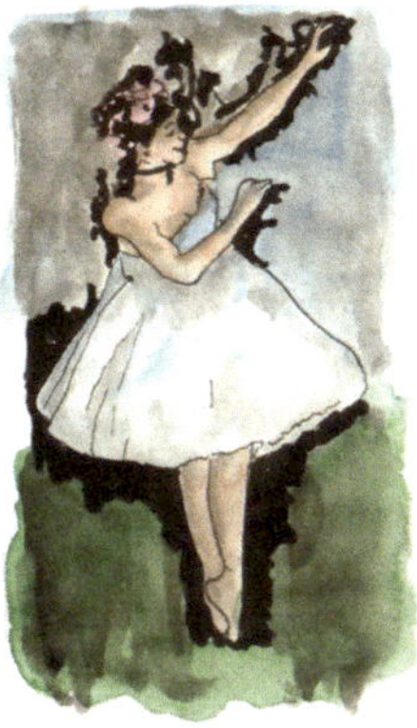

Is it figurative?

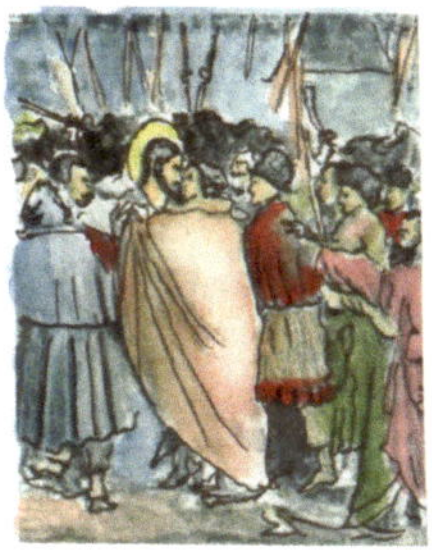

Is it religious?

Is it allegorical (conveying complex meanings)?

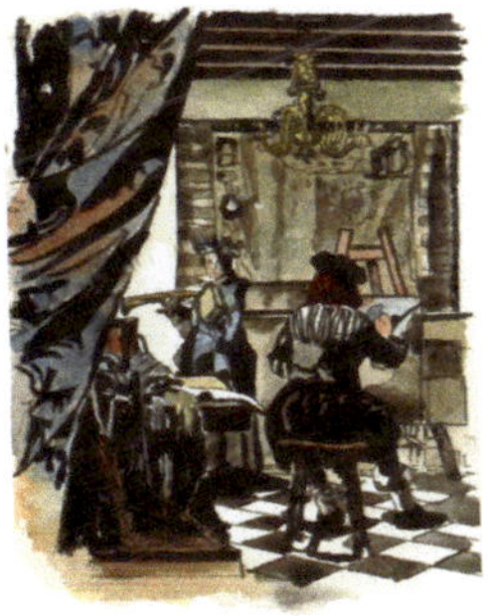

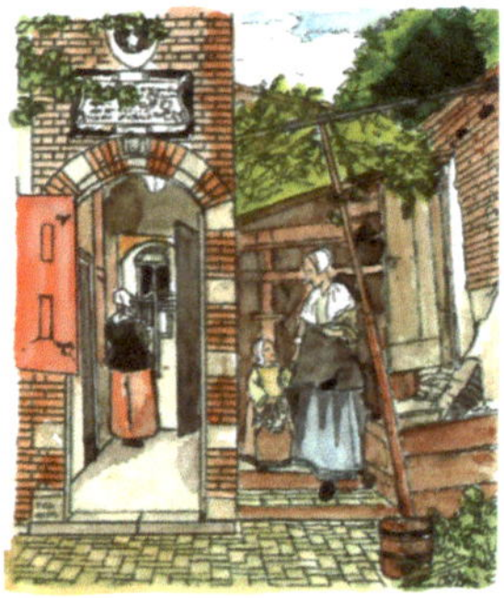

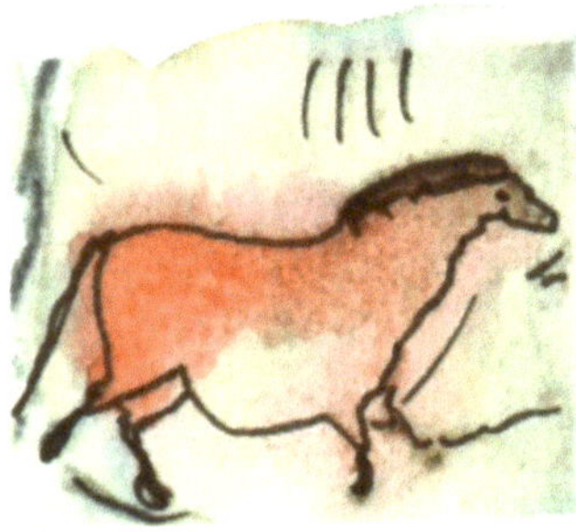

Is it an animal?

Is it a scene of everyday life – a genre painting?

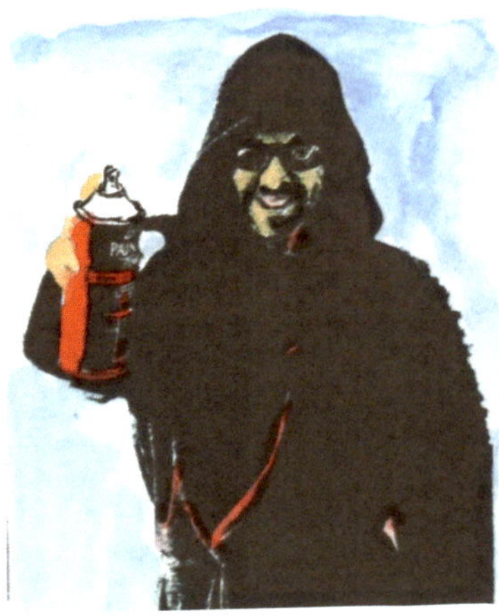

Is it street art?

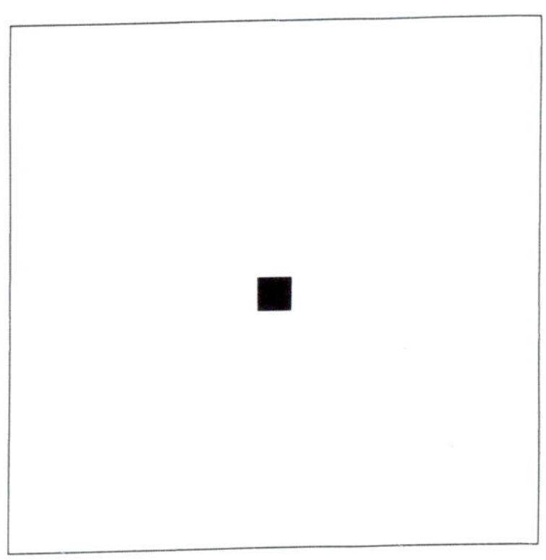

Is it conceptual?

Evolution

Let's ask the picture **"where did you come from?"**

Moving through 20,000 years of people painting pictures and chatting to some of the artists on the way, we'll see how the picture on the wall before you is the product of a long line of evolutionary processes from the caves at Lascaux to our own modern times.

It's quite a journey and reams have been written about art's history. Multitudes of TV series have been produced and many magazines created, university courses and lectures are there for all.

Here we'll keep things simple and to the point but without losing the importance of salient aspects of art or the integrity of its vital contribution to our cultural heritage.

Let's begin our whistle-stop journey through an over-view of the evolution of pictures leading to that work before you.

Pre-History

Pictures are the most certain forms of expression that humankind has achieved. And as such they have been before us since the very dawn of time. It is an indisputable fact that humans have an innate desire to make a mark on the blank surface before them. A cave, a wall, a piece of paper. A canvas.

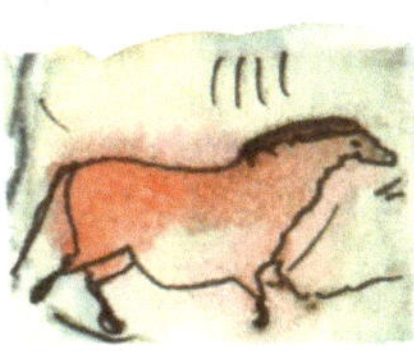

"Nobody knows why I painted animals in their own image, was it for ritual, for illustration, for teaching or pure decoration? Was it for magic? By making a representation I've acquired power over the animal in order to hunt and eat it. My art is therefore aesthetic or practical?"

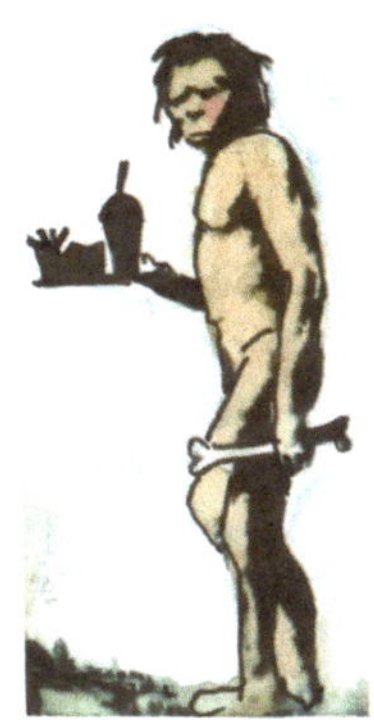

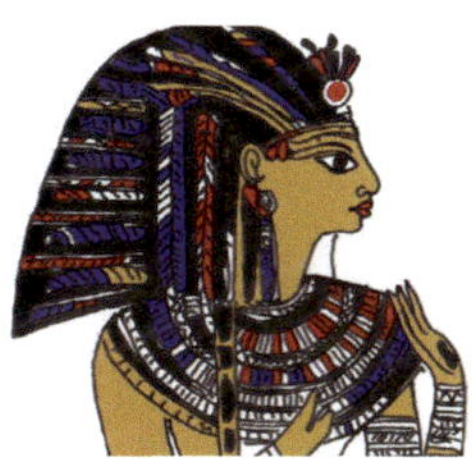

"I was born 5000 years ago. I produced pictorial representations of gods, my leaders, stories of battles and conquests".

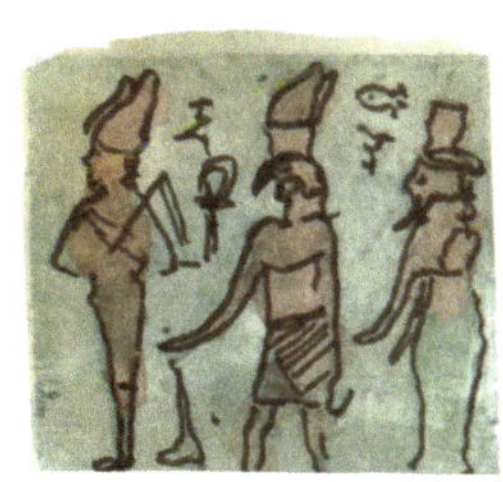

Think how rapidly art styles change today. Ancient Egyptian art styles hardly changed for 1000s of years.

The Ancient World

Western civilisation and its associated art started somewhere in Mesopotamia with Samaria, Babylon, Assyria, but no pictures as far as we know, survive from this era. Similarly with Cycladic and Minoan art apart from the odd sculpture and architecture.

Egyptian art was dominated by sculptures and richly decorated construction, much of which still survives. Gods, nobles and royalty such as the portrait we've just viewed.

From pre-historical art to Ancient Greece. The surviving Greek pictures are largely found on ceramics. From Greece to the Ancient Romans who emulated Greek art to give credibility to their culture. Few examples of pictures remain beyond wall paintings in excavated palaces such as Nero's in Rome and ancient Christian art found in Rome's catacombs.

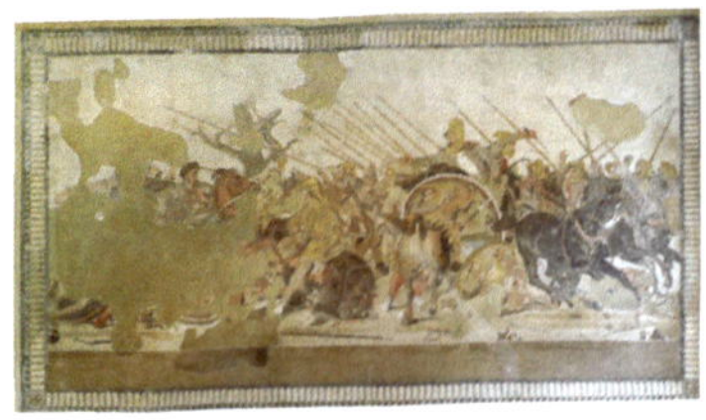

Apelles of Kos 4th C BCE

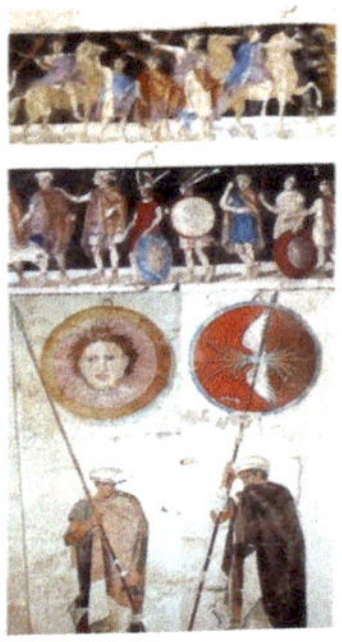

Macedonian tomb fresco Thessaloniki 4th C BCE

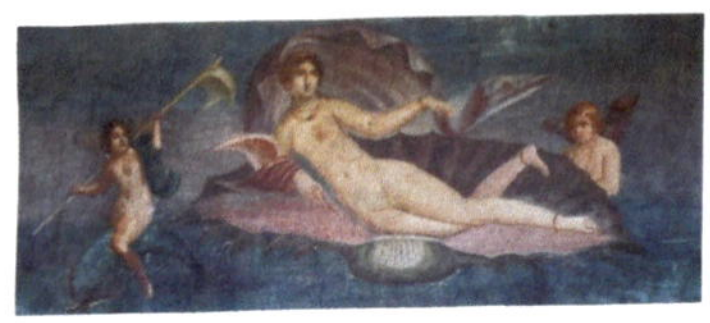

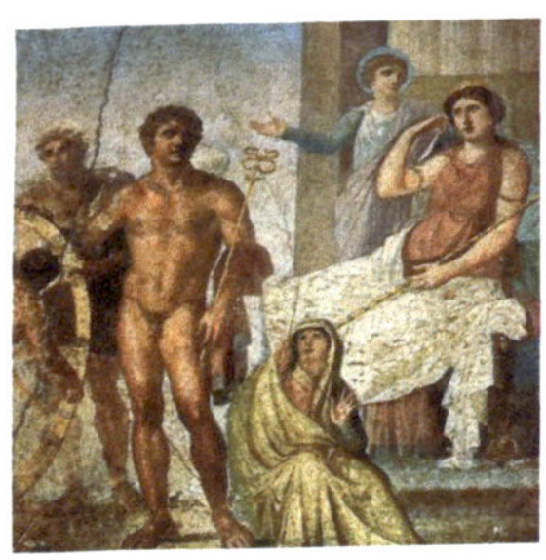

Ancient Roman art. There is little remaining. This example is from Pompeii. *The Punishment of Ixion*

Briefly to set the context, Ancient Rome fell to the Goths in the 5th Century CE and the empire found itself divided between the conquered western world and the eastern world centred on Constantinople, created as the Roman Empire's new capital by the Emperor Constantine in 330 ce. The beginnings of the Byzantine Empire.

In consequence in the western world during the early years following the collapse of the Roman Empire, art as we would recognise it today, did not form such an important a part of life, whereas in the eastern world art flourished, albeit mainly in the form of architecture and with mosaics being primarily Christian divine decoration.

This art form has become known as the Byzantine style and it can be described as particularly formulaic.

Geo-politically, the Byzantine Empire was concentrated in the eastern Mediterranean and over time, with the Italian peninsular loosening its bonds from its pagan invaders and becoming Christianised once again, the artistic influence of Byzantium spread to Italy and so dawned the beginnings of an art heritage leading to the Italian Renaissance.

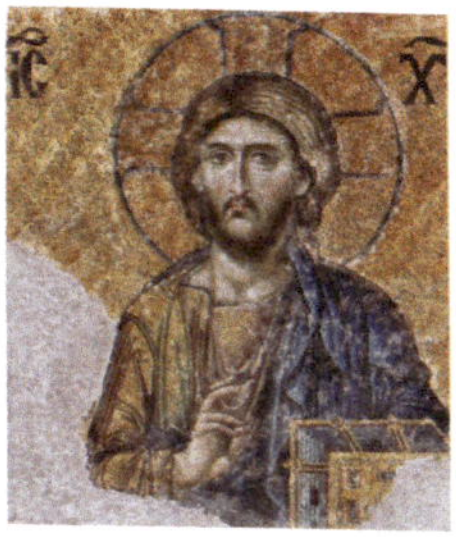

A little taste of the Byzantine and Italo-Byzantine style.

Byzantine Constantinople

Mosaic from Hagia Sophia and the Rabula Gospels 6th C CE

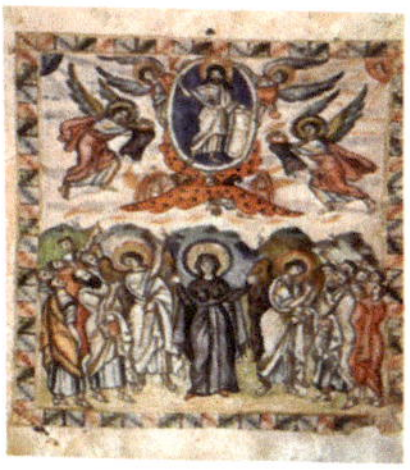

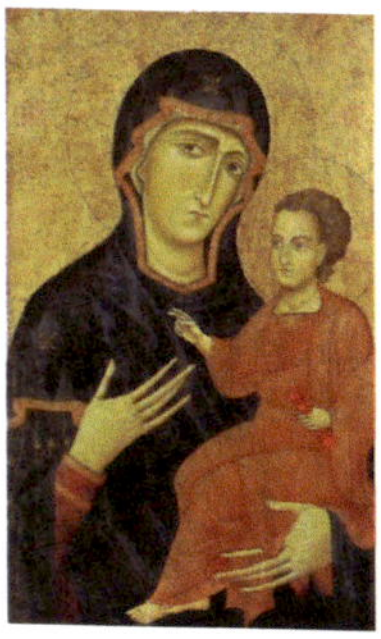

Madonna and Child c1250 CE

Italo-Byzantine

Early Mediaeval

Meanwhile in northern Europe in early mediaeval times after the so-called dark ages, art was practiced by the Carolingians, the Anglo-Saxons and Vikings amongst other cultural societies. These art works were particularly in the form of jewellery such as the King Alfred Jewel, and Viking boat and weapon decorations as evidenced in the UK by the Sutton Hoo burial site. If there were pictures created, there is very little evidence now available.

However, within these societies, Christianity's abbeys and monasteries thrived and this led to the opportunity for art to flourish in the form of beautiful illustrations of the Bible and manuscripts.

The Lindisfarne Gospels. Thought to be the work of the monk Eadfrith, produced around the years 715–720 in the monastery at Lindisfarne, on the north east coast of England. It is considered one of the finest art works of its time bringing Mediterranean, Anglo-Saxon and Celtic elements together.

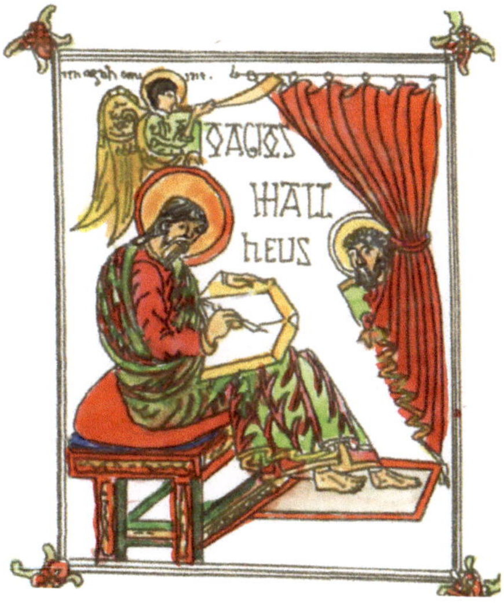

The works were for reverence, for salvation, worship and education.

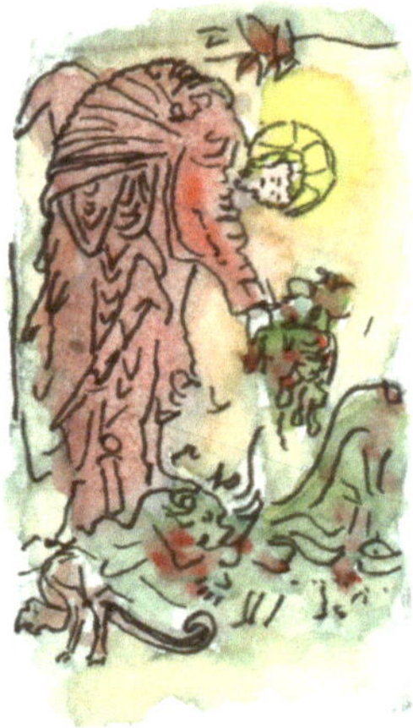

This is known as the Winchester Style. It found its way all the way to Rome and back again to England from the 10th to the 12th Century.

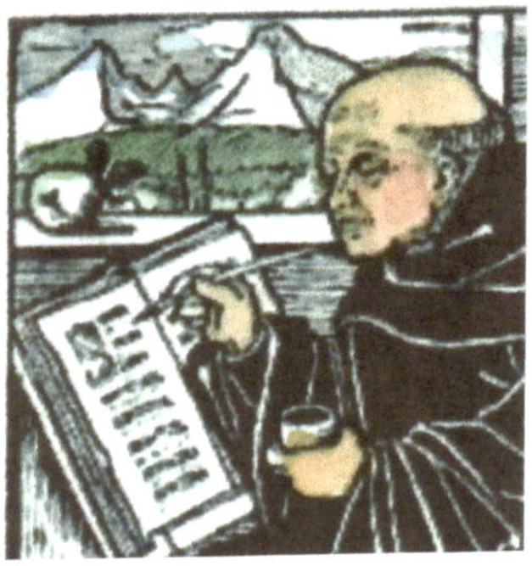

Italian Renaissance

The Byzantine style influenced the early Renaissance Italian artists such as Cimabue, Giotto and Duccio. The Catholic Church was the principal source of commissions resulting in what the Church wanted: Biblical pictures with colours and subject matter in the form dictated. The Church was in charge. Collective representations as a rule formed part of a mystical complexity within which people's emotional and passionate elements were scarcely allowed any free thinking in order to obtain any personal mastery.

The Catholic Church did not need a modern PR agency. It commissioned the very best image makers to visualise its propaganda and marketing and from there control the flock. The Catholic creed harnessed the power of the picture.

Art became an intermediary between the natural world and the world of spiritual presences. A symbol of an emotional state, a means to convey information. A theological dialogue with the congregation.

Amongst the first of the Early Italian Renaissance painters, we find Giovani Cimabue (1240-1302) who has been heralded as the father of Italian painters, establishing the Florentine School and whose works famously adorn the walls of the Basilica San Francisco of St Frances' in Assisi.

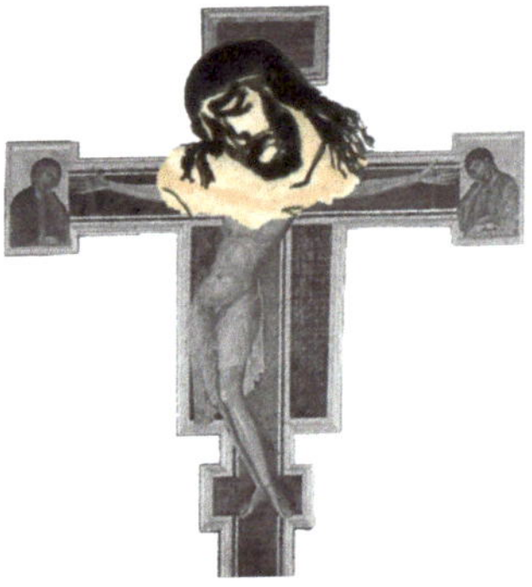

Cimabue's c. 1265 Crucifix in the Santa Croce Church Florence amply illustrates the important contribution he made to the evolution of art.

The Christ figure now depicted broken in mortal agony on the cross, not as in Byzantium as invincible even in death, but as one of us, a human being. The new values of humanism. Naked, contorted in pain. Lifelike. A revolutionary portrayal of human suffering that became of seminal importance and influence on Michelangelo, Caravaggio and even Francis Bacon in our modern times.

Until this time artists were not too concerned with a true representation of the human form. Essentially, they were achieving beauty in design and colour of angels and icons of the holy people almost as symbols.

Cimabue, Duccio and Giotto were inspired to show people as people. How they looked, how they thought, how they aspired to achieve enriched lives and not simply as fallen sinful beings simply waiting for judgement and the hereafter.

So artists started new ways of creating the results desired. The real world, true representation yet not losing that profound belief in the divine.

The Renaissance saw the harmonising of the humanistic secular with the transcendent. These early artist pioneers led the way to a whole new world order.

The Renaissance, the new beginning, the revitalisation of art particularly showing humans as humans in a natural way, had begun.

From Cimabue so to Duccio in Sienna and Giotto di Bondone in Florence, breaking away from centuries of Byzantine iconography in favour of more naturalistic forms with their figures on isometric parallel planes as more accepted by the human eye. Duccio and Giotto also brought real human emotions into their art and their figures were given distinctly individual identities.

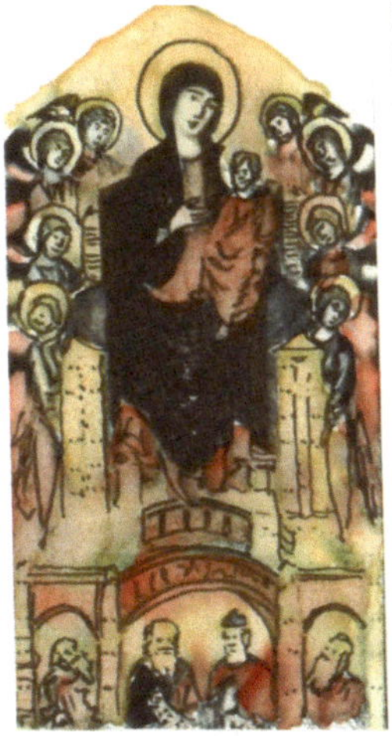

"This sketch of my work is a simple and humble illustration of my magnificent '*Santa Trinita Maesta*' that actually measures 385 by 223 centimetres. It represents a monumental change in art at this time."

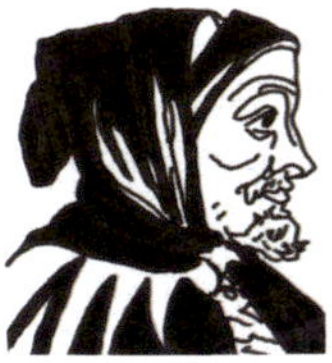

Giovani Cimabue

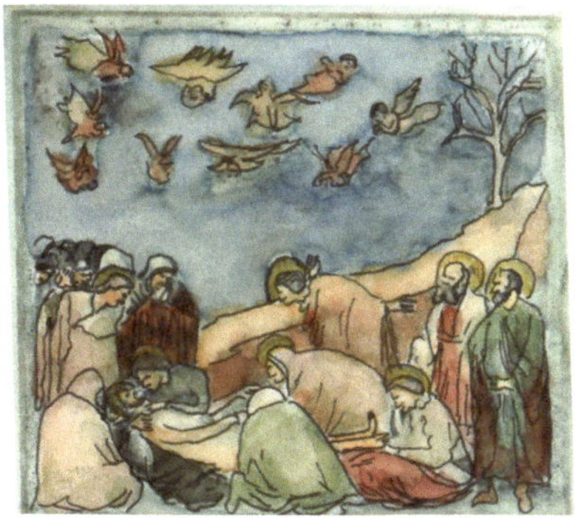

Giotto 1267 - 1337

Lamentation of Christ

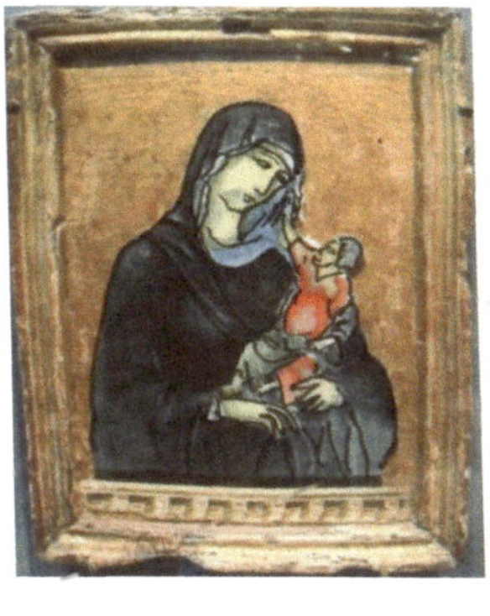

Duccio 1255/60 - 1318/19

Madonna and Child

International Gothic

This is a term coined by art historians to describe a style of painting created across Europe primarily in the quattrocento, the 14th Century and popular within court circles.

Decorative stylisation, use of rich colours and gold. Often spatially illogical complex perspective with finely observed natural details. Elongated and delicately modelled forms of figures. Courtly aristocratic elegance of pose and gesture.

In architectural terms the Northern French and English cathedrals of this time are prime examples. Chartres, Canterbury, Winchester, York and many others. Pointed arches, vaulted crypts and ceilings, buttresses. The style developed through a dialogue between European courts, especially the papal court in Avignon following the schism of the Catholic Church.

Key example artists of this period of art are Pisanello and Giovanni di Paolo.

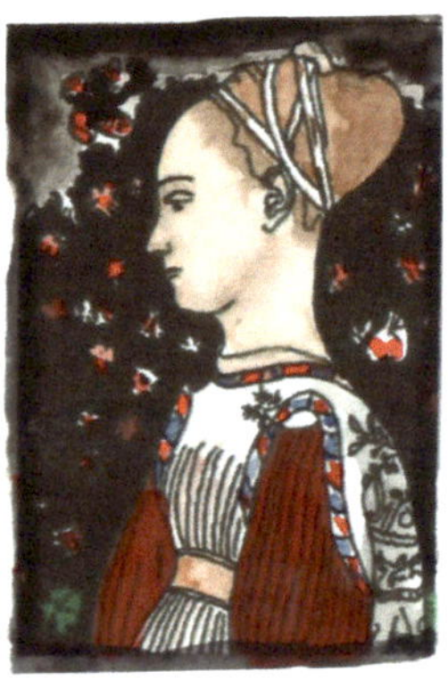

Portrait of a Princess 1449

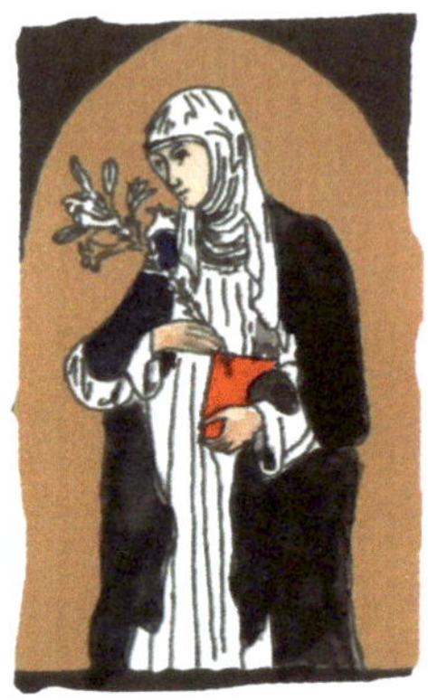

St Catherine of Siena 1475

In the early 15th Century, the development of the pictorial image evolved further, and it is a landmark pivotal moment when the work by Tommaso Masaccio (1401-1428) was created in the Brancacci Chapel, Florence.

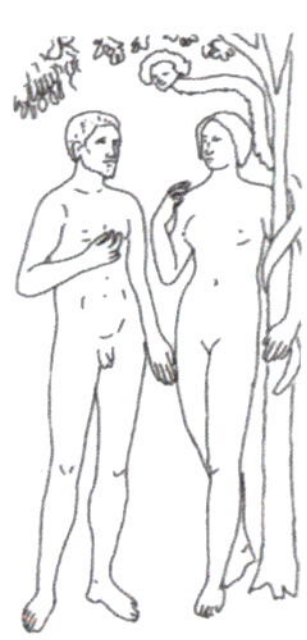

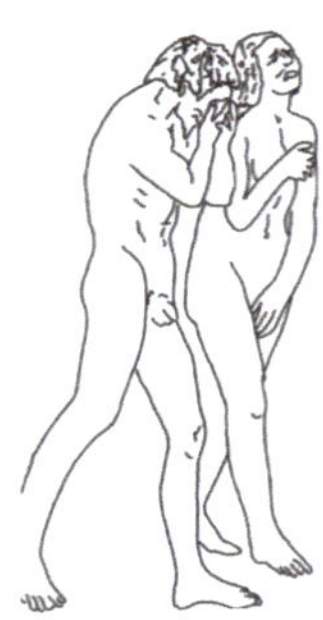

Compare and contrast the styles. Notice the difference in pose, facial expressions, animation and conveyed emotion even with the postures, between Masolino's Gothic Adam and Eve on the left and Masaccio's new order of style on the right. Sketched here without the distraction of colour to highlight the comparison.

Masaccio notably completed the frescos in the chapel started by his tutor and mentor Masolino, evolving to a more natural representational and emotionally charged modern Early Renaissance.

Typical of Masaccio's frescos this picture *The Tribute Money* 1425, contains several parts. St Peter, always dressed in blue and gold, is challenged by a tax collector. He has trouble paying. Eventually he renders unto Ceasar what is Ceasar's. Masaccio's drama symbolically identifying St. Peter as one of us with our own tax debates. It couldn't be more everyday human. A Biblical story brought to our daily life.

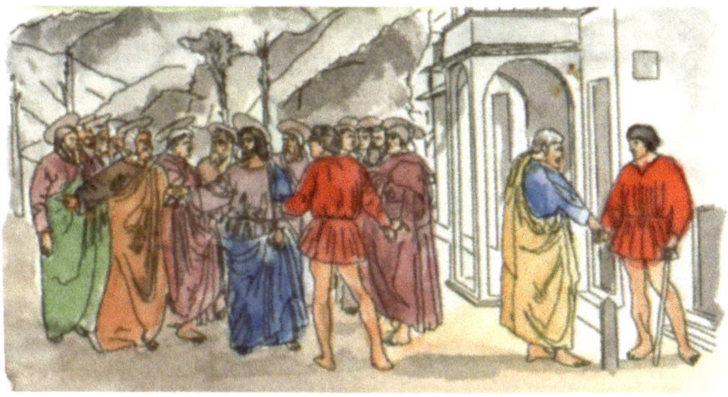

Further around the Brancacci Chapel walls is

Masaccio's *St Peter Baptising the Neophytes.*

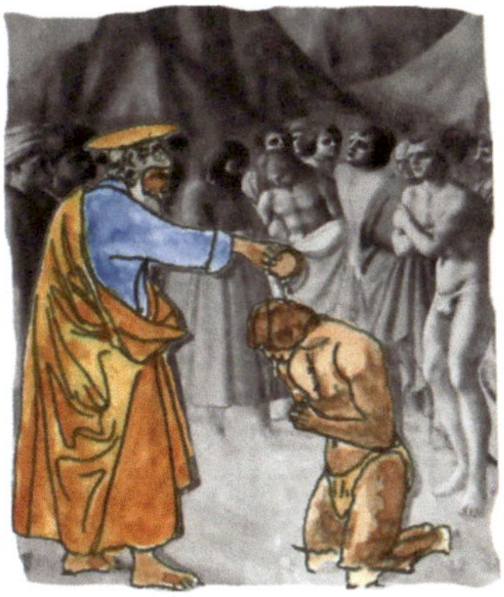

Masaccio's work inspired Michelangelo's realistic human form and that artist's own interpretation of the Biblical story. Its true physiological natural depiction of people as individual human beings with particular identities. Michelangelo with his sketchpad stood before Masaccio's works, in particular *St Peter Baptising the Neophytes,* for many hours in contemplation and from this we can see what an impact Masaccio had on the master.

Filippone Lippi (1457-1504) followed from Masaccio leading through the Early Italian Renaissance.

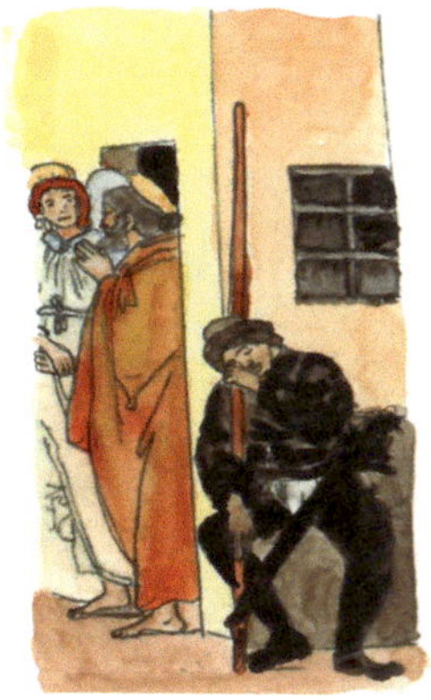

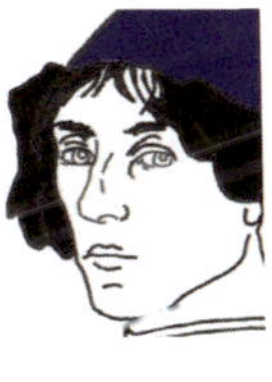

The Liberation of St Peter 1482

Piero della Francesca (1415-1492) represents the second generation of Renaissance humanist painters. He fused geometry, spirituality and perspective and moving around Tuscan towns, he successfully spread humanist art and the 'new age' of painting. Della Francesca died in 1492 the same time as Christopher Columbus discovered the Americas for Europeans. The brave new world was evolving at a pace.

The Baptism of Christ 1440-1450

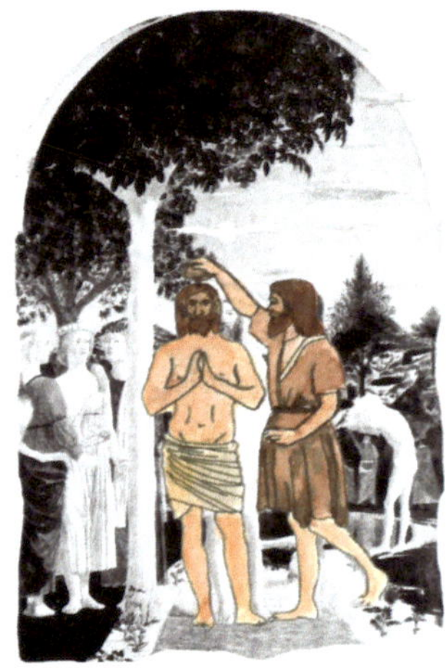

Andrea Mantegna (1431-1506)

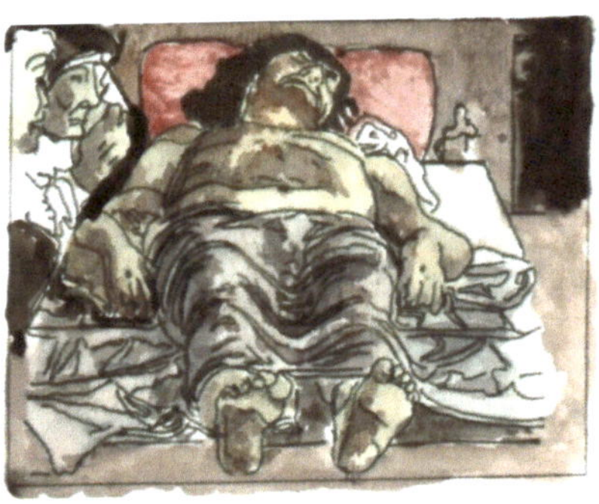

Study this fantastic example of foreshortening. A truly realistic representation of the human condition.

The Lamentation of Christ c1480

Sandro Botticelli (1445-1510). His famous allegories *Primavera* and *The Birth of Venus* provided symbols of the Medici family who ruled Florence and in particular Lorenzo the Magnificent. Botticelli's long career spanned the height of humanism in the Renaissance, through to Mannerism.

Primavera c 1472-1482

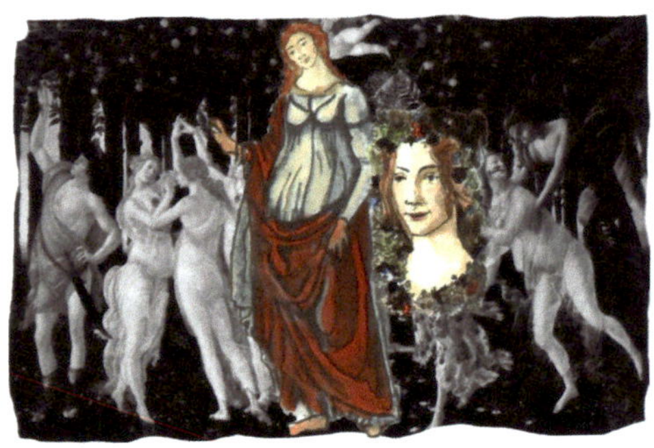

From the Early Renaissance of Giotto to Masaccio, Piera Della Francesca and Sandro Botticelli, the evolutionary process leads onto the High Renaissance.

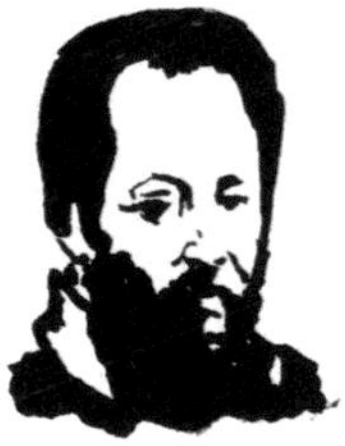

"Greetings. I'm Giorgio Vasari and in 1550 I published my '*Lives of the Most Excellent Artists, Sculptors and Architects*'. Since then, my works have been of enormous influence on art history. I concentrated on chronicling artists in Italy and especially my beloved Florence."

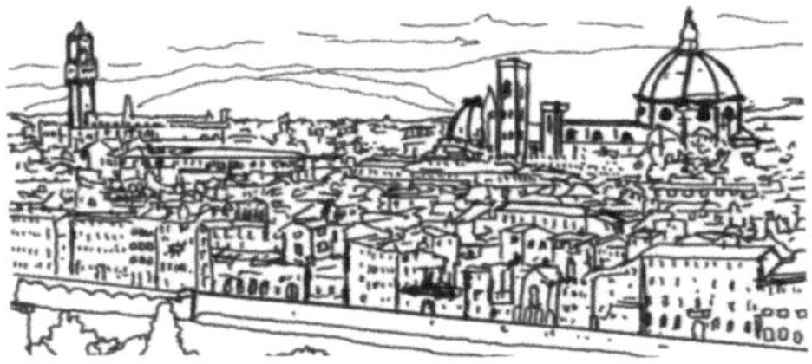

Florence, governed for most of its influential years by the extremely wealthy through the trading and banking Medici family, in particular Cosimo and Lorenzo the Magnificent. The Medici proved to be significant patrons of the arts and scholarship leading to Florence being the flower of the Renaissance.

Renaissance from the French meaning rebirth. Rebirth from the cultural classical times following centuries of little learning and secular debate, the Church dominating behaviour and supressing freedom of thought and expression.

Dante, Boccacio and Petrarch were all there. Intellectual debate, scholarship, literature, printing and art flourished within the world of humanism and wealth. Florence was able to see off many invaders as well as such episodes as the anti-secularist Girolamo Savonarola with his Bonfire of the Vanities. The city saw itself as the ancient classical world reborn deserving of its title as the flower of the Renaissance.

Cimabue and Giotto as we know. Ghiberti, Brunelleschi, Donatello and Masaccio who we've now met. Fra Angelico, Michelangelo, Botticelli and Galileo Galilei. Quite a cast list of emerging personalities in their own right.

Eventually in the late 15th and 16th Centuries, the Italian centre of arts shifted a little from Florence to Rome with the Papacy and Roman nobility in particular supporting the arts.

"In Italy for thirty years under the Borgias, they had warfare, terror, murder, and bloodshed – they produced Michelangelo, Leonardo da Vinci, and the Renaissance.

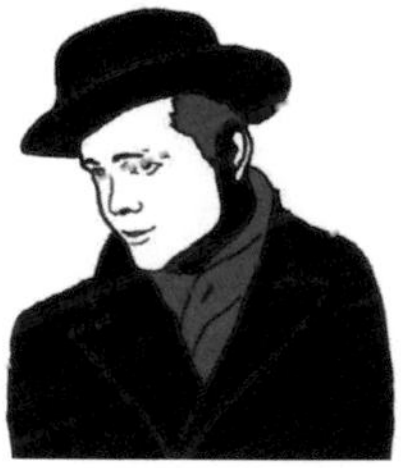

In Switzerland, they had brotherly love and five hundred years of democracy, and what did they produce? The cuckoo clock!"

Well not quite true Harry Lime. Add in the Medici, the Papacy and the Sforzas, and women in Switzerland didn't have the vote until 1971.

*

One of the most famous Renaissance artists and engineers is of course Leonardo da Vinci. Described as a modern polymath he said of painting **"Painting is the sum of all the sciences leading to a knowledge of the world and to a kind of creation of it."**

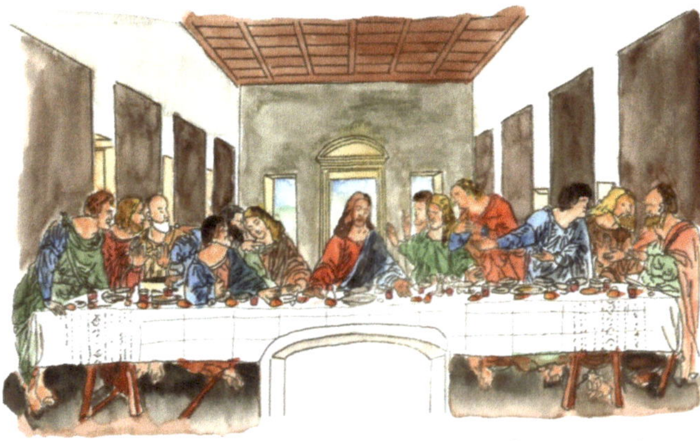

Leonardo is well known for his *Last Supper* painted as a fresco on the wall of the dining room of the former Dominican convent of Santa Maria delle Grazie in Milan. Also we know him as the creator of the *Mona Lisa.*

"I'm Leonardo da Vinci. At the height of the Renaissance, I contributed to the humanism of the arts helping to move away from the pro forma religious works to order".

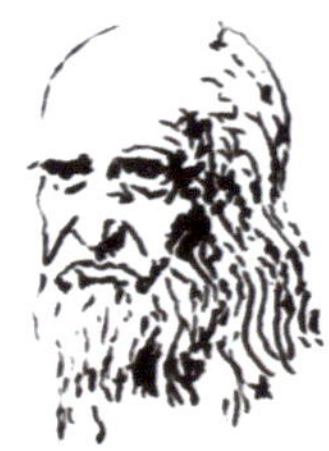

Renaissance historians following the theories of the Swiss social historian Jakob Burckhardt (1818-1892), determined that decisive change in European culture started at this time. Essentially moving from collective values to individualistic humanism.

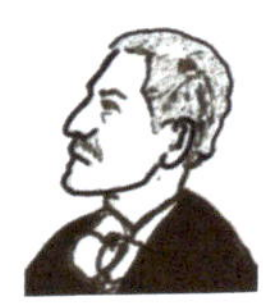

The great chronicler of the age of the Renaissance, he first showed how a period should be treated in its entirety, with regard not only for its painting, sculpture and architecture, but for the social institutions of its daily life as well.

Burckhardt was one of the founding fathers of art history also one of the original creators of what we now recognise as cultural history.

The Renaissance did not only change the fundamental nature of art but altered the conditions under which artists worked, freeing them from the disciplines and inhibitions and allowing more freedom of expression. However, naturally artists had merely exchanged one kind of dependence for another. They could now freely express but only as a marketable commodity. Economic servitude if you will.

Artists now became recognised as professionals as such, far away from the social category that included craftsmen such as carpenters, blacksmiths and masons.

Their market expanded considerably from simply the Church. Artists sought commissions beyond the Church's constraints, for example portraits, flattering of course, and secular historical depictions.

And who would now pay for commissions? The rich of society, nobles, royalty and non-religious establishments such as civic authorities. The artists could now declare themselves as confessing to their humanism and celebrating the humanity of their fellow humankind.

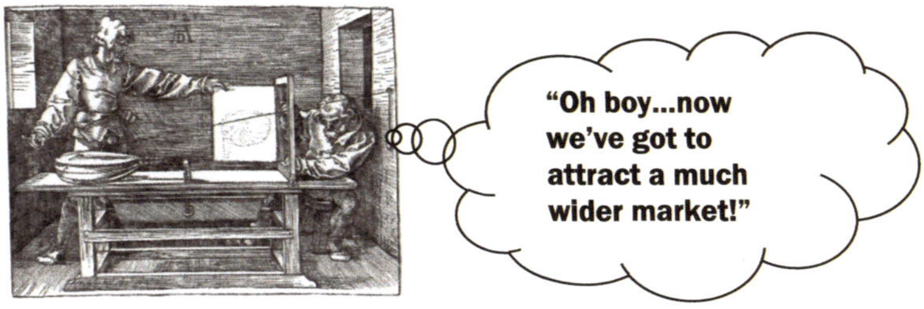

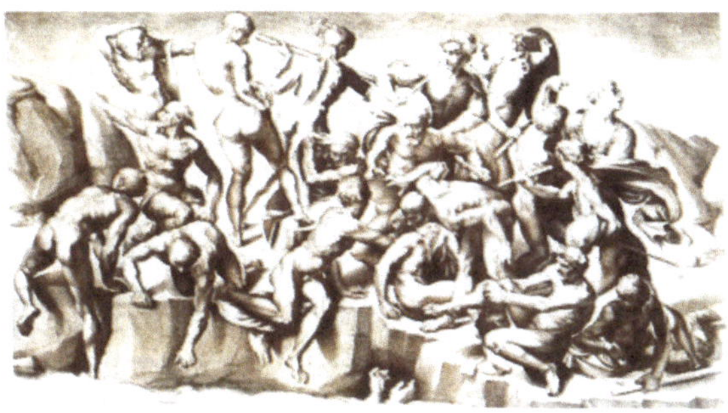

This is a drawing of the Battle of Cascina. A competition put on by Niccolo Machiavelli and commissioned in 1504 by the Florentine hierarchy to see who could depict a battle scene better – Michelangelo or Leonardo. Neither was ever completed. Its subject matter is 'historical'. This is Michelangelo's attempt.

And this is a sketch by Peter Paul Rubens of the Battle of Anghiari by Leonardo. It was painted over many years ago by none other than Giorgio Vasari.

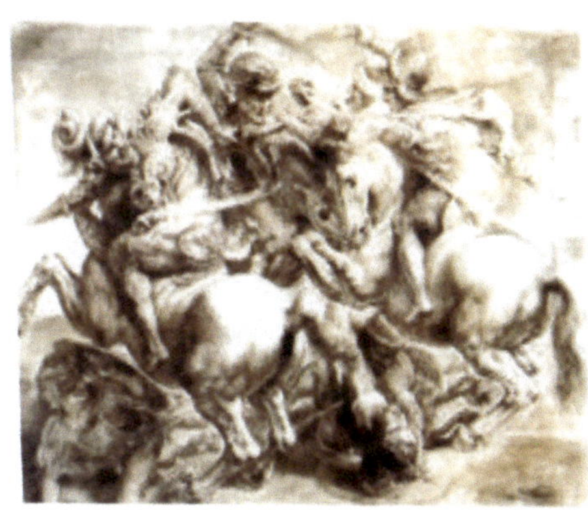

These are examples of amongst the first historical scenes commissioned by a civic authority – the City of Florence. The subject matter: commemorations of battles. Far removed from purely religious matters. This Florentine competition illustrates how well artists were now seen as artists and allowed their own free style in interpretation. The evolution of painting moved on.

"I'm Ambrogio Lorenzetti. I painted my work *Good Government* as a fresco for the civic authority in Sienna in 1340. Much earlier than the above. And it's still there! One of the first landscape paintings? Civic propaganda?"

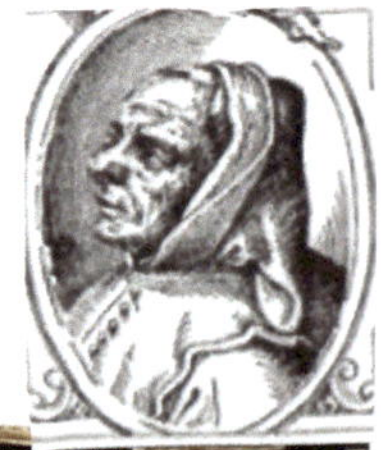

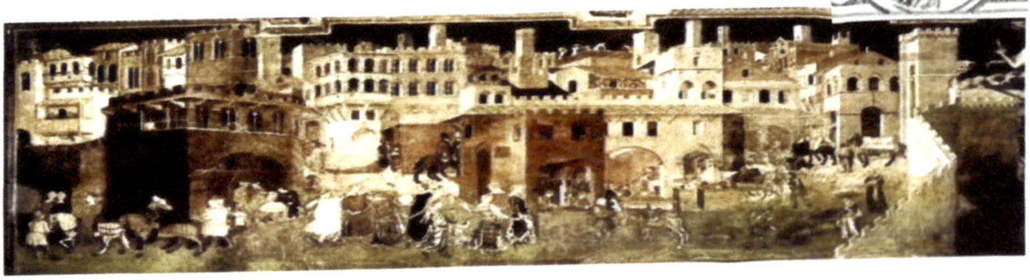

However, of course the Catholic Church remained a significant commissioner of art evidenced by the monumental works ordered by the Popes in the Vatican. Paid for by such financial sources as indulgences. But as we can see from Michelangelo's Sistine Ceiling, the Vatican allowed a far greater degree of artistic interpretation recognising the professionalism of artists to perform with their own discretion albeit still following codified contracts determining broadly what the Church wanted to see.

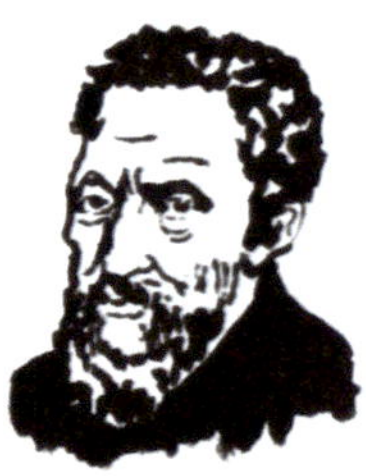

"Masaccio's humanist approach is not a bad idea. Let me see how it could influence me with my Sistine Chapel ceiling"

Look at the realistic and human depiction of the figures, Michelangelo demonstrating his artistic genius without having to strictly adhere as hitherto to imposed constraints in respect of form and content.

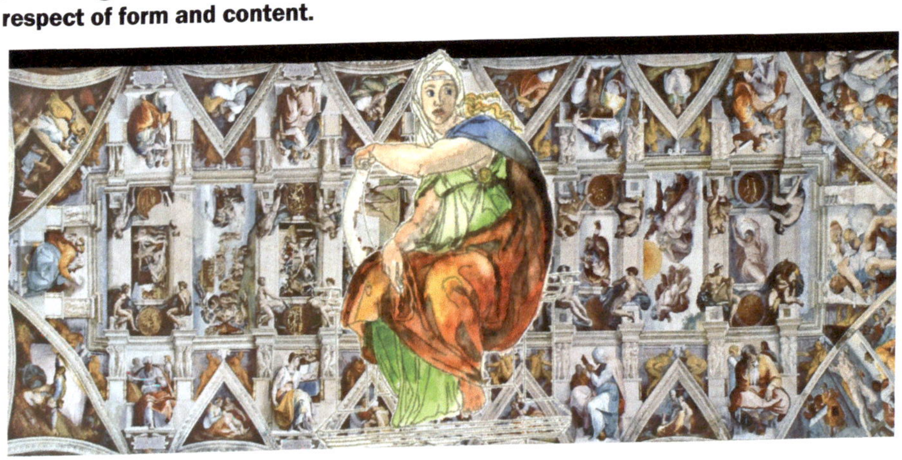

Michelangelo Buonarroti Sistine Chapel ceiling 1508 - 1512

The High Renaissance as epitomised by Michelangelo and Raphael, dramatically evolving on from Duccio, Giotto and Masaccio and the Italo-Byzantine styles. A didactic reaction to the hitherto formulaic art of the Byzantine era.

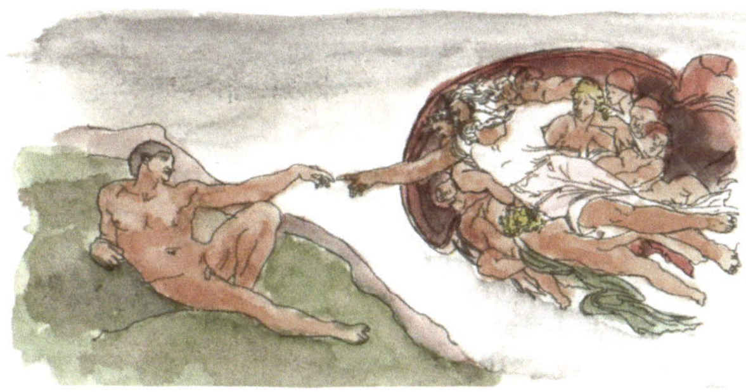

If Adam was created divinely why the navel? Maybe it was Michelangelo's statement humanising his subject even more.

If you could get close to Adam and God on the Sistine Ceiling, you would see how Michelangelo achieved his masterpiece. Each day his assistants would lay down fresh applications of plaster for the master to paint that day. A day's work or '*giornata*'. Adam took four '*giornata*' and God the same. Eight days for this scene alone. 570 days plus for the whole ceiling.

Artists vied with one another in giving their subjects every conceivable accent of originality and extravagance, desiring always to exhibit their own skill and imagination, evolving to the expression of their individual vision.

Michelangelo humanising religious subject matters and artists' works such as Andrea del Sarto's 1512 *Madonna and Child with St John*, adopting an emotional and humanistic approach to religious iconography.

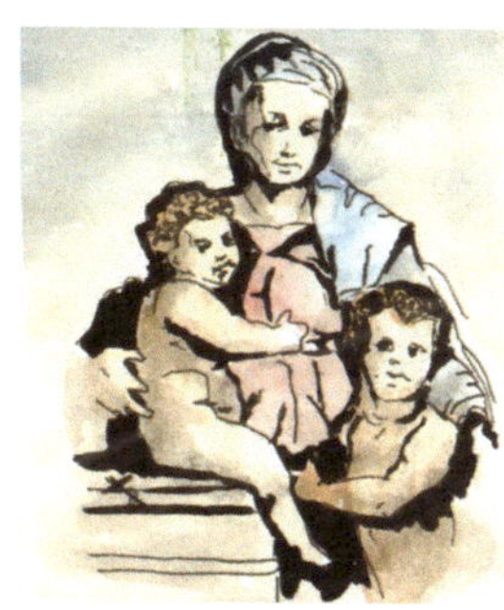

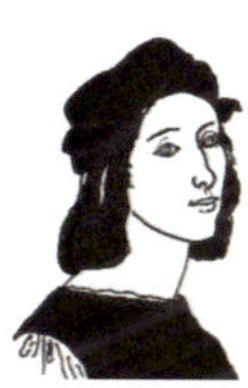

"Consider my *School of Athens* painted as a fresco in the Vatican in 1510. You see a truly revolutionary example of the way art evolved in the High Renaissance. The figures are representational in their poise and postures, a real-world depiction. There is movement here and I used vibrant colours.

Raffaello Sanzio da Urbino. Raphael. 1483-1520

The subject is classical, ancient Athens and the figures are recognisable philosophers not Biblical icons. Humanism at its peak. Also, as you'll see later in this book, my drama is substantially enhanced by the application of the technique of linear perspective, drawing you in to the reality of the scene and almost making you a part of it."

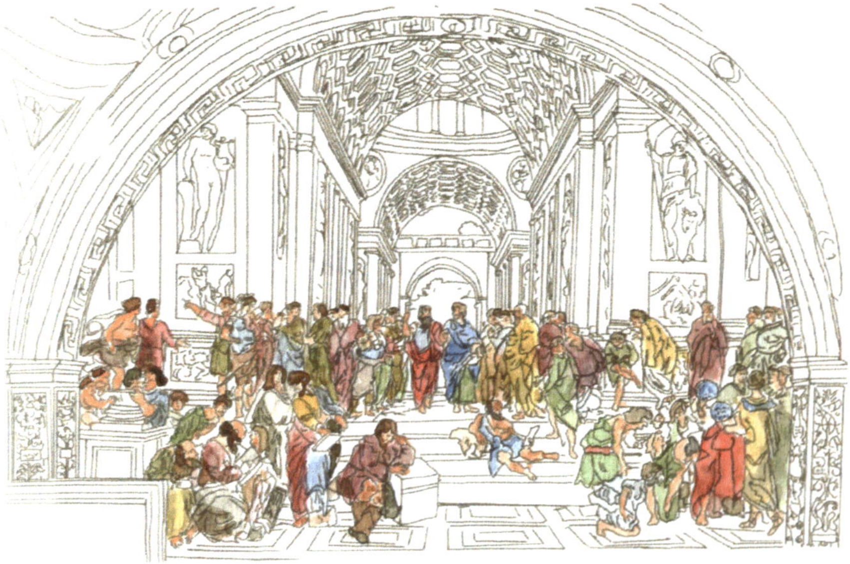

Raphael - Raffaello Sanzio da Urbino (1483-1520)
The School of Athens 1510 - 1511

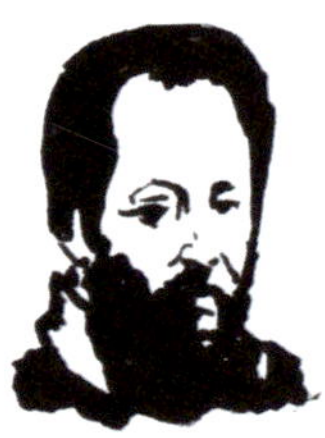

"In my book *Lives of the Most Excellent Painters, Sculptors, and Architects* I prominently describe Michelangelo who I call '*the divine*', a gift from God. Who could better him? How could painters possibly improve on his mastery of art. And that's it – the perfection of art."

With artists in the Italian Renaissance dramatically expanding their freedom to choose their subject matter and the way it was depicted, artists such as Correggio, Raphael and Titian were able to acknowledge in spectacular form, our strongest emotions: love and desire and a deep affection for one another.

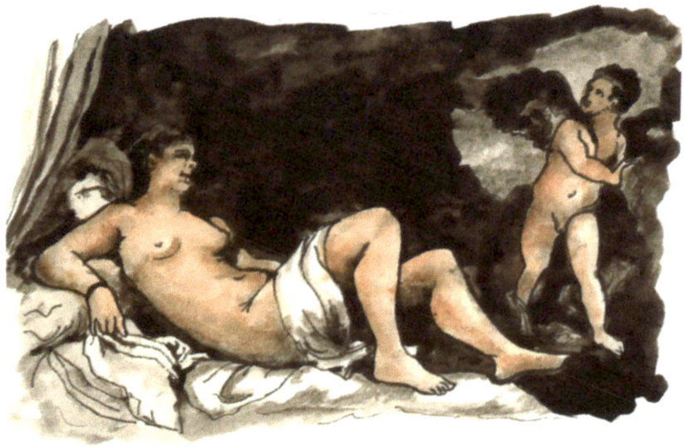

Titian 1488 – 1576 *Danaë with Eros* 1544

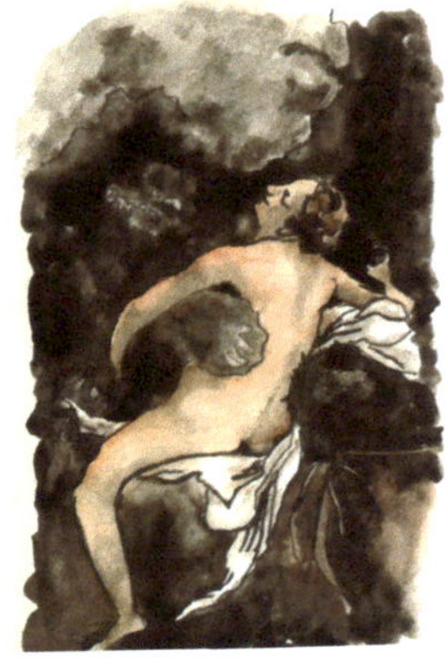

Correggio 1489 –1534. *Jupiter and Io* 1531

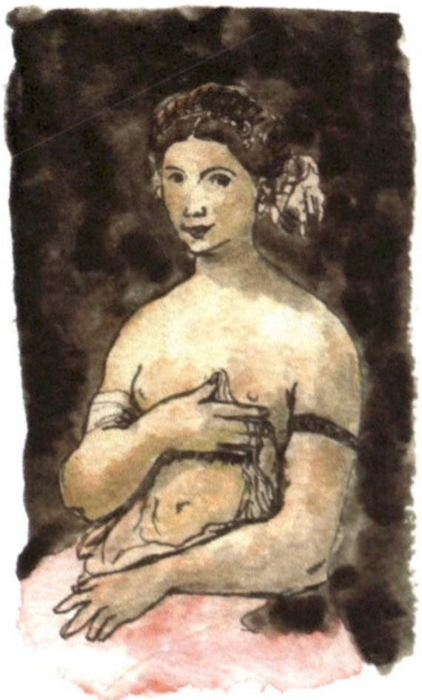

And non-mythological as Raphael lustily painted his real love *La Fornarina* 1519

From the silent fantasising of our desires to the practical depiction of our love - in art. Things had substantially moved on.

"Well, that's about it then!
Quo Vadis.
Where are we going from here?
Do we have a job still?"

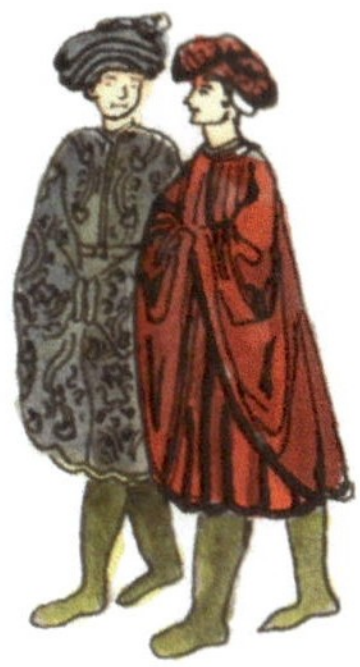

"I know, let's not try and out do Michelangelo's and Raphael's perfection of human form. Let's be good, very good, but move on and fiddle a little."

*

Venitian Renaissance

Colourful. Dynamic. Secular. Classical mythology. Movement.

Artists associated with this region and era are primarily Giovanni Bellini.

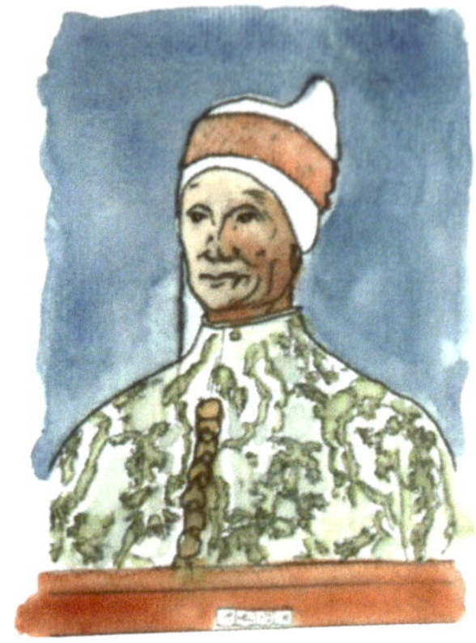

Giovanni Bellini *Doge* 1501

Jacobo Tintoretto (1518-1594) and Tiziano Vecellio, known as Titian (d. 1576)

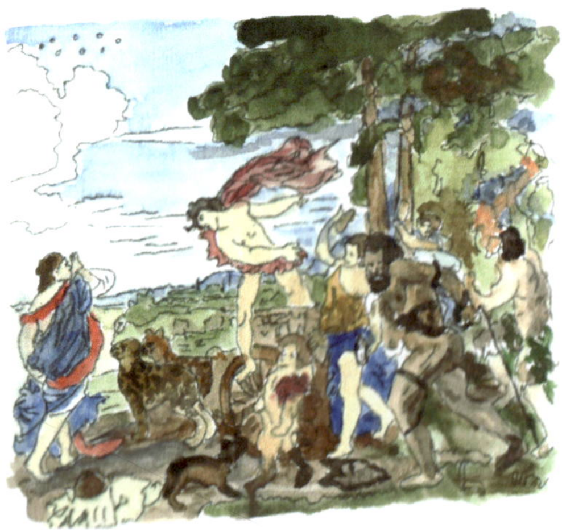

Titian *Bacchus and Ariadne* c. 1520–1523

Much later is Giovanni Antonio Canal (1697 - 1768) or better known as Canaletto.

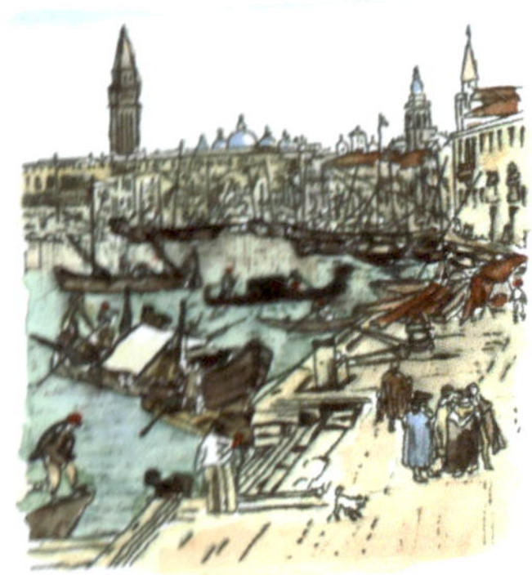

*

Mannerism

Stylized and towards the distorted and artificial, yet elegant and refinded. Complex.

Parmigianino left his native Parma for Rome in the mid 1520s just following the early death of Raphael. He became know as 'Raphael reborn' and consequently he realised he had to distinctly distinguish himself. Mannerist, compelling, idiosyncratic and a move away from the previous classical and geometric perfection of Raphael's Renaissance apogee.

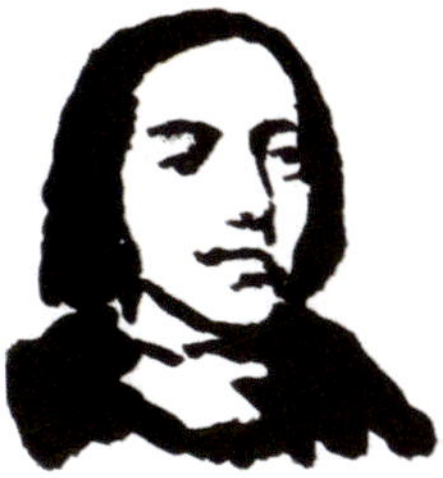

"Has my Madonna an extra vertebra in her neck?

And this is my self-portrait as viewed through a convex mirror. Now that's Mannerism for you."

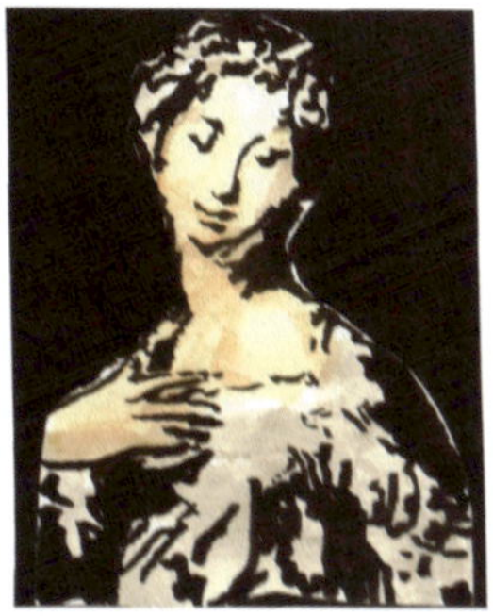

Girolamo Francesco Maria Mazzola
aka Parmigianino
("the little one from Parma") 1503 – 1540

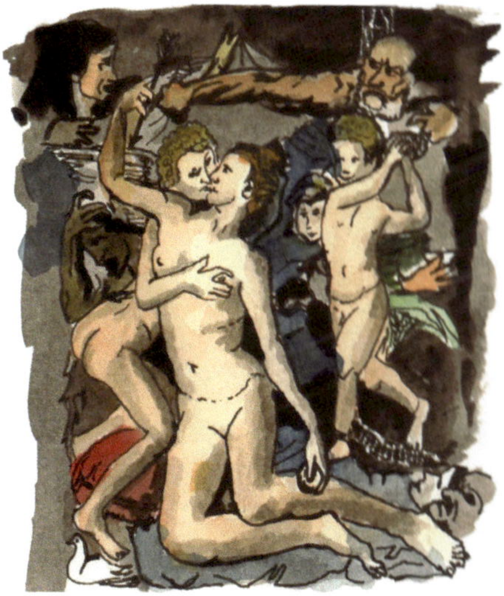

The Mannerist style also beautifully illustrated by Agnolo Bronziono's *Venus and Cupid* painted in 1545.*

From the early 17th Century and through the 18th there was a significant increase in the number of landscapes, genre (that is paintings of ordinary life and people), and animal paintings, particularly in northern Europe.

*

Martin Luther and the Protestant Reformation

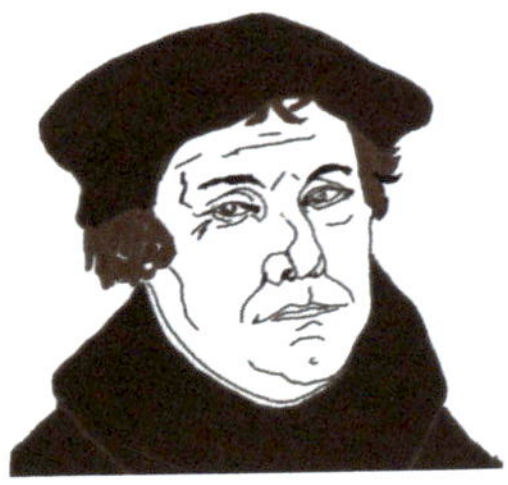

Perhaps it can be described as an artificial intervention into a natural arts evolutionary process, happened in 1517. Martin Luther pins his 95 theses on the church door in Wittenstein Germany in response to the Church's sale of indulgences, strictness of intersessions and other controlling factors.

Martin Luther by Lucas Cranach

So begins the Protestant Reformation and the schism of the Church.

The Catholic Church in an effort to stem the Reformation calls the Council of Trent (1545-1563). The Counter Reformation. In respect of art, artists in remaining Catholic countries were to move their works away from the fancifulness of the High Renaissance and Mannerism to be more based on the scriptures. The Council came up with a set of theological rationales for spending on the arts. In supporting priests' Biblical religious teachings, images were to be clear and readily understandable to the lay public. Realistic and so relatable and emotional in order to engage and encourage piety.

Artists such as Caravaggio rose to the occasion for example with his *The Taking of Christ* 1602.

Baroque

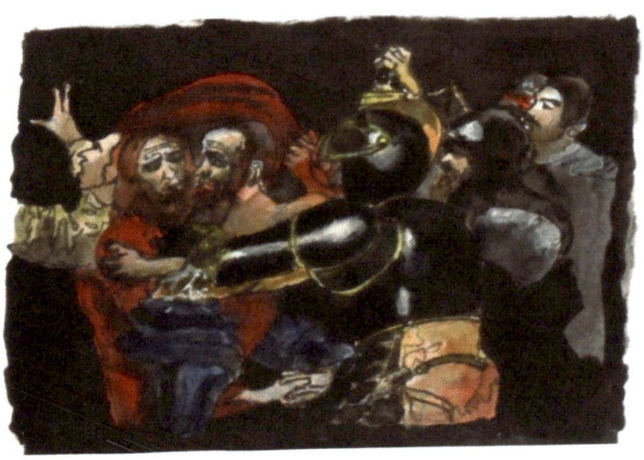

Dramatic, lavish, with emotions exaggerated. Highly detailed and easy to understand and interpret. Movement into mass. The odd, whimsical or extraordinary. To Jakob Burckhardt the Baroque style was the degeneration and disruption of the Renaissance.

Caravaggio's work was passionate, raw and showed poetic realism drawing from everyday life for his scenes and figures. In 1606 at the peak of his career he killed a rival and had to flee to Naples to escape execution. From Naples to Malta and Sicily, returning to Naples where he met his death in 1610.

Caravaggio became a major influence on subsequent artists with not only his genre approach to his depictions but particularly his use of dark backgrounds and shadows.

Chiaroscuro and tenebrism meaning of 'dark manner'. The contrast of light and dark to stage the drama. The viewer always drawn into the scene whether directly as holding a lantern, or as if standing in the street before the drama.

The highlighting of his figures and the drama of the scene created a strength of form and composition that few artists were able to emulate so successfully as Caravaggio in later periods. His approach is now known as 'Caravaggesque'.

*

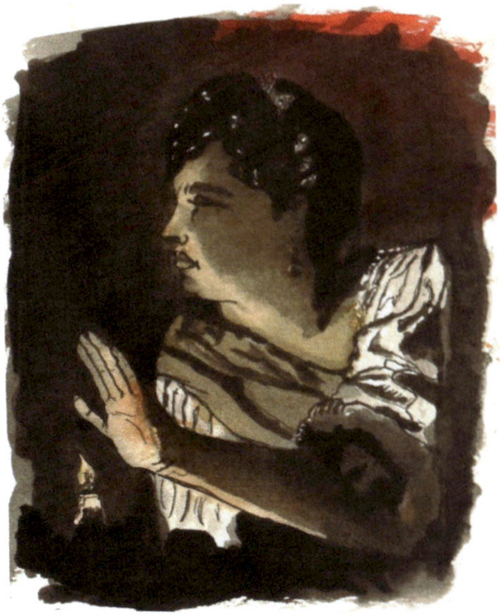

Religious painting almost disappeared in the European Protestant countries. However, even in Catholic countries such as Italy still under the strict governance of the Church, artists such as Artemisia Gentileschi (1593-1656) were able to concentrate on secular themes inspired by the ancient and classical world.

Artemisia Gentileschi

Detail from

Guiditta e la Fantesca

1625

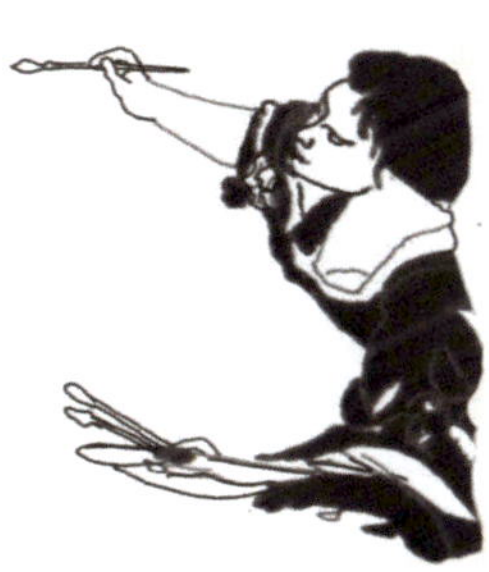

"Men have codified art. They are the privileged ones in creative art's narrative that objectifies women and women's bodies. We are usually shown as submissive, naked or with a child to please the gaze of the male. But I managed to get around this misogynistic culture by focussing on women as brave and heroes. And I became the first woman to be accepted into the Accademia delle Anti del Disegno."

In northern Europe, Peter Paul Rubens worked in the Baroque period.

Based in Antwerp he was influenced by a host of artists amongst which were Caravaggio, Titian, Michelangelo, Leonardo da Vinci, Pieter Bruegel the Elder. Rubens received international patronage from royalty and the nobility and was one of the most successfully recognised artists of his time.

Sumptuously fleshy nude figures dominate his work, scenes of movement, animation and almost debauchery. 'Rubenesque'. A complete contrast to fellow Dutch painters such as Pieter de Hooch and Johannes Vermeer who concentrated on clothed, genre everyday people and scenes as we shall see later in The Dutch Golden Age.

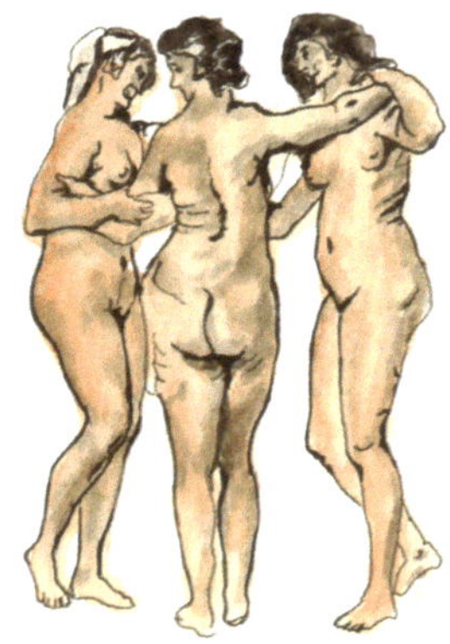

Detail from Ruben's *Three Graces 1630-35*

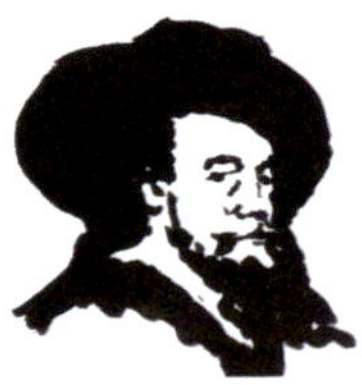

Peter Paul Rubens 1577-1640

*

Northern Renaissance

Meanwhile let's step back a little in time and consider the magnificent work of Jan van Eyck. One of the prime movers of the Northern Renaissance.

This was at a time and location ruled over by Philip the Duke of Burgundy and his benevolent reign ensured that peace, security and prosperity could be maintained. The cities of this region traded heavily and became rich enough that large commissions could be afforded especially as a means of securing one's place in heaven or at least avoid purgatory. Van Eyck's patrons for his *'Adoration of the Lamb'* were the mayor of Ghent and wealthy trader, Jodocua Vyd and his wife Elizabeth Borluut.

Once thought to be the inventor of oil paints, van Eyck was one of the first artists to exploit this new material. One theory is that the use of oil paints was inspired to depict flesh more realistically as up until this time, no real achievement had been secured to paint human flesh sensuously. With oils, broad brushstrokes could be used creating an immediacy and almost tactile, touchy feely.

Oil has a permanent lustre as can be seen by van Eyck's work which after all of its history of looting and theft as well as its various restorations, looks as good as new. Modern acrylics lose their immediacy. Watercolours of course were also a much later invention.

Egg tempera, with a little oil as used by Leonardo da Vinci on his *Last Supper,* we now know was a mistake on that particular surface in that particular situation given its serious deterioration almost even upon completion. If Leonardo had used oils on a more forgiving surface, that would have been a different story.

The *Ghent Altarpiece* or *Adoration of the Lamb* was painted in 1432. An early period at the beginning of the Northern Renaissance.

Art historians have reflected that an Italian artist by the name of Antonello da Messina, saw one of Jan van Eyck's works belonging to King Alfonso V of Aragon at the Court of Naples.

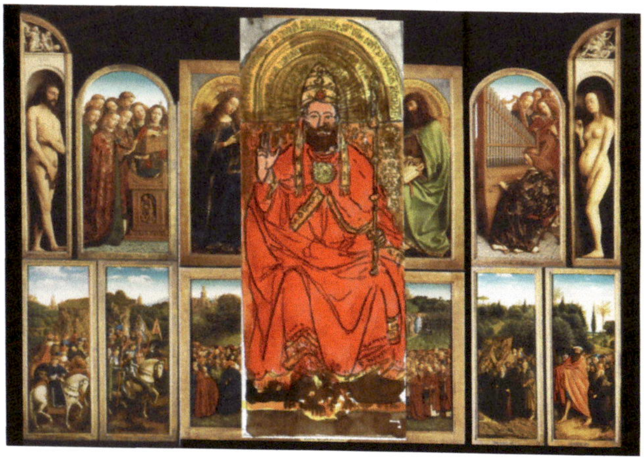

So inspired was he by the technique of oil painting rather than the traditional egg tempera, that he learned the secret of how to make oils work and became one of the first Italians to master the van Eyck approach. He took his knowledge to Venice where, so we understand, he shared his knowledge with the Bellinis and thus contributed to becoming a major influence on the use of oils in the Italian Renaissance.

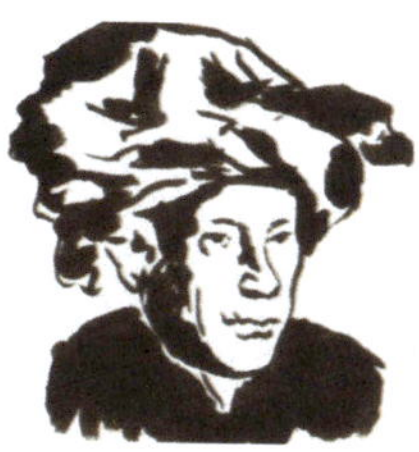

Jan van Eyck 1390-1441

"Many attributed the invention of painting with oils to me. I certainly took full advantage of them.

The Adoration of the Lamb or *Ghent Altarpiece* is my masterpiece although it was started by my brother Herbert who unfortunately died before he could finish the work.

Notice my inclusion of the two patrons of this work, Jodocua Vyd and his wife Elizabeth Borluut. So begins the inclusion of true portraiture to eventually become a genre in its own right."

In northern Europe, Hieronymus Bosch (d. 1516) was an important influence on Pieter Bruegel the Elder, and even Salvador Dalí with his earthy and enigmatic scenes in his *Garden of Earthly Delights* (1515) showing the paradise of Eve's garden through to his evocative monsters.

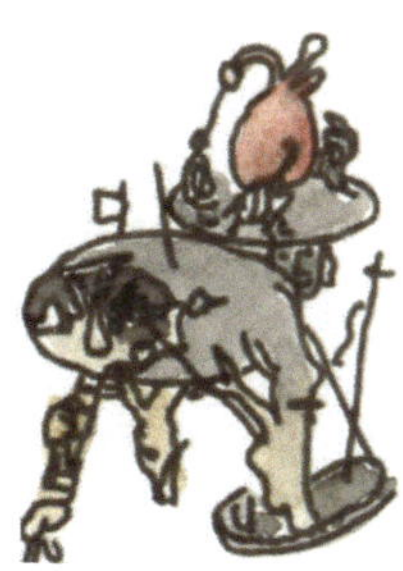

Another significant artist of the Northern Renaissance was the committed intellectual Albrecht Durer of Germany (1471-1528).

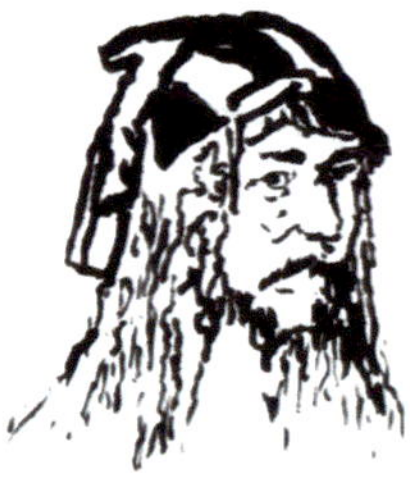

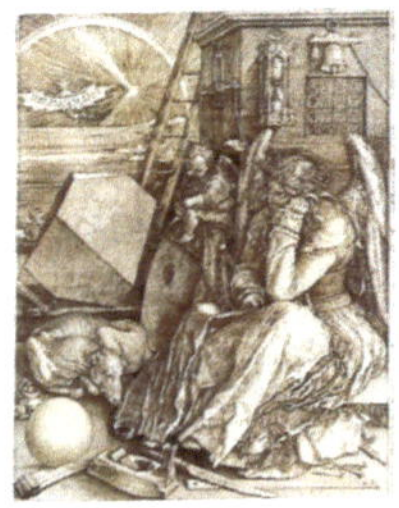

Melancholia 1514

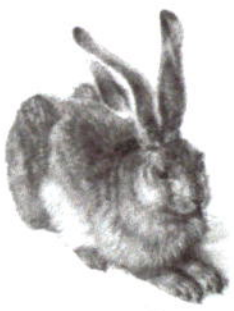

Young Hare 1502

Lucas Cranach the Elder, also based in Germany (1472-1553) became another leading artist of the Northern Renaissance.

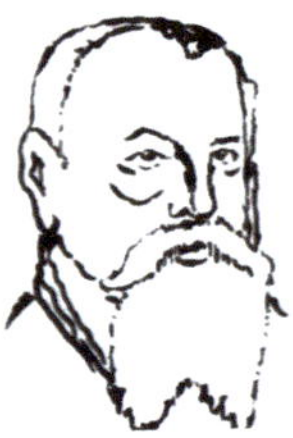

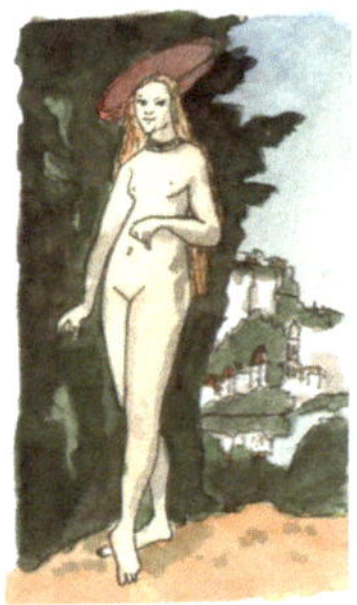

Lucas Cranach the Elder

Venus

1529

Pieter Bruegel the Elder and his son the Younger, concentrated on paintings of ordinary people and ordinary scenes. Pieter Bruegel the Elder 1525/30-1569, focussed on a range of paintings depicting the lives of peasants as with this famous of all his works, *The Peasant Wedding.* 1560. The beginning of the Dutch Golden Age, centring on ordinary people in ordinary scenes.

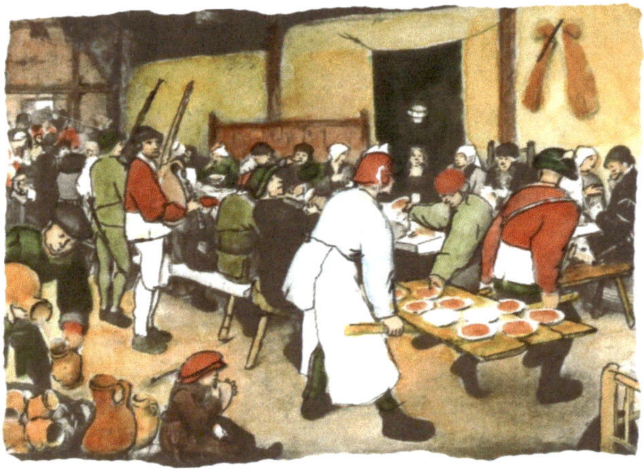

And it was at this time that landscape art became a recognised subject. Pieter Bruegel the Elder pioneered the subject following the Antwerp painter Joachim Patinir's lead in being possibly the first to specialise in landscapes.

The painting here, *Hunters in the Snow* (1565) beautifully illustrates the contrast between the fun of skating on ice with the seriousness of survival during the winter months with the exhausted hunters returning bowed over, followed by their weary dogs. Man up against nature. Domesticity. Joy and playfulness. The everyday. Distinctly Northern Renaissance with its secularity and humanist approach.

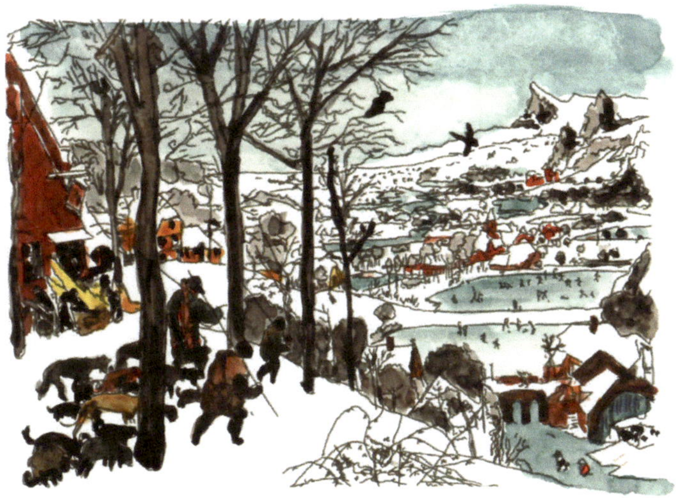

And so, with the Italian and Northern Renaissance, we now see the next step in the evolutionary process, Baroque Classicism. Art becoming more art for art's sake.

*

Meanwhile in England

The evolutionary progress of the Northern and Italian Renaissance never really involved England. However, secular art did develop there in the 16th Century in the form of portraits of the court and aristocrats.

Few examples of religious works as found in this time in Catholic countries were evident in England at this time of King Henry VIII and the Reformation and establishment of the Church of England.

Henry's court received many ambassadors from the European mainland as did Elizabeth I's reign albeit in attempts to overthrow the Protestant establishment and the nation's first secret service under Robert Cecil and Francis Walsingham helped scupper the threat of Catholic resurgence under the powerful and wealthy leadership of Phillip II of Spain in 1588.

Hans Holbein the Younger (1497-1543) moved to England in 1526 under the patronage of Sir Thomas More. He then moved to Italy but was forced back to England during the Reformation.

He became a court painter for Henry VIII and is most well-known for his painting *The Ambassadors* in 1533.

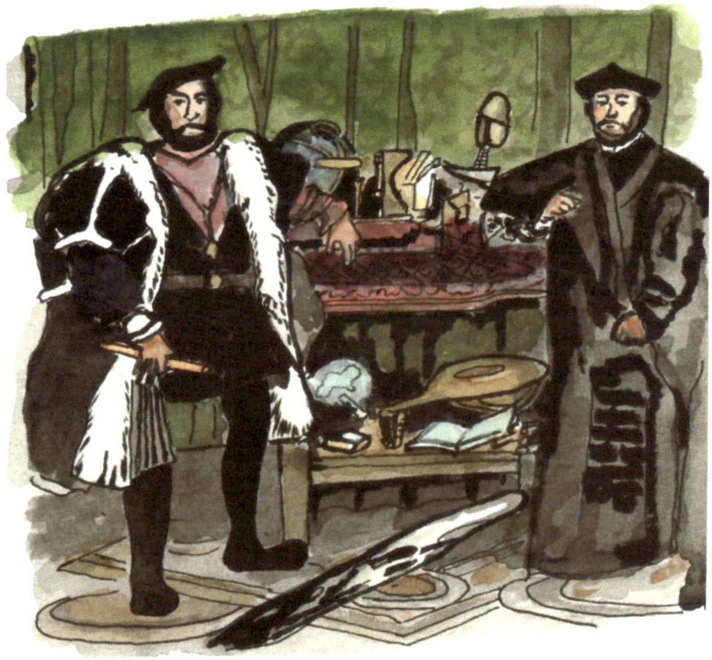

Anthony van Dyke (1599-1641) became one of the most important artists of his time. From Flanders, he became a court painter in England as is particularly well known for his portraits of the English King Charles 1.

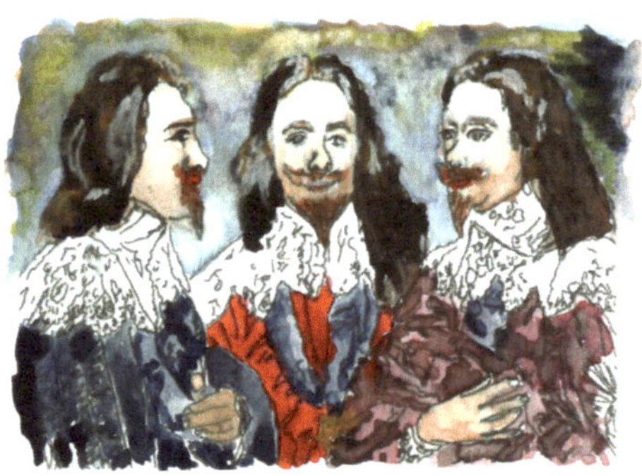

Charles I in Three Positions 1636

*

Baroque Classicism

And so to Baroque Classicism which is particularly associated with artists such as Claude Lorraine (1600-1682) and Nicolas Poussin (1594-1665), where the drama of the Baroque was mixed with the proportionality of the Classical. It was Baroque Classicism that largely influenced the early classical mythological paintings of JMW Turner before he moved on to his impressions.

The addition of classically dressed and posed figures in many of these landscape works enabled the pictures to be elevated to a higher classification in respect of the then hierarchy of art, from mere landscapes.

Lorraine's landscapes became the model for landscape artists until the modern age of art.

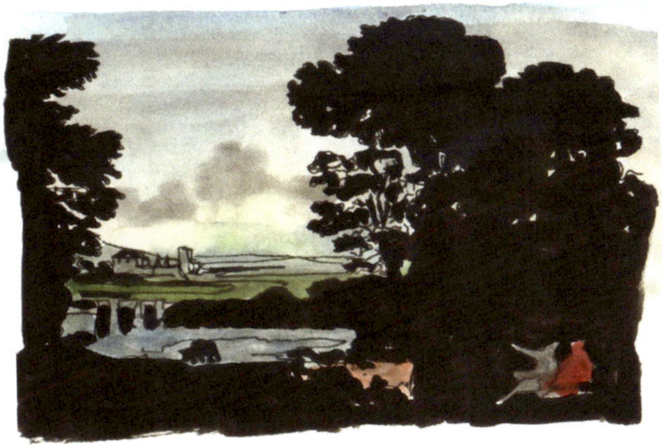

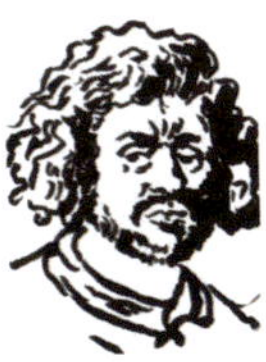

Claude Lorraine 1600-1682

"Did you know that rich people would wear 'Claude' spectacles that changed the landscape they were viewing to look like one of my paintings?"

Nicolas Poussin painted in the court of Louis XIV, a circumstance of extravagance and paradoxical luxury, cultured and sophisticated.

Poussin was also an intellectual artist as shown in his composition, figures and melding of mythological classical tales.

Perhaps his work is one of the highest examples of 17th Century Classicism which led to 200 years of Classicism being the par-excellence in France. 'Academic art' wholly supported by the Académie royale de peinture et de sculpture, the Paris Salon, originating in 1667. That is until the dramatic impact of Édouard Manet as we shall see later.

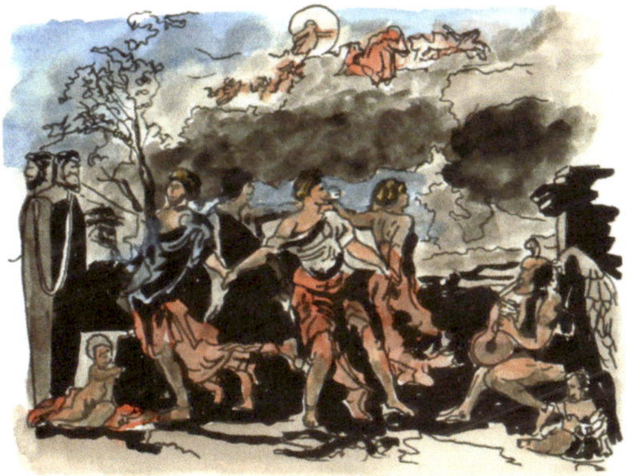

Nicolas Poussin

A Dance to the Music of Time 1636

*

Dutch Golden Age

And remaining in the far north of Europe we see the dawn of the Dutch Golden Age.

From Baroque to Allegorism where the viewer reads into the picture to determine the storyline and what is going on.

Johannes Vermeer (1632-1675) a loved and respected artist, his few works are today highly sought after gems.

The everyday, the miracle of light and perspective. Greater attention paid to detail and domestic routine but nevertheless of great importance. Allegorical, inviting the clues to be spotted and interpreted.

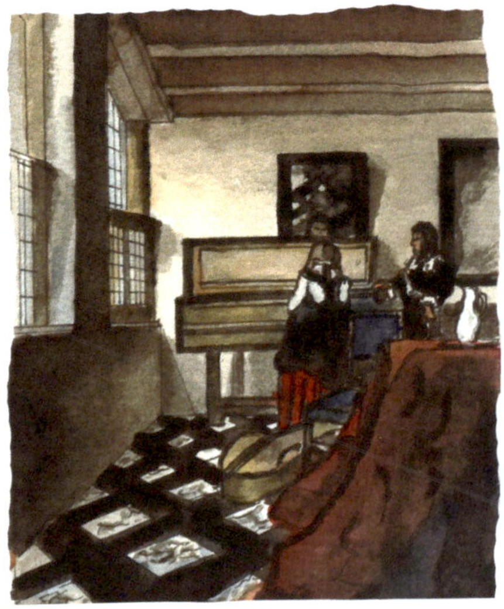

Johannes Vermeer 1632 – 1675
The Music Lesson 1662 - 1665

Similar to Johannes Vermeer's genre approach, is the work of Pieter de Hooch (1629-1684)

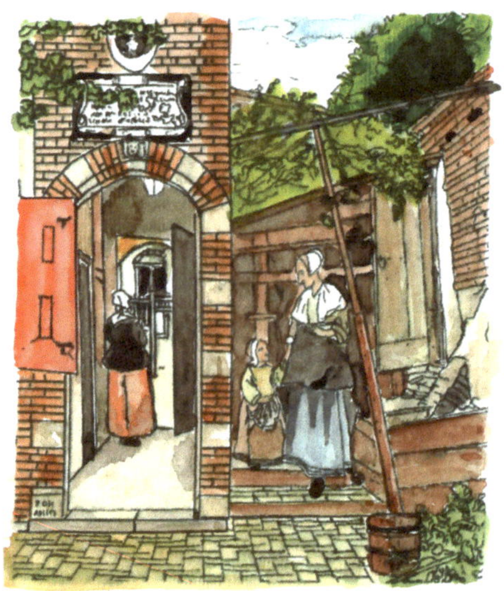

The Courtyard of a House in Delft 1658

This beautiful seascape was painted by Hendrick Dubbels, a Dutch artist in 1650.

Shipping Becalmed Offshore

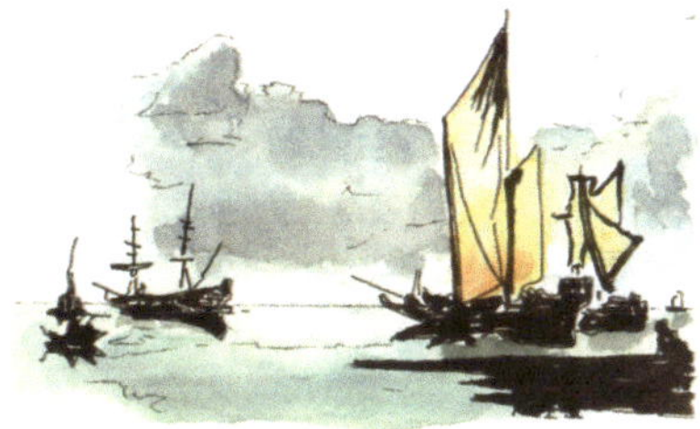

The Dutch Golden Age and its maritime and domestic scenes were also a significant influence on JMW Turner. Consider the 'impersonality' of the Dutch maritime pictures compared to Turner's attempt to empathise you with the fear and excitement of the human experience, drawing and inviting you into the painting.

Born in Leiden the Netherlands in 1606 and dying in Amsterdam 1669 Rembrandt Harmenszoon van Rijn is one of the most well known and loved artists of all time.

Timeless, personable, soul fulfilling. An excellent example of Dutch secular humanism and the art of the genre.

He is particularly well known for his self-portraits chronicling the aging process we are all victims to.

One of his most dramatic historical pictures many consider is *Nightwatch* painted in 1642 at a time of unrest in the region due to the struggle for independence from the rule of the Spanish Hapsburgs.

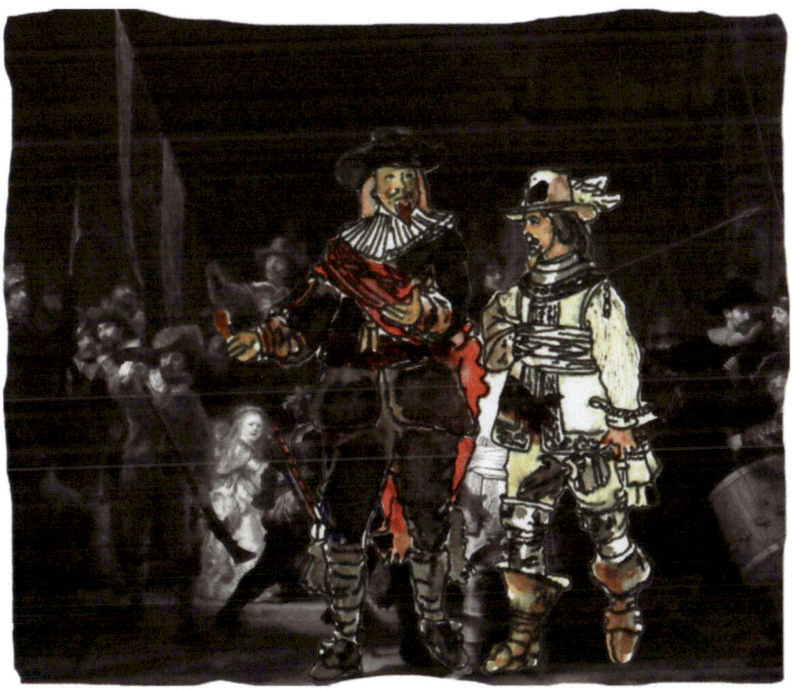

Spanish Golden Age

Contrast the Dutch Golden Age with the Spanish Golden age. This was a time in Catholic Hapsburg Spain. Consequently the most important patron of art and culture during this time was King Philip II (1556–1598).

One particular example from this era is the *Rokeby Venus*. This depicts the goddess Venus lying on her side with her back towards us looking into a mirror held by her son Cupid. It was painted c. 1647–1651 by Diego Velázquez (1599-1660).

One of the more controversial paintings on display in the London National Gallery. An obvious nude with overtures of drawing in voyeurism. Velázquez has not even presented his Venus with facial detail to give her some identity and dignity.

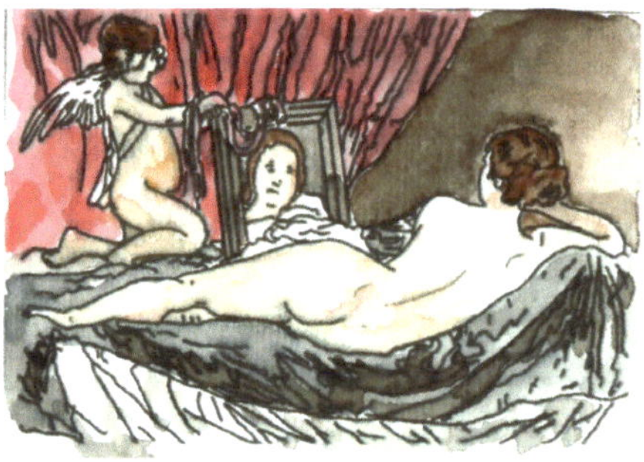

*

A mention of Rococo.

Largely evidenced in France's 'Ancien-Régime'. Elegant and light, peaceful with natural settings. Aristocratic imagery. Elegantly refined erotica and galante capturing the lifestyles of the pleasure-seeking upper classes having fun. Youthful and feminine, happiness and graceful. Rococo is particularly associated with Louis XV and his mistress Madame Pompadour. The French Revolution followed shortly.

Whilst Rococo is largely exemplified by architecture, artists making their name during this period were Jean-Antoine Watteau, François Boucher, Jean Honoré Fragonard and Jean Baptiste Chardin.

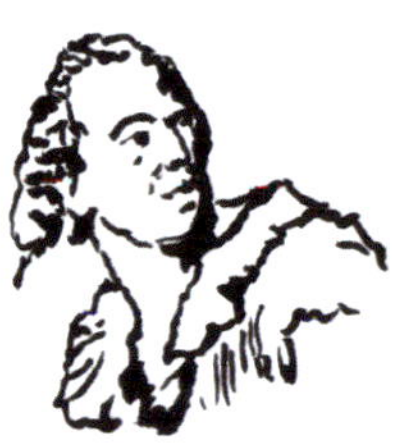

Jean Honoré Fragonard

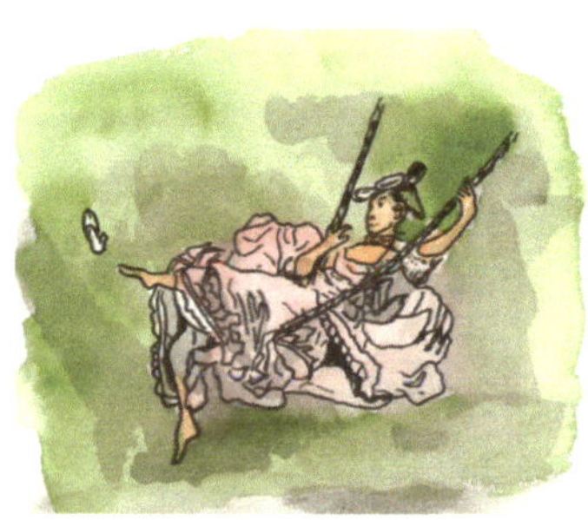

The Swing 1767

Jean-Siméon Chardin is known for his reserved chronicling of everyday life such as his *House of Cards.*

A painter in Paris he nevertheless concentrated on the ordinary. Antithesis of prevailing academia, flamboyant art, ostentatious and courtly life, although he did exhibit in the Salon, Chardin basically followed on from the style and approach of the Dutch Golden Age of daily life and attention to detail. Observant of middle-class life and rich in human values.

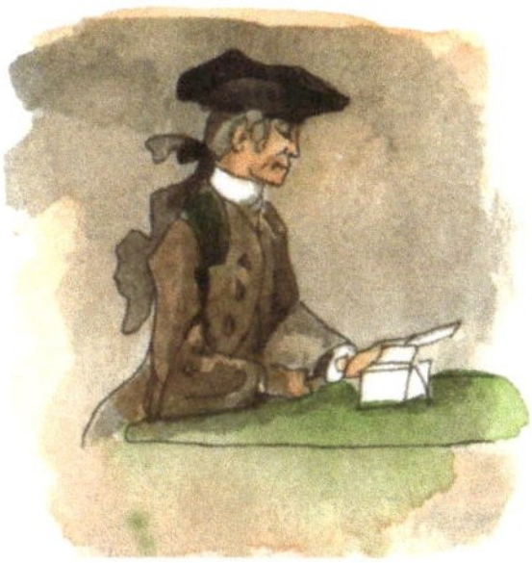

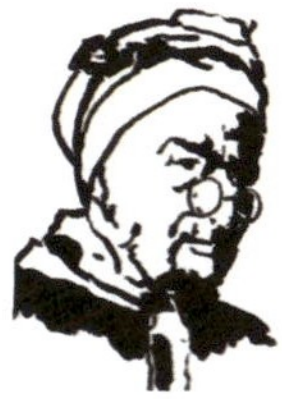

"I concentrated on genre paintings, that is paintings of ordinary folk in everyday life. Similarly to my Dutch colleagues."

Jean Baptiste Chardin

1699-1779

*

Meanwhile in England, in 1750 in complete contrast to Rococo's depiction of the aristocratic debauched lifestyle, we see William Hogarth's (1697-1764) *Rake's Progress, The Madhouse.* A sombre depiction of the Rococo lifestyle being ruined by the wrong decisions. To William Hogarth this was the affirmation of life even in the presence of death.Social realism and satire. Provocative criticism of social norms. Reflecting the aristocracy in *Rakes Progress* to street life behaviour in *Gin Lane* and the ruination of many.

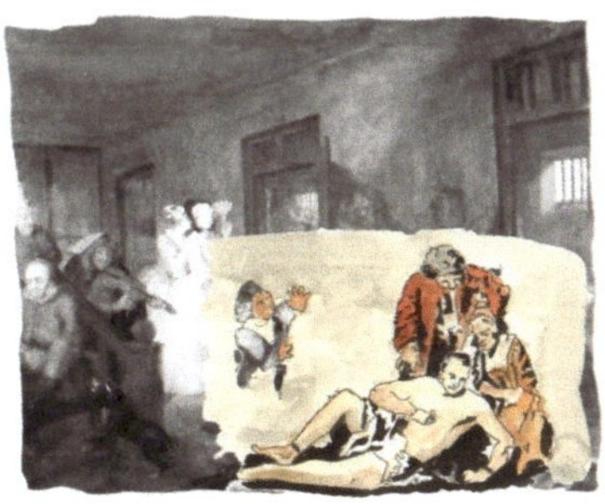

Detail from *Rake's Progress* 1732 - 1735

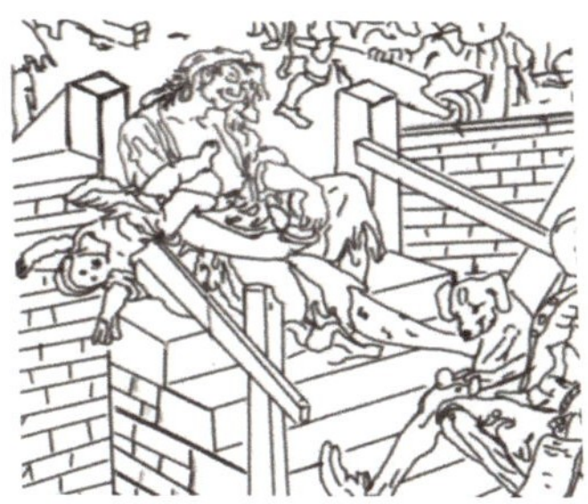

Detail from *Gin Lane* 1751

Hogarth was responding to the fiction and drama of his age. He said that he wished to compose pictures on canvas similar to that seen on the stage. **'I have endeavoured to treat my subject as a dramatic writer; my picture is my stage, and men and women my players, who by means of certain actions and gestures are to exhibit a *dumb show.*'**

*

The Enlightenment

At this point it is worth considering what the Enlightenment's huge difference made to society, the role of the church and economics.

The Enlightenment, 17th and most of the 18th Centuries, also known as the Age of Reason, is particularly associated with the Scottish Philosopher David Hume, the English John Locke and Thomas Paine as well as the French Philosophies: Voltaire, Diderot and Rousseau.

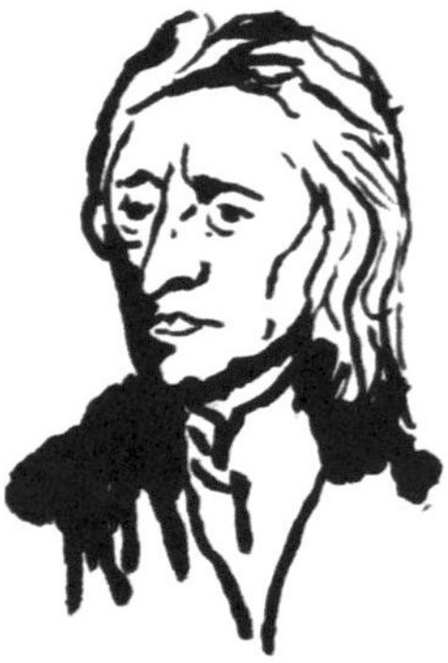

John Locke FRS

1632 - 1704

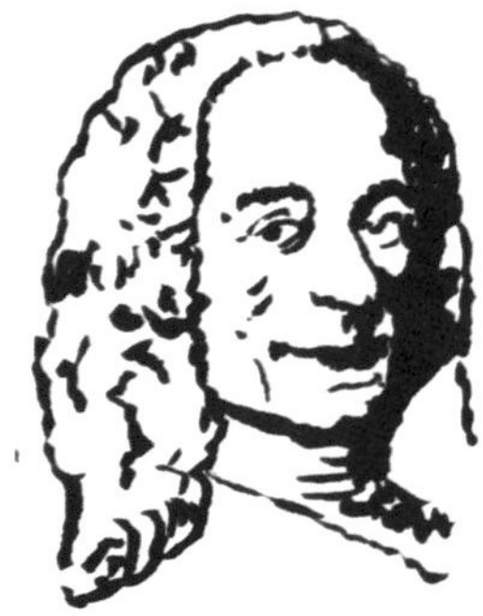

Voltaire (nom de plume) François-Marie Arouet

1694 -1778

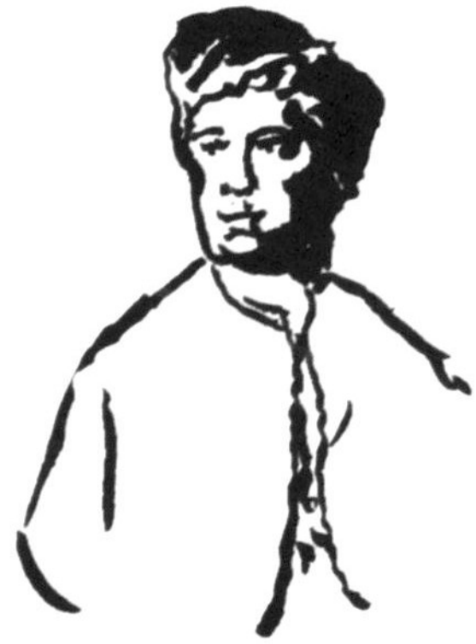

David Hume

1711 - 1776

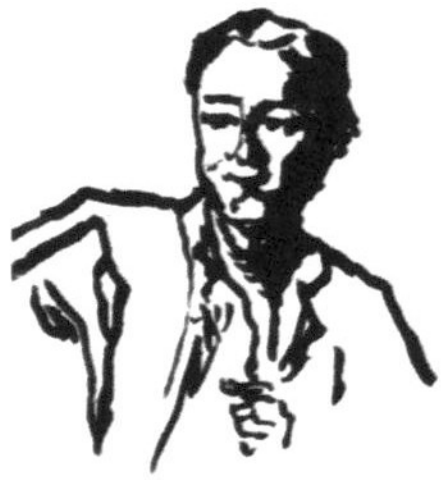

Denis Diderot

1713 -1784

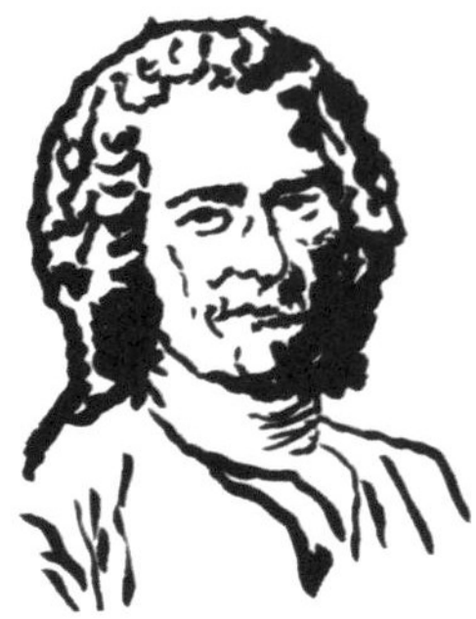

Jean-Jacques Rousseau

1712 -1778

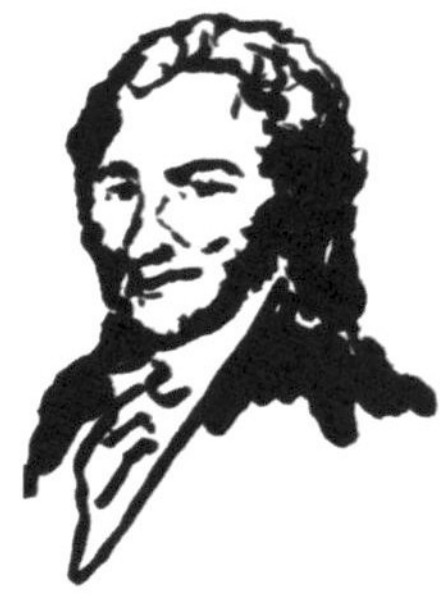

Thomas Paine

1737 - 1809

The philosophy of the Enlightenment criticised all forms of traditional, feudal and religious authority, replacing fear and superstition with consent and truth and thus promulgated a social order based upon natural law and reason and the realisation of a universal humanity.

Immanuel Kant defined the Enlightenment as mankind's emergence from self-incurred immaturity and that people should have the courage to use their own understanding of themselves and the world.

Leaving artists more or less free to do their own thing but necessarily appealing to whoever could afford it or whatever organisation was interested, for commissions unless the artist was from a wealthy enough background to be self-supporting, or quite content to live poorly, thereby being really free to indulge as avant-garde.

And so, for example in England we have the Age of Enlightenment captured by artists such as Joseph Wright of Derby (1734-97).

"I attempted to illustrate to mankind the Enlightenment, science, technology and education being the way forward in the modern world."

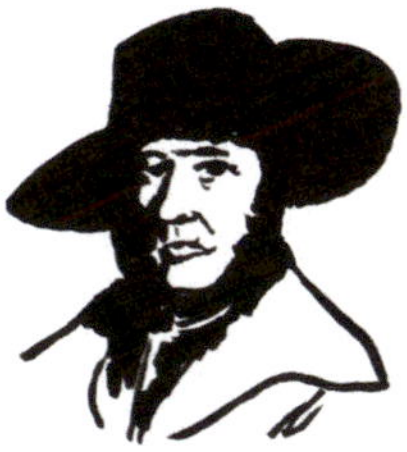

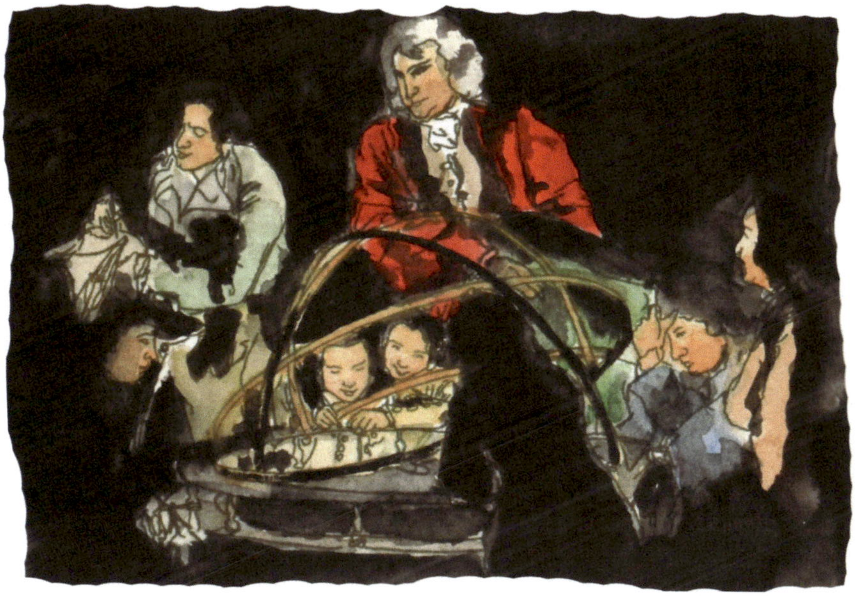

A Philosopher Giving that Lecture on an Orrery, in which a Lamp is put in the Place of the Sun 1766

*

Neo-Classicism and Academicism

In France in the late 18th and into the 19th Century we witness the significant influence of the Neo-Classicism and Academicism as evidenced with the works of Jacques-Louis David and Jean August Ingres. A serious swing against Rococo. It codified and many would say straight-jacketed art to strict rules and regulations aimed at perfecting the image and the way it was portrayed. For instance, fine brush strokes and the painting's surface finished almost glass paper smooth.

The Académie des Beaux-Arts was the art body responsible for artists only being able to gain respectability by having their works hung at the Salon, the official art exhibition of the Académie des Beaux-Arts in Paris.

Jacques-Louis David is a good example of the expected meticulous exactitude and with pictures such as *The Oath of the Horatii* and even with *Napoleon Crossing the Alps*, an antidote to frivolity and gaiety.

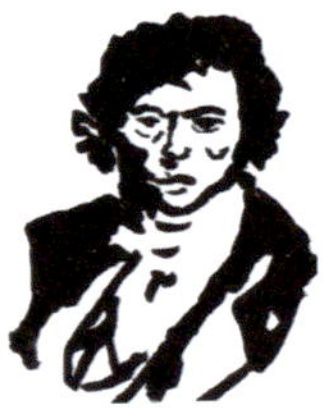

Jacques-Louis David
1748-1825

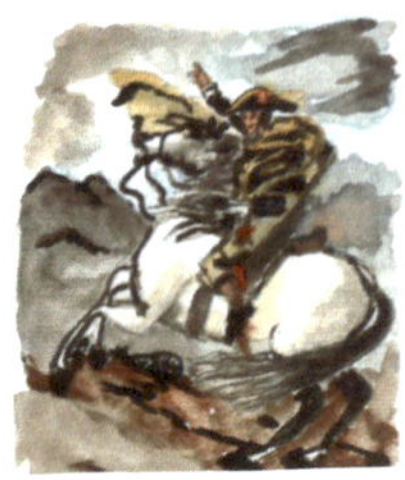

***Napoleon Crossing the Alps* 1801**

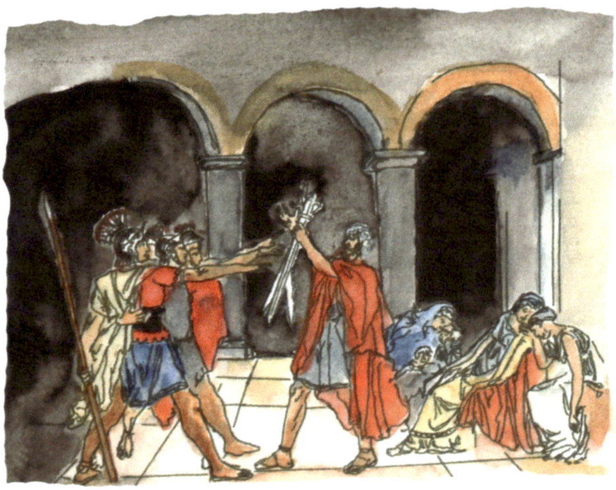

***Oath of the Horatii* 1784**

*

Era of English Portraiture

The 18th Century was the time of Joshua Reynolds (1723-1792) and Thomas Gainsborough (1727-1788)

Portraiture at its highest achievement. Merchants, aristocrats, landed gentry, these two artists were highly sought after owing to their exactitude of figurative and physiognomic detail.

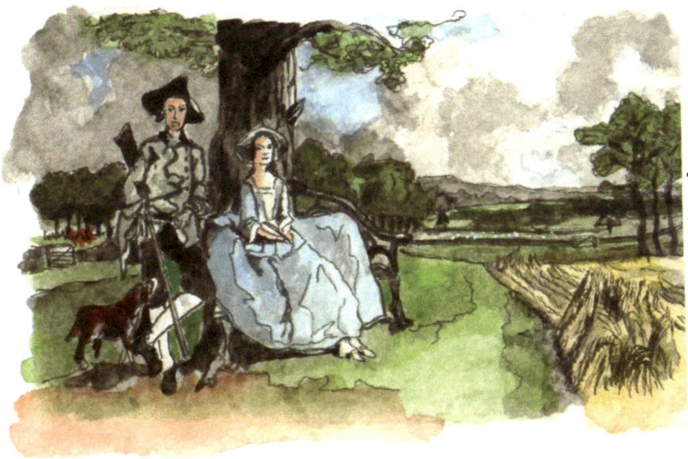

Thomas Gainsborough
Mr and Mrs Andrews
1750

*

Romanticism

In the early 19th Century, at the time of the Napoleonic Wars, landscape painting took prominence in British Romanticism art.

Romanticism was not a style but a way of thinking as it emphasised an appeal to the viewer's emotions and imagination, rejecting the Enlightenment's order and reason. Light and contrasts were used for dramatic effect. Nature in a sense a refuge from life.

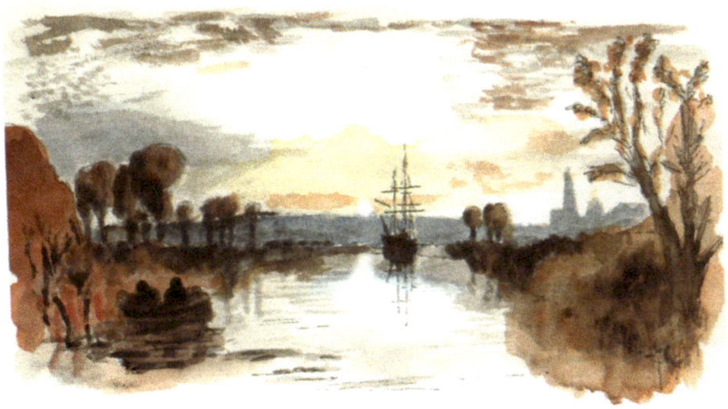

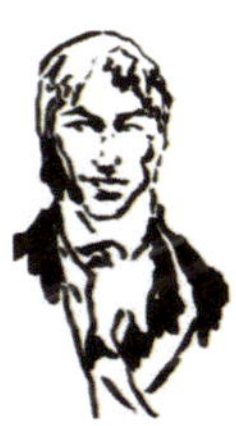

Joseph Mallord William Turner 1775-1851

"My classical paintings after Claude Lorraine are awe-inspiring, but please remember me for my works countering the Industrial Revolution and the impressionistic use of my materials and brushes. This is my 1828 *Chichester Canal*"

"Many people look at my pictures as beautiful images of England, but I was deeply disturbed at the effects of the Industrial Revolution and the increasing resentment of the peasant classes to the structural status quo of society. There is more to my paintings than meets the eye."

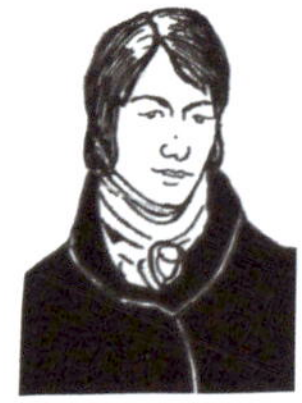

John Constable

1776-1837

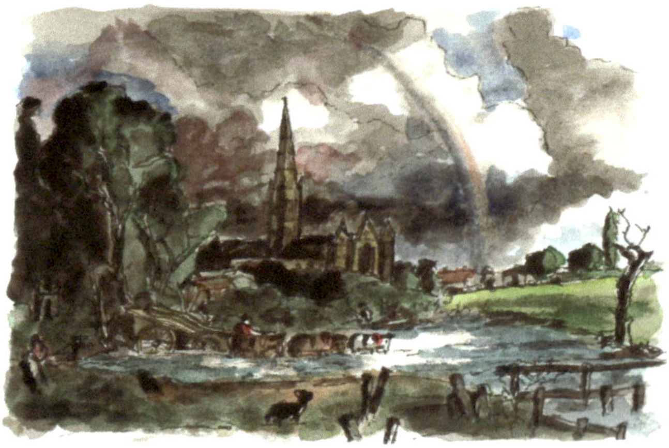

Salisbury Cathedral 1831

And in Germany we see the strength of the Romanticist movement evidenced by Caspar David Friedrich (1774-1840).

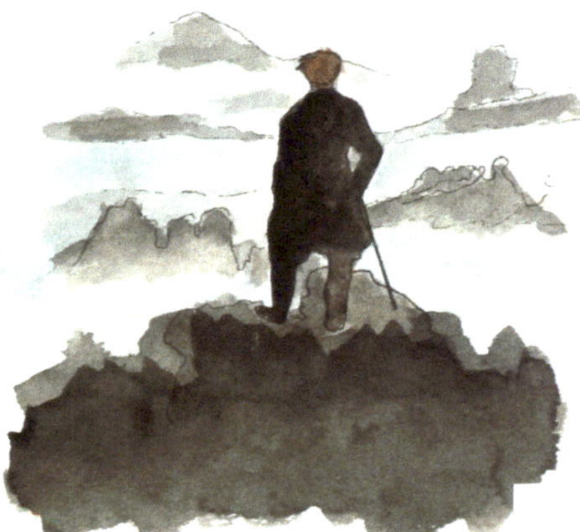

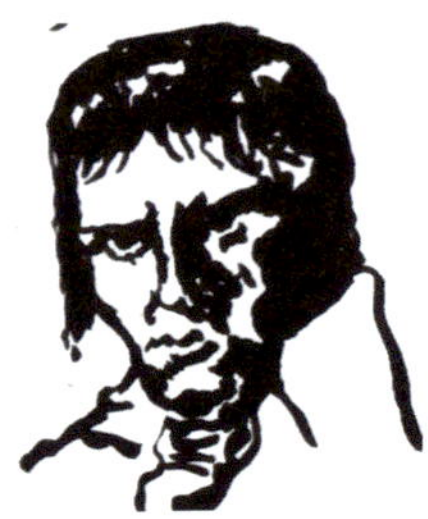

"I am a German Romanticist. I painted my *Wanderer in a Sea of Fog* in 1818. It reflects my approach of following the idealism and concepts of Immanuel Kant. Mystical and helplessness before nature"

With the Romanticists, nature evoked powerful emotions – fear, terror, love and joy: all being dynamic dramas of the human experience.

Turner and Constable reflected what was perceived as beautiful and artistically appropriate at the time. Vision and vitality, responding directly to what they saw, with free expression in their brushstrokes, colour and composition, capturing weather, seasons and light with their deliberate intensity.

Both Turner and Constable provide painterly delight far removed from the simple conceptual and political. Sensuous with vast inclusive themes. These artists engage us and immerse us with intensive pleasure.

The late 18th and early 19th Centuries saw war and revolution, political turmoil and reform as well as rapid industrialisation. All metaphors for change and uncertainty as well as the joy and pain of the human story.

It can also be considered why in many of their works, the figures are small and not a central feature. At a time of riots and political uncertainty, were these artists acknowledging the essential existence of peasants and labourers yet because of the threat they may have felt about them, they were kept at a distance?

Meanwhile in France the Académie des Beaux-Arts in Paris continued to be the dominant determinant of high art, whilst in the UK a powerful new movement saw a deliberate break from past dictates.

*

Pre-Raphaelite Brotherhood

Formed in 1848 by Dante Gabriel Rossetti, John Everett Millais and William Holman Hunt, the Pre Raphaelite-Brotherhood, the PRB, reacted against the formal painting conventions and teachings epitomised by Royal Academicians.

The PRBs advocated a return to a more natural style as they perceived being before Raphael and the Renaissance.

Mediaeval naturalism as opposed to highly formalised and stylised *'grandiose disregard of the simplicity of truth, the pompous posturing of the Apostles, and the unspiritual attitudinizing of the Saviour'* William Holman Hunt.

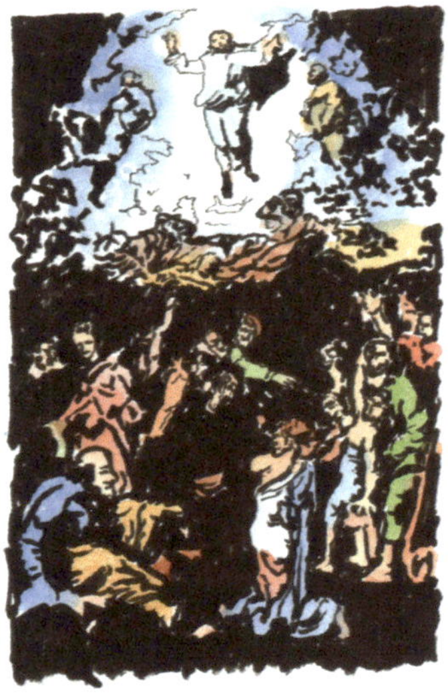

Supported by their principal proponent John Ruskin, the PRBs created an enormous stir in the Victorian art world that would not be the same again.

Look at these contrasting examples. Stylised posturing compared to natural reality.

Raphael *Transfiguration* 1516-20

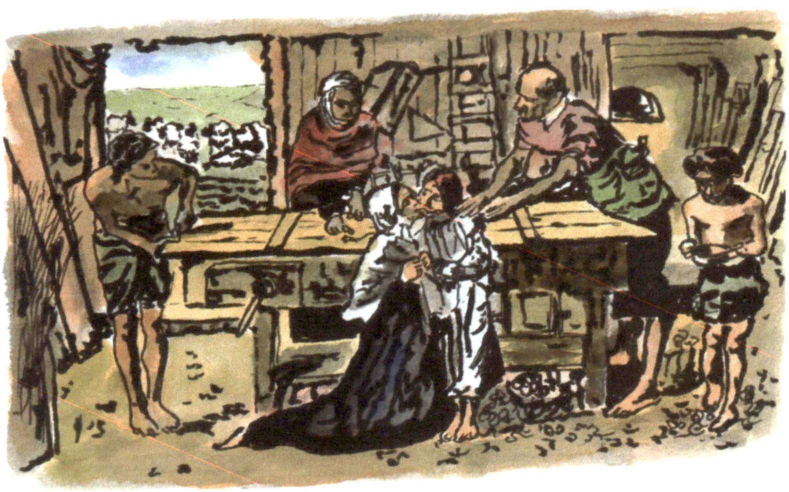

John Everett Millais *Christ in the House of His Parents* 1850

*

Beginnings of Modern Art

Returning to France, the academic art world witnessed the arrival of Édouard Manet.

Le Déjeuner sur l'herbe was rejected by the Salon in 1863. It was subsequently exhibited in the Salon des Refuses. A revolutionary new exhibition opportunity for those refused by the Academic Salon.

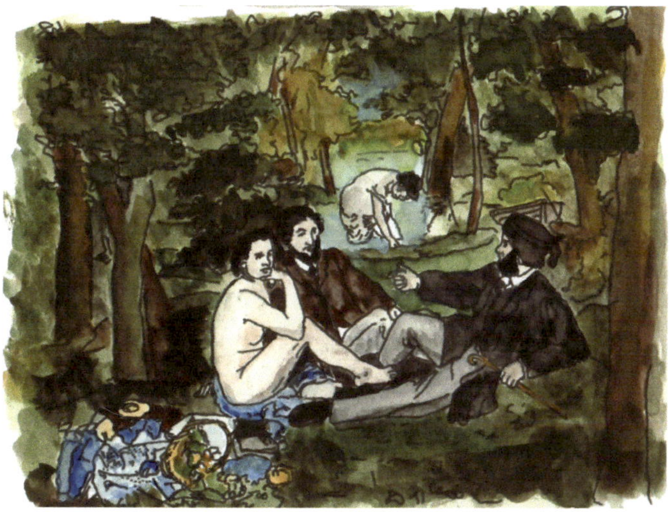

It depicts a nude woman sitting with two fully dressed dandies. She is staring directly at you and has the poise, appearance and attitude of an 'ordinary' woman who you would not normally expect to see depicted naked in a public park. An affront to the art world's sense of propriety, it caused notoriety and controversy.

Strong and obvious brush strokes. No real sense of perspective. Even unpainted areas of canvas. Layers of light and dark with colour so used in contrast to the stultifying conventions of academic normality.

Such controversy sealed Manet's name and like JMW Turner and later the PRBs in the UK, the French art world was never the same again.

Edouard Manet's subsequent 1863 *Olympia* sparked even greater controversy.

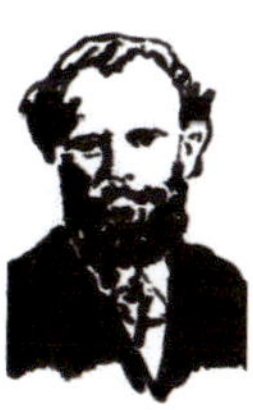

"Look at my *Olympia.* Realistically raw, brazen, unabashed, brutally factual, even obscene yet sublime. Think of yourself gazing at this figure.

Many people think of me as being one of the fathers of modern art. I certainly moved away from the traditional academic Salon and started to change society's attitudes and preconceptions and cultural assumptions, particularly in the way women were depicted and considered."

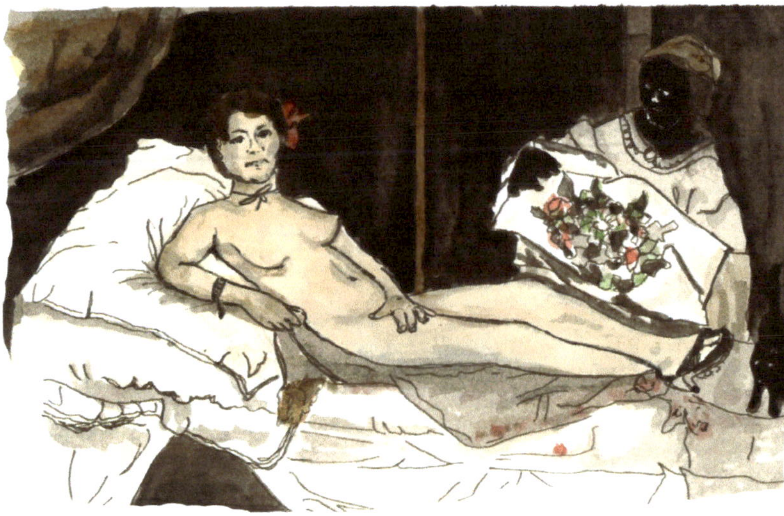

Again, a nude. This time obviously a prostitute, but rather than being demur and hiding her assets, she is looking out directly from the canvas at you, the viewer. Displaying herself as a purchasable commodity.

'Immoral and vulgar' was the response.

From this point in the two centres of the western art world, painting evolved more rapidly in terms of subject matter, composition, style and technique than ever seen before. The flood gates were opened to what we can now term the avant-garde.

Manet had visited Madrid Spain for a brief period. Brief because he couldn't get on with the food or heat. He journeyed there as he was so impressed with the work of Spanish artists, and particularly Francisco Goya. Displays of contrasting light. Realistic images of the human form away from the stylised perfection of the Greek and Roman ideal of beauty so evidenced at the Salon.

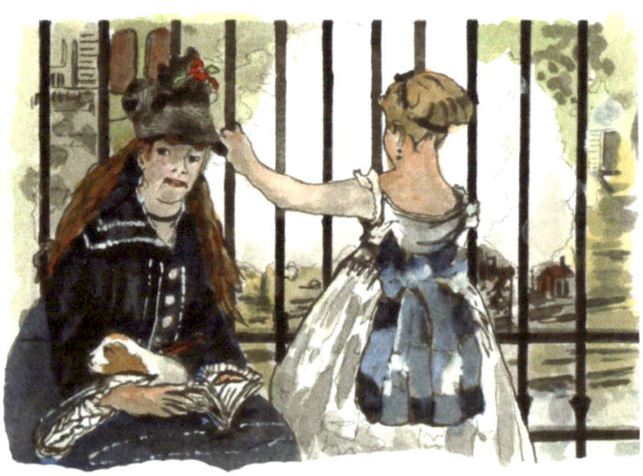

Édouard Manet

The Railway or *Gare Saint-Lazare*
1873

This picture caused yet another sensation for Manet. It was considered as symbolizing the rapid change occurring in Paris at the time, transforming life as it was known, accelerating into the modern uncertain age. Study the railings separating the figures with the railway, the old separated from the new perhaps? Look at the young girl yearning to be a part of the modern, yet her older companion preferring to remain static reading a book almost as a distraction from what is going on around her?

*

We now move on to how the Impressionists came about.

In 1863 the French Salon refused submissions as we know by Édouard Manet and also amongst others, Gustave Courbet and Camille Pissarro.

These artists set up their own exhibition nearby at the Salon des Refuses. This exhibition attracted such an enthusiastic following that the Emperor Napolean III formally endorsed the event in order to enhance his popularity with the average viewing public.

In 1869, Claude Monet and Pierre-August Renoir decided that they wanted a day out in the fresh air. Living in Paris it would have taken quite a time to journey to the countryside so instead they arrived at a parkland in the city's suburbs, La Grenouillére (the Frog Pond) and here they set up their easels and opened their paint boxes.

La Grenouillére could have been described as seedy and down and out, but nevertheless it was a most popular place of relaxation and recreation for the ordinary folk of Paris.

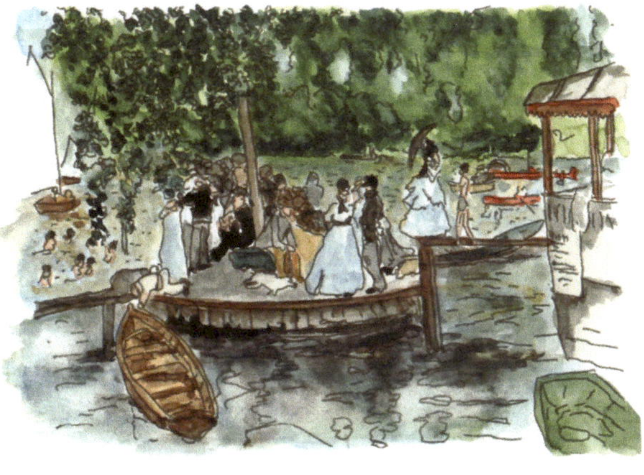

Pierre-August Renoir *La Grenouillére* 1869

With the sun, the activity, the movement and life and enjoyment all around them, the artists were in their element.

The resulting day's work was an unparalleled invention. The solid, unyielding physical world of water, people, buildings and even a dog was broken down into obvious broad, bold, rapid, staccato strokes of contrasting colours black, white, blue and green.

So was born **Impressionism.**

In 1874 the Société Anonyme was formed, and the Impressionists began exhibiting their own works away from the Salon. Derided for some time but eventually Impressionism became to be accepted. The Salon began losing popularity.

*

It's worth a thought at this point of the influence of photography.

From the mid-19th Century its development grew exponentially.

People associated with the invention and development of photography are Thomas Wedgewood, Nicéphore Niépce, Louis Deguerre and Willian Fox Talbot, and that's only the first half of the 19th century.

Look at paintings before the onset of photography and then when photography was really taking off.

Ask yourself: when did Impressionism start to take prominence? With Turner of course but as a generally accepted term with the Impressionists, in the 1860s. When did Cézanne work on his binocular view of still life, people and landscapes?

Photography was making tremendous progress in this era but it was monocular, that is from a single eye.

Where did that leave painting?

There was obviously still demand as there is today, for paintings of landscapes, still life and portraits.

With the progress photography was making, artists of an avant-garde disposition were then given a much greater opportunity to move on from pure representation.

Realistic depictions to greater experimentation. Artists did not have to simply concentrate on figurative narrative realism, they could experiment.

Was photography challenging painting? Not really. It simply provided another medium to capture an image and left artists to use their skills and techniques to illustrate the soul and character of the sitter, to use their artistic licence in respect of their interpretation of a subject matter - not a simple capturing of a face or a scene. To give us another dimension, another way of looking at things, to challenge our perspective, to look at the world and all within it from the uniqueness of the artist's interpretation.

Look at a photograph and a painted portrait and ask: can a photograph capture the soul and character of the subject in the same way as an artist can? Why is it that even today people visit photographers for their portrait picture but the demand for painted portraits is undiminished, at least for those who can afford them?

*

United States in the 19th Century.

The United States was emerging as a country following its War of Revolution against British imperialism.

In respect of the arts there is not a great deal to be aware of in terms of the evolutionary story of western art. However, what is worthy of note are four artists in particular.

James A. Whistler who is particularly well known for his painting *Whistler's Mother* 1871, although he painted this work in Chelsea, London.

Thomas Cole (1801-1848) painted spectacularly wonderful landscapes of the open, unpopulated scenes across the then known part of the nation. Symbolic of an emerging nation with a growing pride in its heritage.

Similarly, Emanuel Gottlieb Leutz painted the iconic *Washington Crossing the Delaware* in 1851.

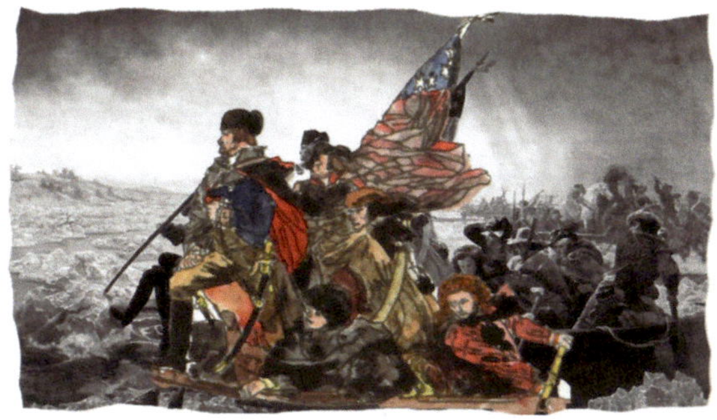

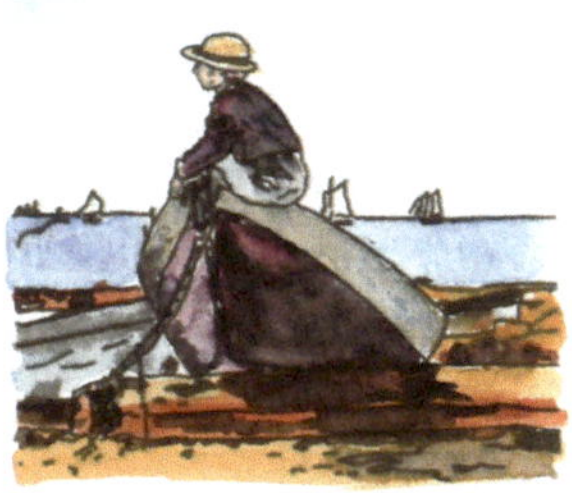

Winslow Homer (1836-1910) painted evocative seascapes in his home area of New England, whilst Mary Cassatt and John Singer Sargeant joined Whistler by leaving the United States and continuing their careers in Paris and London.

Winslow Homer *Waiting for Dad* 1873

It was not until the middle 20th Century that American art particularly came into its own with dramatic force and consequences as we shall find later.

*

French Realism

This period is particularly associated with the artists Gustav Courbet (1819-1877) and Jean-François Millet (1814 - 1875). These artists painted realistic representations of ordinary people in ordinary situations such as Millet's *Gleaners* painted in 1857.

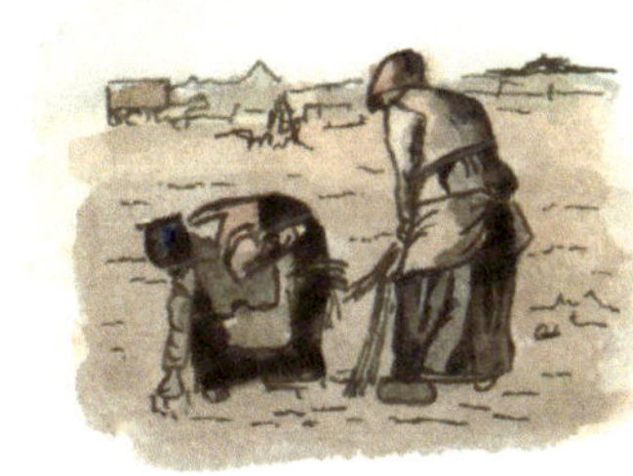

*

Impressionism

And so we return to Impressionism, reflecting the life and spirit of the age. The beginning of la Belle Epoque and the Gilded Age in America. Following the Franco-Prussian War of 1870-1871, peace, wealth and dynamic cultural creativity and experimentation. Democracy on the rise, authoritarianism on the decline, for the time being at least.

1870 and 1871. The French humiliated at Sedan. Paris besieged by the Prussians. People ate rats and dogs and froze in the winter. A deal. The Commune emerged. Riots and street violence. Thousands killed or incarcerated. Napoleon III fled to England. The dynasty collapsed.

And what did it produce? Édouard Manet. Impressionism. The belle epoque. Berthe Morisot, Pierre August Renoir and Claude Monet and the world was turned on its head with the birth of modern art.

The devastation, desperation, slaughter and instability of these years proved salutary to those avant-garde artists attempting to make sense of the situation and circumstances they found themselves in. Impressionism, the brief transience of life resolved on the canvas by the capturing of the ephemeral light, far removed from the hitherto solidity of fine art.

Following the gloom of 1870 and 1871 and the morbidity and concentration on classical, religious and mythological themes so prevalent as accepted fine art particularly at the Salon, Impressionism emerged with light, joyfulness, joie de vie, frivolous even and acknowledging existential fragility. A supreme dialecticism.

Years later Sigmund Freud summed up this emotionally fragile psychological state with the term, transient value. It's where we become aware of the unavoidable transience of things: life, nature, the seasons moving on and we therefore increase our perceived value of what matter to us. As we value things that are scarce, like life, thereby their value enhances.

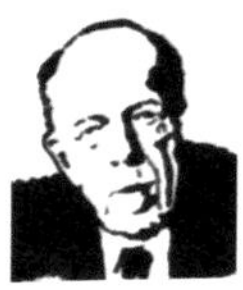

"It took some time before the public learned that to appreciate an Impressionist painting one has to step back a few yards and enjoy the miracle of seeing these puzzling patches suddenly fall into place and come to life before our eyes." Ernst Gombrich

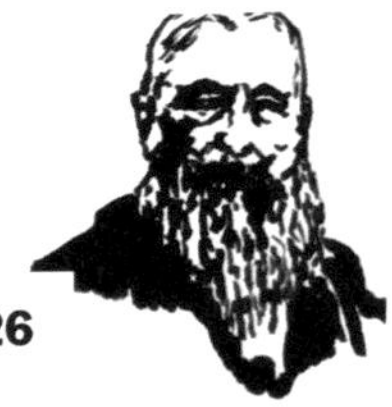

Claude Monet 1840-1926

"Our movement, the Impressionists may be considered one of the most important movements of art overall. Colour and the capturing of light and movement to the fore."

The return of the open dynamic brush strokes from the Salon perfectionism. Movement. Everyday scenes and people. Rapid capturing of light. No concentration on perspective, capturing the experience of the viewer and often painted outside the studio, plein-air.

Pure colours. Layer upon layer of iridescent colour. A vibrant flow of life and with *Impression Sunrise* below, almost spectral.

One of the first major Impressionist works Claude Monet's *Impression Sunrise* invited a newspaper reporter Louis Leroy writing for the French satirical newspaper Le Charivari, to use the term an 'impression'. The intention indeed was to satirise, but the term stuck and became the accepted and almost revered title for the movement.

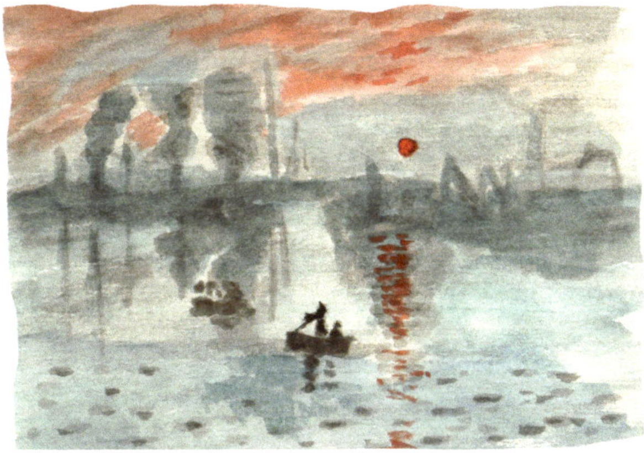

Claude Monet *Sunrise* 1872

From this point the evolution of art moved forward at a breathtaking pace. Modern Art was nurtured still further from Manet's instigation.

Claude Monet and the Impressionists were influenced by JMW Turner. We know that Monet was in London escaping the French-Prussian War in 1870 and the Siege of Paris 1871. We know that he visited an exhibition of Turner's work whilst in London.

So, was the Impressionist movement inspired by Turner's works such as *Rain, Steam and Speed* (1844)? Maybe.

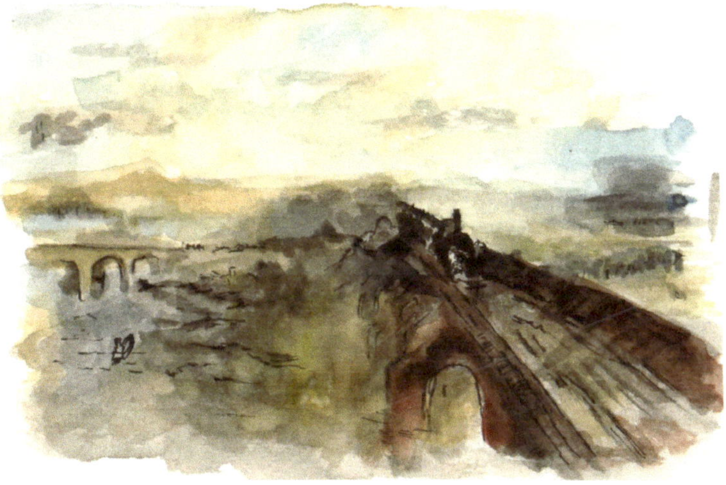

JMW Turner *Rain, Steam, Speed. The Great Western Railway* 1844

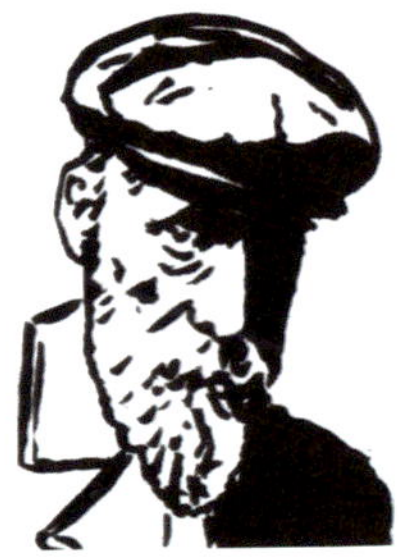

"Claude Monet and I achieved an interpretation of light and not merely a replication, or representation of the scene. An impression.

It could be said that we conquered light."

Pierre-August Renoir 1841-1919

"I'm Berthe Morisot and I'm one of the early pioneers of Impressionism. I lived in Paris during the years of the Siege and Commune and that experience significantly influenced my work. I came out of this time absolutely disgusted with my fellow men, even with my best friends. How as a demoralised artist could I respond? I concentrated on human relationships particularly mother and child. The impressionistic fragility of my work reflecting the flux and transience of life particularly symbolised by my concentrating on images of the especial vulnerability of women, babies and girls painted and conveyed by the capturing of light itself."

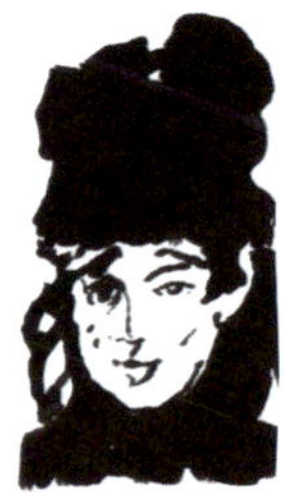

Berthe Morisot 1845-1895

Detail from her portrait painted by Édouard Manet 1872

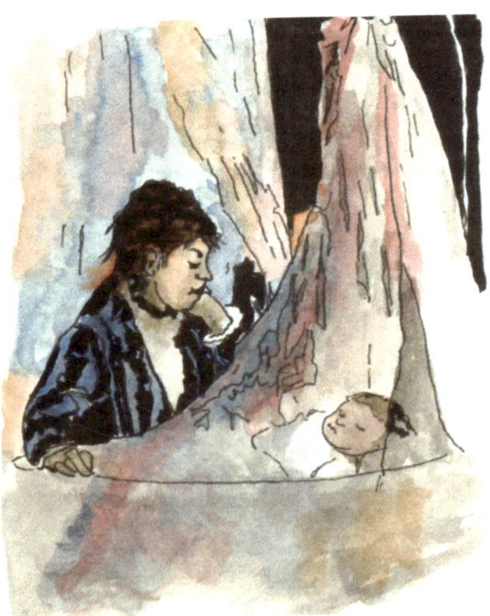

The Cradle 1872

Similar to Berthe Morisot's painting of her sister Edma with her new born in *The Cradle* showing the deep emotional bond reflecting the loving relationships between people and especially within the family, was also a familiar theme with the American artist Mary Cassatt (1844-1926)

***The Child's Bath* 1893**

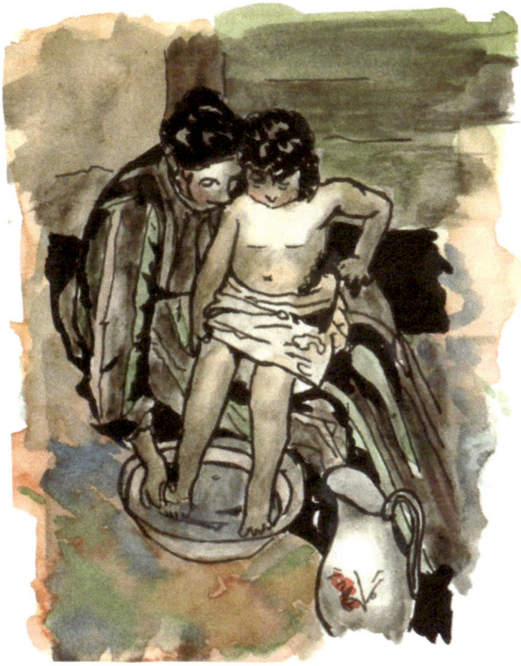

However, the academic world carried on with its formalised paintings for the time being even though the Salon declined in its power and influence in the 1880s.

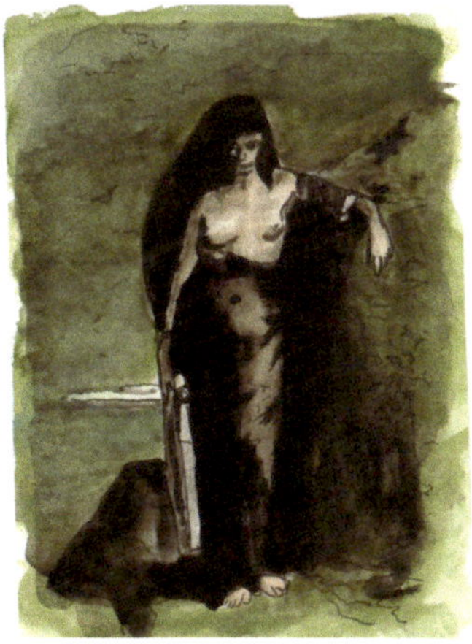

Charles Mengin 1853-1933

***Sappho* 1877**

Fantasy, ancient images and divorced subjects from reality, almost flawless perfectionism in its display: covering up what's true and perhaps even unacknowledging that it is a work by a human. Édouard Manet, John Constable, JMW Turner and others had brought back that human touch, proudly broadcasting that the painting was actually achieved by a person and not some sort of divine perfect creation.

*

Vienna Succession

Gustav Klimt (1862-1918) and Egon Schiele (1890-1918) are two principal artists representing this era.

The Vienna Succession was a free association of artists opposed to the official academic organisations.

Gustav Klimt's seductive and mysterious females, his nudes and charming male figures evoke an end of an era, the Hapsburg Empire in decline and the dissolution of monarchies across Europe leading to World War 1, The Great War.

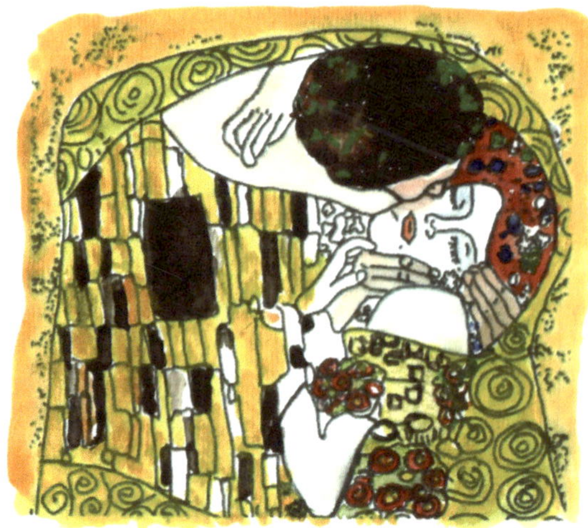

Klimt *The Kiss* 1908

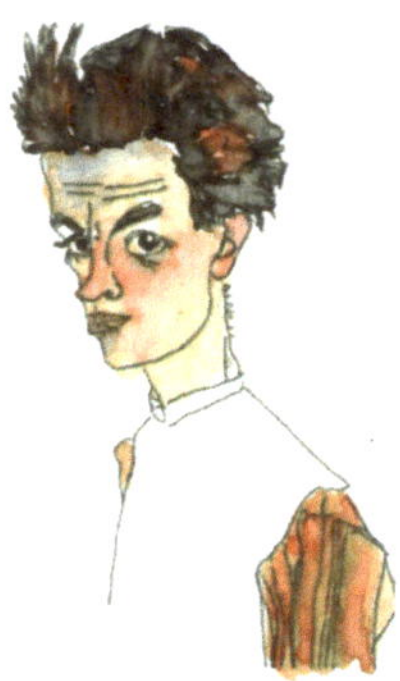

Self Portrait with Striped Shirt 1910

Egon Schiele influenced and was influenced by Expressionism.

*

Post Impressionism

At the end of the 19th Century a decisive game changer was dropped by artist Paul Cézanne in France. One of Cézanne's techniques was to acknowledge that we enjoy a binocular vision that is seeing with two eyes rather than a monocular view, thereby giving deeper dimensions to how we see things from different viewpoints. This distorts the tradition of linear perspective singular vanishing points.

Consequently because of this and further crucial changes that he made, Cézanne has subsequently been placed alongside Manet as being another father of modern art.

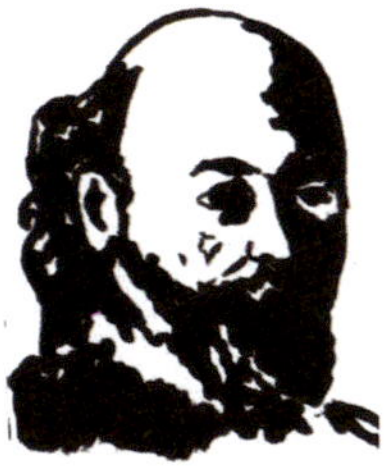

Paul Cézanne 1838-1906

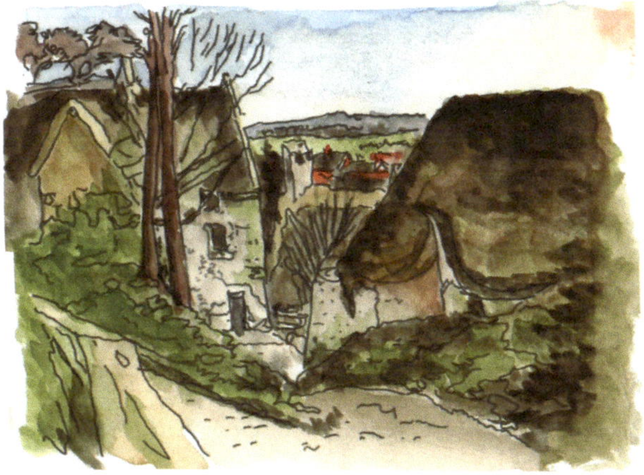

The Hanged Man's House
1873

"I've taken the impressionistic transient approach and mixed it with the solidity of the actual scene: the landscape and still life. And I'm not merely copying what I see with two eyes but attempting to represent the sensations I feel"

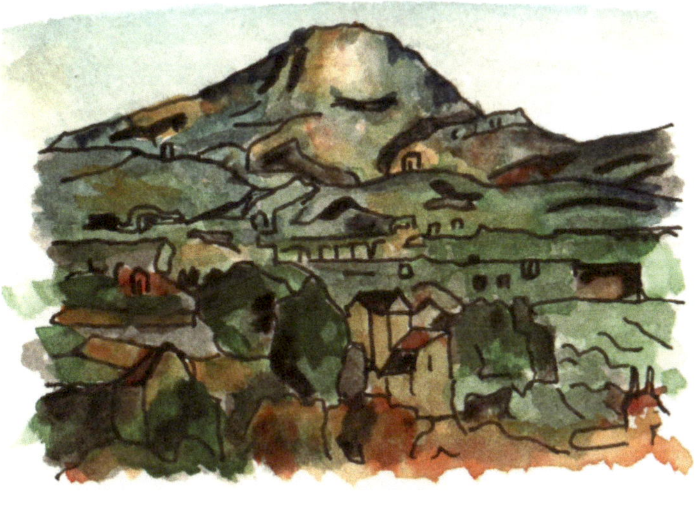

Mont St Victoire 1895

Breaking conventional rules of perspective, rapid and small brush strokes, emphasising plains of colour, blended the fluidity and light concentration of the Impressionists with the solidity of the object and the landscape and buildings and plants, Cézanne took centre stage in yet another evolutionary step forward.

Meanwhile, whilst Cézanne was making a name for himself, quietly working away first in Paris then in Arles South of France, there emerged yet another artist of significant importance, Vincent van Gogh.

*

Casting away all pretence of emulating the accepted norms and styles of art Vincent brought to his canvasses light, movement and a deeply personal interpretation of the world.

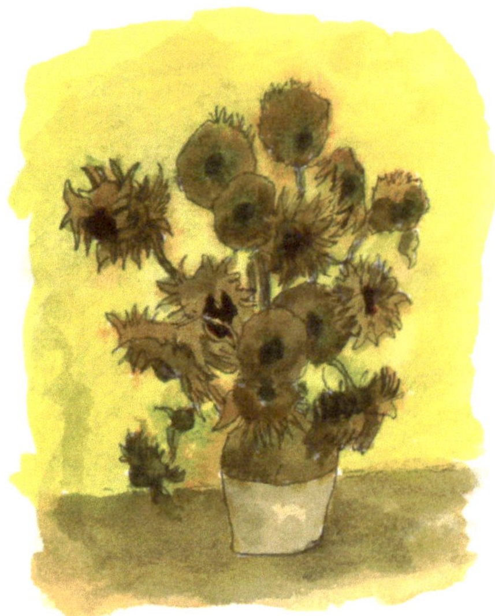

Vincent van Gogh 1853-1890 *Sunflowers* 1888

In 1888, Vincent was joined in Arles by his close friend Paul Gauguin. Vincent was hoping to establish an artists' colony in the town, but this turned out to be a pipe dream.

Gauguin had made a name for himself in the Brittany village of Pont Aven where he and his followers developed a movement we now term as Symbolism and this together with his work on cloisonnism and synthetism made Gauguin a major feature in avant-garde art.

These artists accentuated the expressive impact of individual sensations by completely excluding an objective reference to reality.

Symbolism – the inclusion of items symbolising various meanings for example St Michael fighting the Devil below. Cloisonnism – flat areas of colour and bold outlines and synthetism - neither form nor colour predominate but each has an equal role. All as can be seen in his work *Vision After the Sermon* 1888.

Whilst they continued their close friendship for many months eventually Gauguin found Vincent's behaviour and adherence to his own style too much to bear. Gauguin returned to Paris in January 1889 but on the eve of his departure Vincent cut off part of his ear. Gauguin was mortified and sat by Vincent's bedside until he felt compelled to leave.

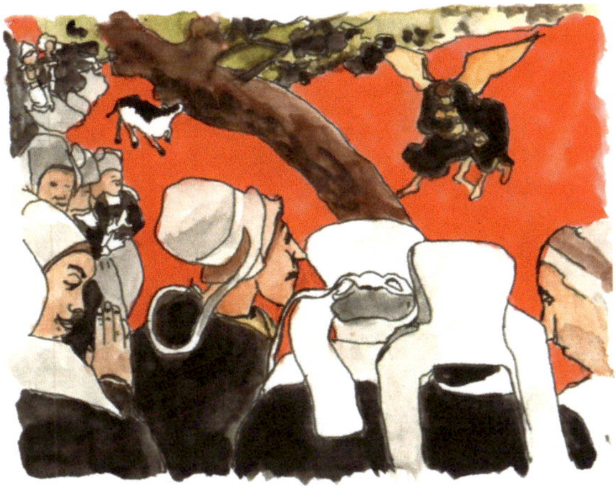

Vincent shortly after admitted himself into a sanctuary where he completed many of his most famous works before allegedly committing suicide.

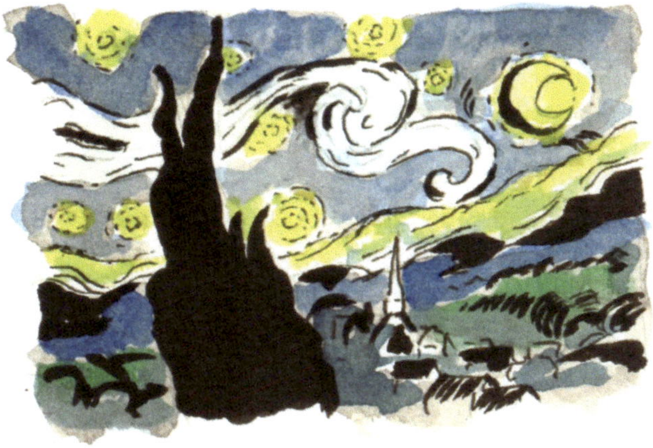

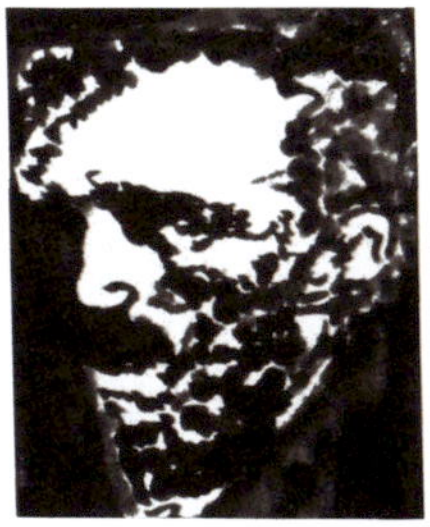

Vincent van Gogh 1853-1890

"Maybe I was insane, maybe not but I certainly painted to maintain my sanity."

Paul Gauguin travelled to Tahiti occasionally returning to France. Gauguin's style of symbolism, cloisonnism and synthesism was richly developed in Tahiti and mark him out as a genius in the evolution of Modern Art. A major step forward in the avant-garde.

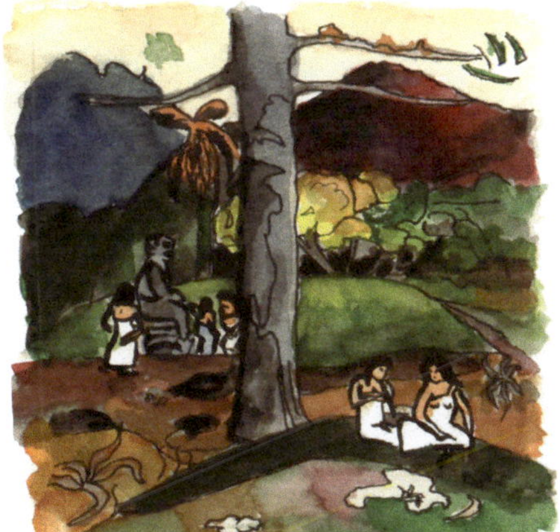

Paul Gauguin *Mata Mua* 1892

It is important to mention at this point that the Impressionists and artists such as Paul Gauguin and Vincent van Gogh were deeply influenced by art coming from the country recently opened to trade in the mid-19th century, Japan.

Initially arriving in Europe in the form of wrapping paper around various goods, the style of Japanese art inspired many artists of the time. Works such as by Utagawa Hiroshige (1797-1858). Clear lines. Bold colours. No obvious reference to perspective.

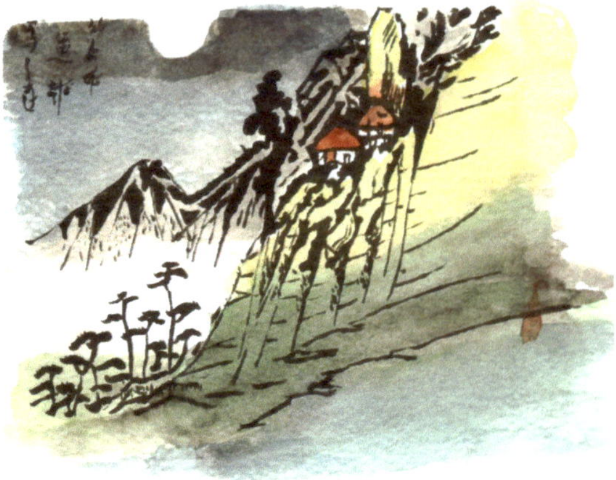

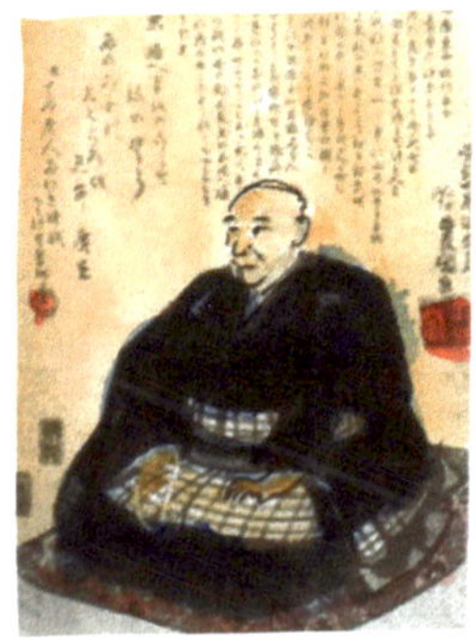

Reflections of the Moon in the Rice Fields of Sarashina in Shinshu.
Woodblock print

And Katsushika Hokusai's 1831 *The Great Wave off Kanagawa*

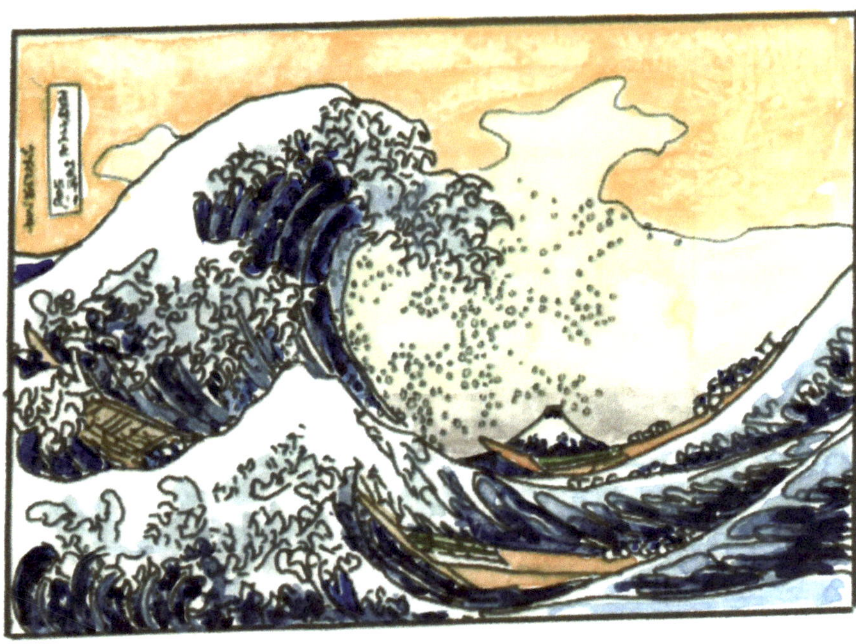

Japanese artists such as Hiroshige and Hokusai were following the style of imagery known as *ukiyo-e.* There is a school of thought that the *ukiyo-e* style was actually influenced by the import of prints of pictures from the Dutch Golden Age. The Dutch were the only European country to have significant trading posts in Japan during the 16/17th Centuries.

*

It was the London Bloomsbury Group's artist and art critic Roger Fry who termed artists such as van Gogh and Gauguin as Post-Impressionists at an exhibition he organised in 1910, and this event further enhanced the Post Impressionists' prestige in the avant-garde world of art.

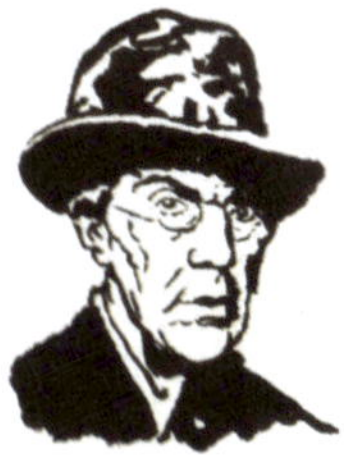

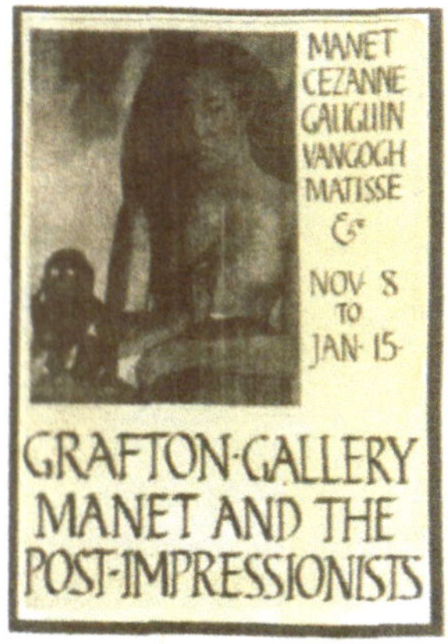

*

Meanwhile in the UK and USA, the Arts and Crafts Movement blossomed. Taking the decorative arts to a high level of prestige and importance, restoring man-made crafts from the machinery of the Industrial Revolution and the factory dominance of products.

Two principal proponents of the Arts and Crafts movement were William Morris in the UK and Louis Comfort Tiffany in the USA.

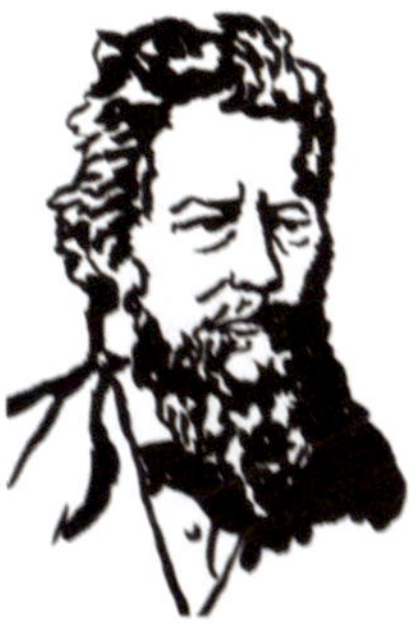

William Morris
1834-1896

"We really made an enormous contribution to the decorative arts for the day-today enjoyment of all. Household goods, lighting, wallpaper and jewellery. Also, architecture, ceramics and furniture."

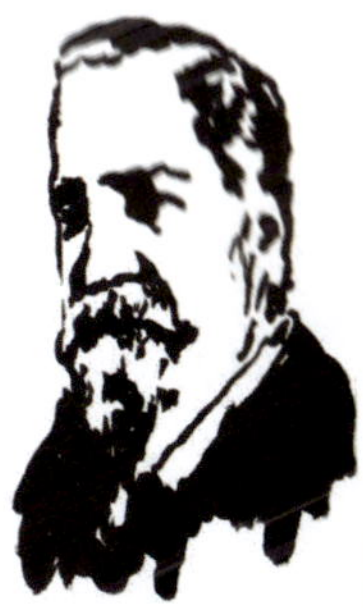

Louis Comfort Tiffany
1848-1933

*

Now that we've arrived at the end of the 19th century, perhaps it's time for gathering some definitions. But before we start let's set a little context.

Flat Earth or Round

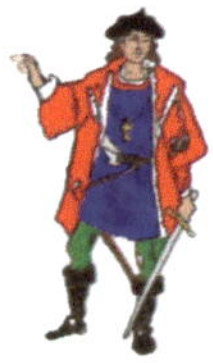

Christopher Columbus sailed the Atlantic Ocean and became the second European to discover the Americans in 1492. Maybe the Viking Leif Erikson was the first. However, the point is that doubts began that the Earth was not flat even though that thought had been theorised by the Ancient Greeks and Romans many years before.

The proof came with Ferdinand Magellan who started his journey in 1519, and his surviving crew returned in 1522 (Magellan was killed in a battle in the Philippines in 1521) having become the first Europeans to circumnavigate the globe without falling off the edge.

The Earth was round after all.

This forced a rethink of dramatic proportions. People had the opportunity to now turn previous concepts, ideas and hitherto received wisdom completely on their head.

And that's what Modern Art and Modernism is about. Enabling you to turn previous rules, traditions and what was recognised as art around and think and see things differently from a new and fresh perspective.

Open up your mind and indulge in new ways of perception and concept thinking and see if Modernism and Modern Art becomes more attainable and fulfilling.

*

Modern Art and Modernism are terms that cover art from the mid-19th century to our recent times where we now have Post Modernism. What do these terms mean?

Modern Art is the definitive term to cover particular art movements from roughly that of JMW Turner to the 1970s. For example, Impressionism is Modern Art.

Modernism is the broad term applied to the trends and movements, philosophy, approaches of culture, literature, music, architecture and design as well as art from again the mid-19th Century to the present times. However, there are also schools of thought that apply the term Modernism to post-World War II culture and again to the beginnings of Post Modernism.

Departing and breaking away from traditional art conventions, Modern Art and Modernism emphasised innovation, and how art should be understood. Essentially redefining what art is all about. The avant-garde. It rejected the prevalence of the natural and academic in art that is, realistic depictions and Royal Academy and Salon purities in favour of experimentations and issues of human experiences and art.

Art moving away from true representation towards abstraction with more of a focus on colour, shape and line.

The artist's personal vision and emotional experience to the fore. Subjective interpretation rather than objective reality.

Furthermore, Modern Art and Modernism show enormous style diversity for example from Impressionism to Abstract Expressionism, a world of difference in style and approaches.

Modernism reflects the complexities of a rapidly changing and uncertain world. Influenced by technological advances, societal, economic, secular changes and new foundations of philosophical thought.

Advocates felt they were in a brave new world completely different from the past; thus, art had to move forward and find its own identity with the artist and their vision pivotally central. What is art? The representation of reality? The unconscious, states of mind, spiritual, emotions, social functions? Dreamlike? Discovering the fundamental truths – whatever they are? For example, with Surrealism.

In other words, anything goes, and anything went.

Post Modernism: that definition will be covered when we reach that stage.

*

Cubism

Central to this evolution is the movement Cubism. The artists especially featured with Cubism are of course Pablo Picasso and Georges Braque.

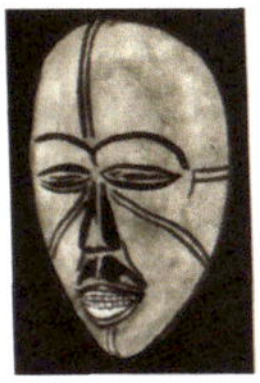

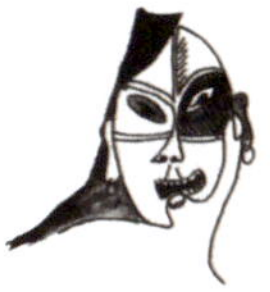

Detail from Pablo Picasso's

Les Demoiselles d'Avignon 1908

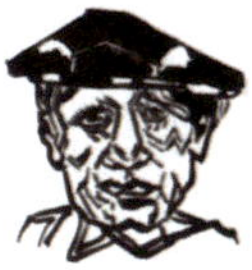

"I'm considered one of the greatest artists and indeed in terms of the avant-garde my Cubism, together with my friend Georges Braque has been placed on a pedestal. I did create a great business from my works. I later moved to very serious political and social conscience works, for instance my *Weeping Woman* and *Guernica*."

Pablo Picasso 1881-1973

Look at the influence of Picasso's hobby of collecting African art together with the 'cubist' 'plains of colour' buildings and landscapes of Cézanne and you can see how it all developed. A new way of depicting form in space as if from binocular multiple viewpoints and breaking things down to geometric shapes.

As Picasso could have said **"this is how I see things: things are always moving. How can you fix a face in one spot. Look at it from moving your angle of viewing and you can see what I'm getting at. Cézanne's binocular viewpoints"**

The western art avant-garde had firmly rejected the academic world, and nothing would be the same again.

Georges Braque

The Guitar: Statue d' Épouvante

1913

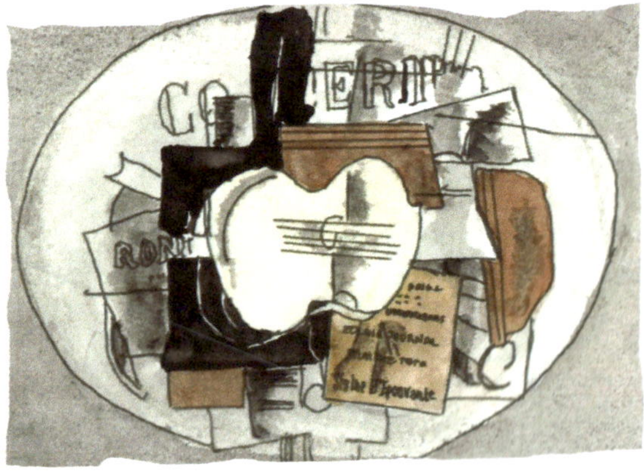

The Dialectic

Let's take a little breather and consider the philosophy of Georg Wilhelm Friedrich Hegel.

Briefly and in as simple terms as possible, Hegel maintained that the history of man's development, including art history, is based on the premise of dialecticism.

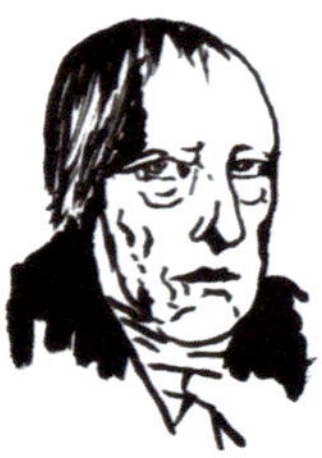

"We start off with the situation as it is, what we'll call: the THESIS. This is reacted against and this we'll name: the ANTITHESIS. This then settles down to an agreed outcome we'll now refer to as: the SYNTHESIS"

Georg Wilhelm Friedrich Hegel 1770 – 1831

What Hegel was basically getting at was the human desire to move on from what is accepted and established to something different, maybe even revolutionary, in contrast to. This then again eventually becomes established and accepted and in due course is once again reacted against. A dialectical cycle keeping things on the move, forever developing and evolving.

"Art is what is has become the fashion to call a dialectical activity; it confronts one thesis, say that of reason, with its antithesis, say that of imagination, and evolves a new unity or synthesis in which the contradictions are reconciled." So stated Herbert Read, an influential British art historian in his book *Art and Society* published in 1936.

We now see this dialecticism particularly prevalent in Modern Art and Modernism: forward, change, establish, forward, change, establish and on and on.

*

Moving further into the Modernism of the 20th Century

So, into the 20th Century we journey with the history and influences of the Renaissance, Mannerism, Baroque and Rococo. We've seen various movements such as the Romanticists the PRB and the Impressionists. Symbolism and Cubism. And so forth.

All paving the way for any style, technique and movement. Anything can be called art. Any creative outcome is avant-garde. The doors are open like never before.

Let's continue to enjoy our conversation with those pictures in front of us, adventuring into our own times to explore their evolutionary history and what brought them to where they are now.

*

Expressionism

Herbert Read: "Expressionist art is an art that gives outward release to some inner pressure, some internal necessity. That pressure is generated by emotion, feeling, or sensation, and the work of art becomes a vent or safety-valve through which the intolerable psychic distress is restored to equilibrium."

In pre-World War I Germany and the succeeding Weimar Republic, Expressionism attempted to portray emotions, moods and ideas purely from a subjective angle. Distorted perspectives, violent contrasts, exaggerated angularities. Harshness of features lines and colours. Perhaps even instabilities reflecting the artists' own emotions. Expressionism.

The particular movements associated with Expressionism in Germany were the Die Brücke, the Berlin and Dresden Secession and Der Blaue Reiter groups and in Paris, the School of Paris.

Edvard Munch of Norway is attributed with being part of the Expressionist movement.

Ernst Ludwig Kirchner was a leading German Expressionist.

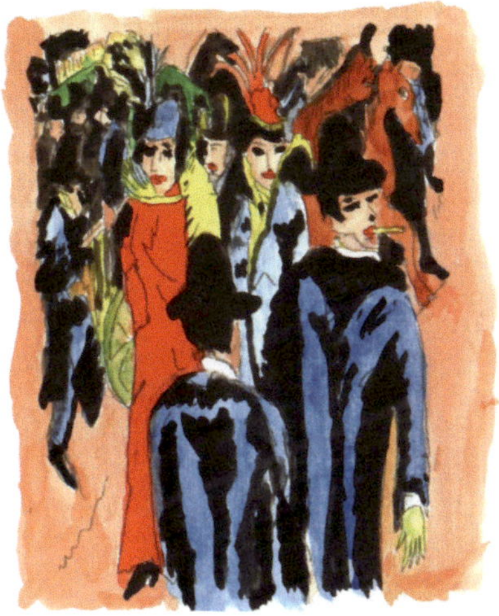

Ernst Ludwig Kirchner
***Berlin Street* 1913**

*

Fauvism

The fauves or wild beasts. Deliberately disturbing the viewer visually and emotionally by employing vivid colours and dramatically fierce brush strokes. Henri Matisse's *Femme*, modelled by his wife Amélie Parayre.

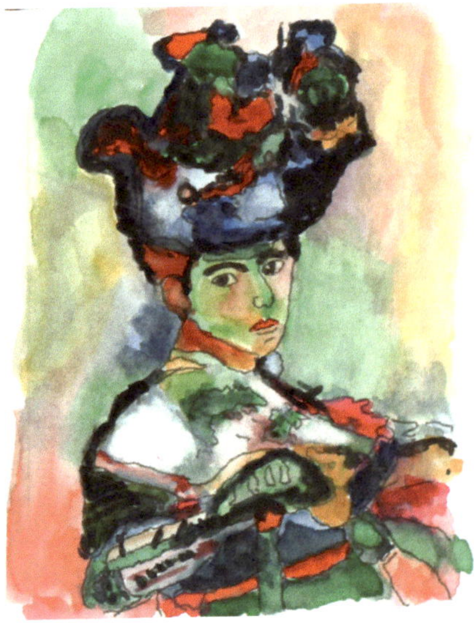

Henri Matisse

Femme au Chapeau

1905

*

Constructivism and Suprematism

"Following the Russian Revolution I attempted to make order out of chaos. I'm proud that my work *Black Square* is considered to be the first completely non-representational painting, upsetting conventional concepts of art language and subject matter. I'm told that *Black Square* is one of the most important works of the 20th Century."

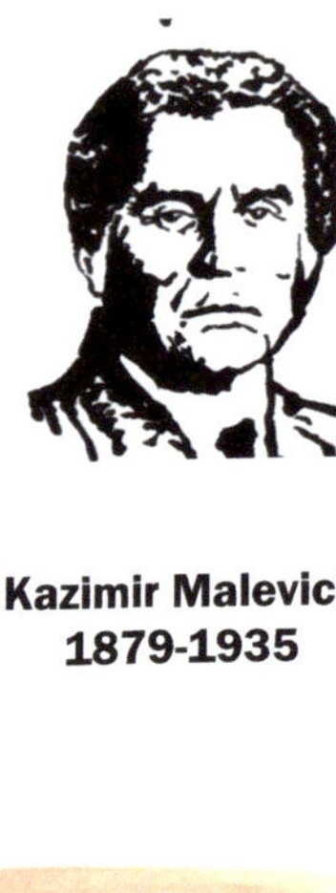

Kazimir Malevich
1879-1935

Vorticism

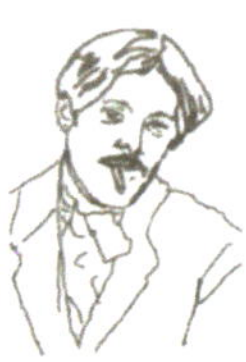

"I'm Wyndham Lewis and I painted my *Vorticist* in 1912 and I started the Vorticist movement"

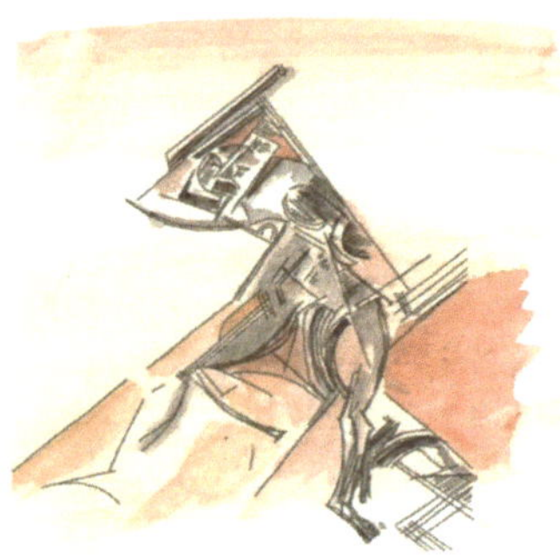

The Vorticism style was about the same time as the Italian Futurists, following the early days of Cubism. Can you spot similarities in style – the angularities? Horizontals and verticals? Mechanistic images? Movement – that is no single plane of the objects depicted? Influenced by Cubism and as we saw, that from Cézanne and African art.

*

Italian Futurism. Capturing the modern era with its speed, sound, electricity and excitement as well as bold colours. Cubism to depict motion.

The Italian poet Filippo Tommaso Marinetti proposed its raison d'etre with his 'Manifesto of Futurism'. **"We say that the world's magnificence has been enriched by a new beauty: the beauty of speed. Time and space died yesterday"** All fine but then Marinetti went on to say: **"War is the highest form of modern art"** He soon changed his tune during WWI.

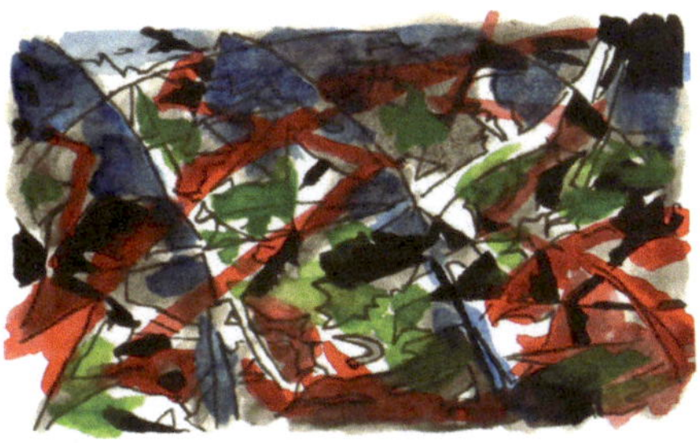

Abstract Speed and Sound, 1914

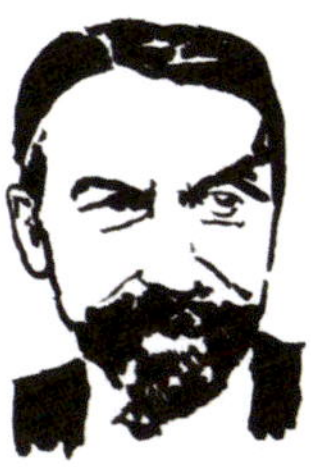

Giacomo Balla 1871 – 1958

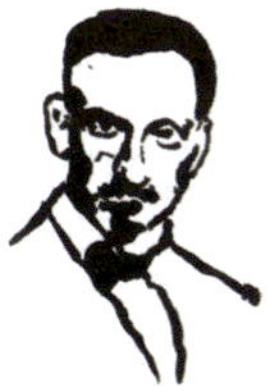

Luigi Russolo

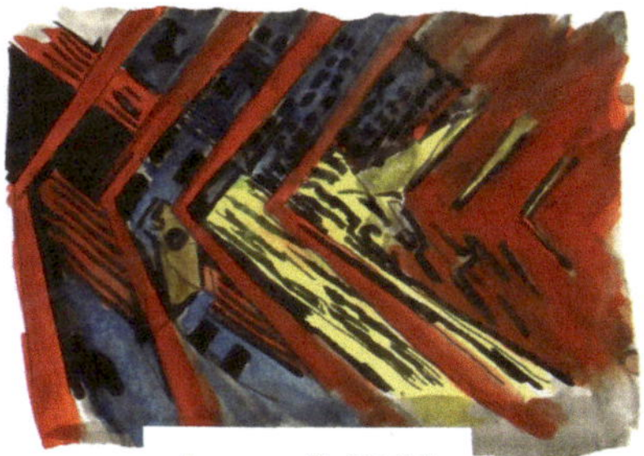

La revolt 1911

*

Dadaism.

Anti-war and the bourgeois. Political and satirical. Often appearing as nonsense.

Following The Great War, World War I, a group of artists previously resident in safe Zurich, inspired other artists such as Marcel Duchamp and Georges Grosz to create nihilistic works undermining social, political and cultural orthodoxies in reaction to the slaughter of World War I.

It became an international movement.

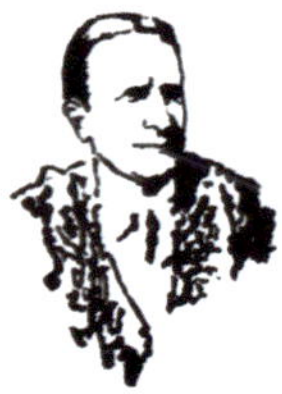

"Bonjour. Marcel Duchamp here. This is a small part of my 1915-23 early Surrealist work called: *The Bride Stripped Bare by her Bachelors, even.* Subject matter? Be brave and look it up!"

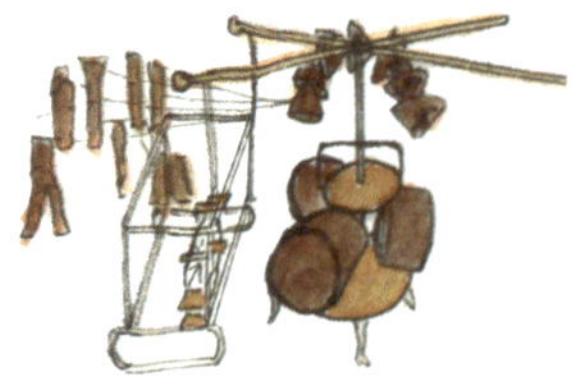

Marcel Duchamp is also well known for his *Fountain*.

Monday 2 April 1917. New York. Marcel Duchamp walks near Central Park to Broadway and 5th avenue.

The Frenchman visits a store: J L Mott Iron Works.

He rummages. He buys. A urinal. He returns to his studio. He turns the urinal over and signs it R. Mutt 1917 (after Mott) and calls it the *Fountain*, a ready-made.

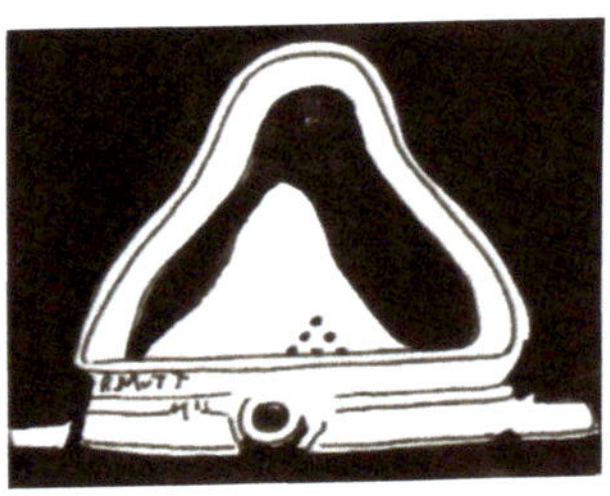

This was an idea 'from' an artist as opposed to a work 'by' an artist. AN IDEA!

He is a member of the anti-art establishment Society of Independent artists.

They're holding an exhibition. He enters his *Fountain*.

It's a critique of the money greedy speculative art collectors. Exposing a bogus, he's challenging the very notion of what constitutes a 'work of art' as decreed by art academics and critics and the self-elected and largely unqualified arbiters of taste.

'If an artist said something was work of art, having influenced its context and meaning, then it was a work of art'.

It's caused a revolution.

The rest is history. The *Fountain* was removed as bad taste. It disappeared but not before the photographer Alfred Stiglitz (husband of the artist Georgia O'Keeffe) photographed it and it became notorious. The power of an idea – you cannot un-invent them.

It was a legitimate work of art and as such documented. Stiglitz's photograph secured its longevity. It is now considered the first avant-garde conceptual ready-made work of art.

*

And with George Grosz's *The Grey Day* 1921, we have a plump affluent architect, a young disabled ex-soldier and a wall being built to separate? New industry re-building a new Germany whilst the past walks by on its stick.

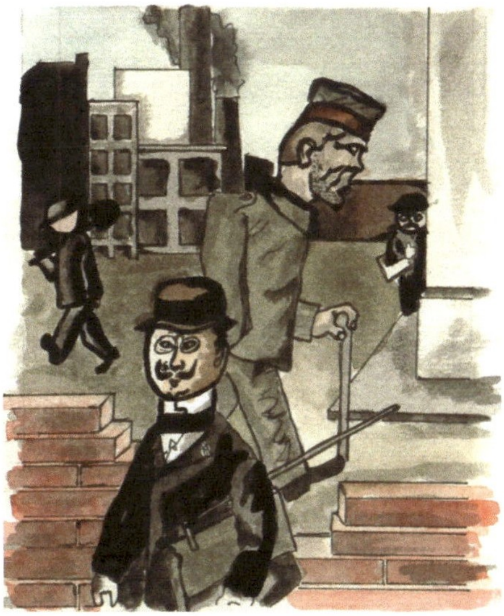

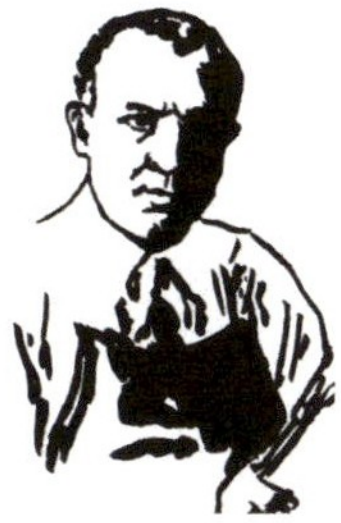

George Grosz
1893-1959

"Nihilism of the deformities of society: Dadaism"

*

American Modernism

Meanwhile in the United States, modern art was quietly moving on a pace, and the artist Georgia O'Keeffe has been attributed with playing a pivotal role in the evolution of American Modernism and its relationship with the avant-garde movements of Europe.

Works such as this by O'Keeffe can be seen to reject history and conservative values such as realistic depiction of subjects with innovation and experimentation with form for instance the shapes, colours and lines that make up her work. O'Keeffe gave her subjects an emotional aura viewing the harmonisation of shape and choice of colour.

O'Keeffe painted her original art works until well into her late age and *'Music, Pink and Blue No.2'* is one of her earliest and is an example of a forerunner to what became her most distinctive style.

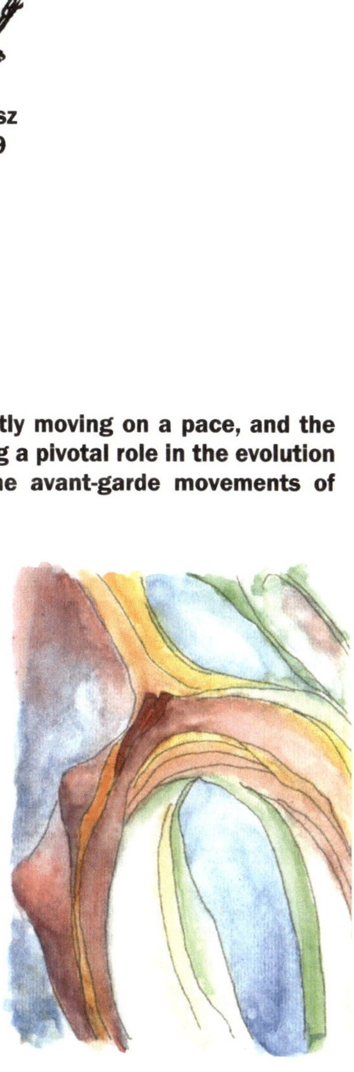

Music, Pink and Blue No. 2 1918

*

Neo-Plasticism

Primary colours and angularities to create balanced forms. An attempt at order and restoration between the wars.

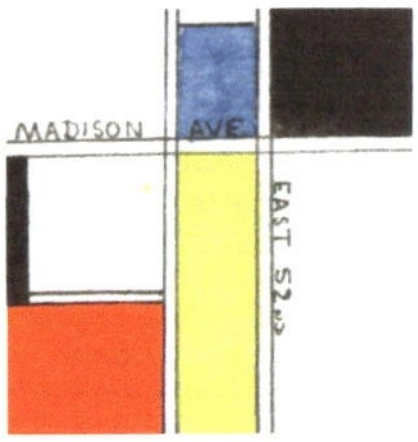

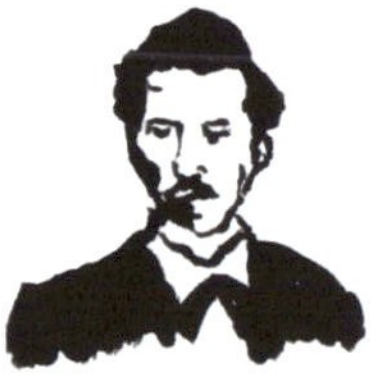

"I painted my *Composition in Blue and Yellow* in 1935. What does it remind you of? An aerial view? You work it out, for me it's a geometric."

Piet Mondrian 1872-1944

*

Abstraction

No reference to reality. Completely without any figurative images. Patterns and splashes of colour and line only. This movement is best exemplified by the artist Wassily Kandinsky.

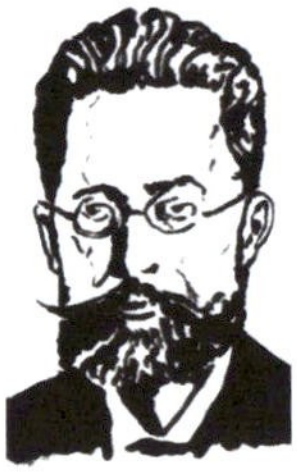

"I have a neurological anomaly called synaesthesia. When I see colours, I hear music. When I smell a flower, I can taste it too. My senses all lead into one another. My abstract works, it's painting taste or music"

Wassily Kandinsky 1866-1944

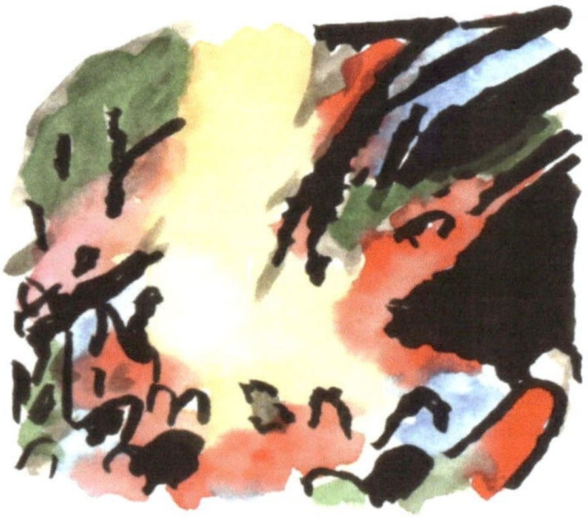

*

Bauhaus

A school established in Weimar Germany in 1919 to unify avant-garde visual art with architecture and design. Walter Gropius was its leader, and he managed to escape Nazi Germany where Bauhaus was frowned upon and via London ended up as an influential resident in The Berkshires New England.

*

Surrealism

Thought's dictation, psychic automatism where artists expressed the actual functioning of thought and the absence of any control exercised by reason and devoid of any influence from the aesthetic or moral concerns.

Spreading across the globe from Paris in the 1920s and 1930s. It aimed to tap into the sub-conscious to release culture from conscious thought, logic and reasoning.

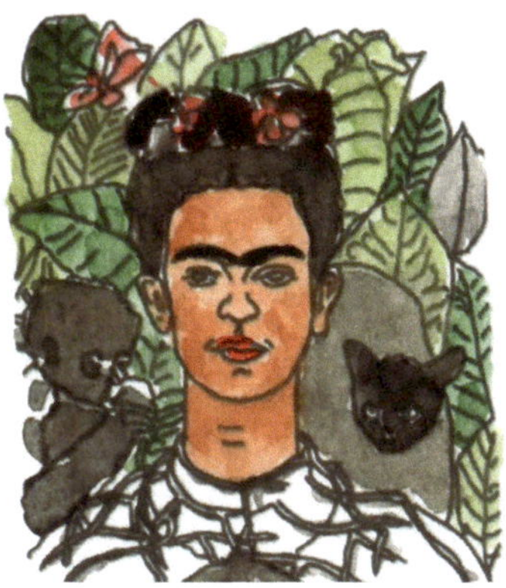

The French poet André Breton gave the cause its foundations with his 1924 manifesto on Surrealism: "...the superior reality of forms of associations hitherto neglected in the almightiness of dreams, in the disinterested play of thought..."

André Breton recognised the Surrealist aspect of the work of Frida Kahlo and invited her to exhibit in Paris, which she accepted.

Sir Roland Penrose (1900-1984) was an influential British Surrealist painter.

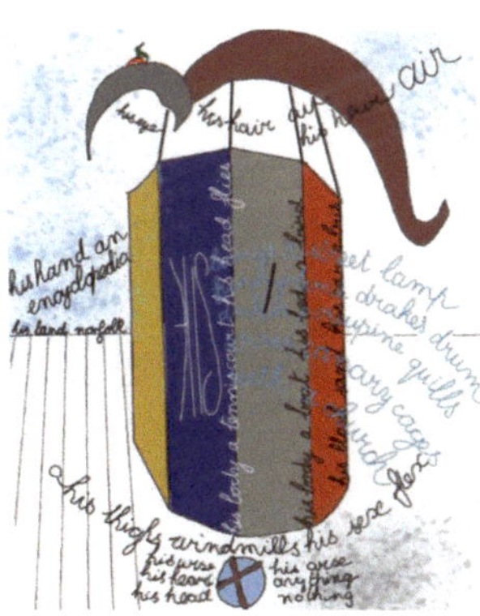

***Portrait* 1939**

But it is Salvidor Dali who we particularly associate with Surrealism.

"Salvador saying hello to you. I'm scratching myself with a part of my *Metamorphosis of Narcissus* painted in 1937. Subject matter – Surrealist dream imagery."

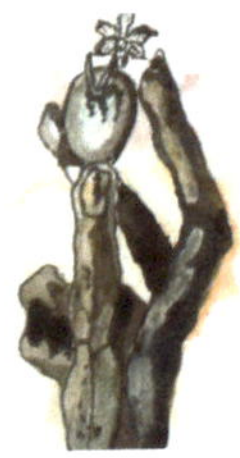

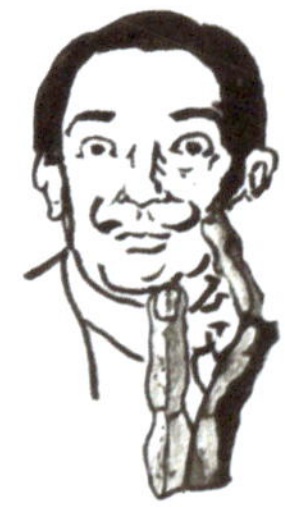

Salvidor Dali
1904-1989

Perhaps Francis Bacon could be included in the movement?

Although whilst not strictly Surrealist, pictures such as this could be interpreted as exploring the subconscious with its fantastic and distorted creatures. Francis Bacon 1945 *Three Studies for Figures at the Base of a Crucifixion.* Subject matter: apparently Bacon based these figures on an Ancient Greek myth and influenced by Cimabue's *Christ on the Cross.* They were to form only a predella to his additional crucifixion painting which never materialised. Imagine these menacing figures forming the platform to a modern crucifixion interpretation. Terrifying.

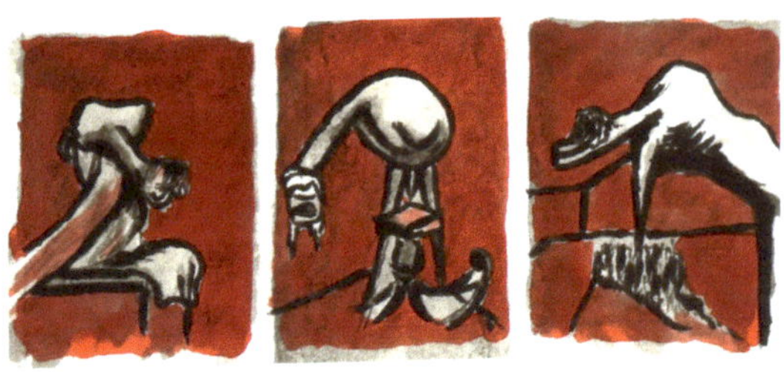

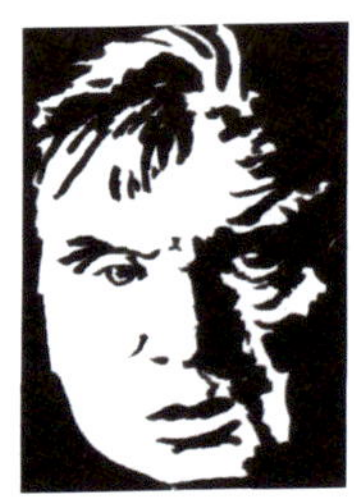

Francis Bacon
1909-1992

*

Existentialism

Jean-Paul Sartre and his partner Simone de Beauvoir, philosophers and feminists living in Paris France after WWII postulated that human life was essentially without meaning. We are all nauseatingly responsible solely for ourselves. We are individually completely alone and totally free to make our own decisions.

Not really an art movement although sculptors such as Giacometti it is said, attempted to follow the existentialist philosophy with his works.

*

Abstract Expressionism

It was at this point that together with Wölfflin, Read and Gombrich arguably one of the most influential art critics of the 20th century rose to prominence. Clement Greenburg.

Sitting comfortably in New York, just before Europe was involved in the Second World War, Clement Greenburg maintained that it was the positive effect of the Enlightenment that led to the social attitudinal circumstances that allowed the avant-garde to exist: freedom of expression.

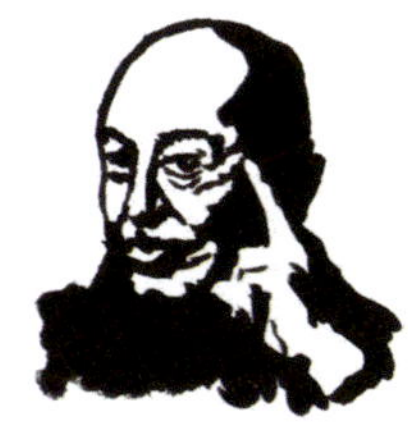

Greenberg went on to say that industrialisation led to money in ordinary peoples' pockets, people who found that they wanted a slice of culture that had previously only been the domain of the wealthy or in earlier times, the Church.

This led to the production of kitsch – because these ordinary people couldn't afford avant-garde art, but they wanted their slice of culture. Or maybe they simply didn't appreciate the avant-garde.

So, what did Greenberg mean by kitsch? *"Kitsch – uses for its raw material the debased and academicized simulacra* (definition: representation or imitation of a person or thing) *of genuine culture ..."*

By which we presume he means top rank avant-garde culture, which most of us cannot afford.

...Kitsch is vicarious experience and faked sensations. Kitsch pretends to demand nothing of its customers except their money – not even their time."

Kitsch is a German word meaning a low concocted form of culture and as Greenberg was writing in 1939 this was at the time of Soviet and Nazi repression of Modern Art and Modernism in particular.

After World War II Greenberg promoted the view that America was the guardian of Modernism as epitomised in the works of Pollock, Newman, de Kooning and Still. '*Medium specificity*' that is art works purely about the medium, for instance the paint and canvas itself, in contrast to post Renaissance attempts at perspective and visual representational illusion. So not kitsch, but the true sense of modern-day avant-garde.

That is what the American art world was now contributing whilst the rest of the world was recovering from the devastation of the War and Paris being the former centre of the art world, would never recover.

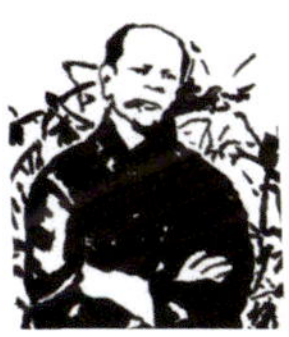

Centred particularly in New York City, its artists tried to express their emotions through abstract works.

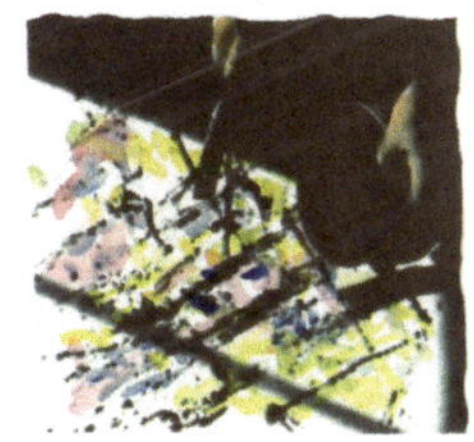

Jackson Pollock (1912-1956) used his drip technique. The focus was on the creation of the work as well as the end result. **"Energy and motion made visible"**. Jackson didn't title his works but simply numbered them so that the viewer would not be distracted from the work's final appearance.

Mark Rothko used broad areas of colour to ingrain into our emotional psychology.

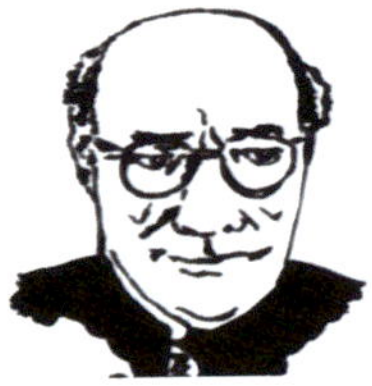

Mark Rothko 1903-1970

Barnett Newman used monochrome plains of colour.

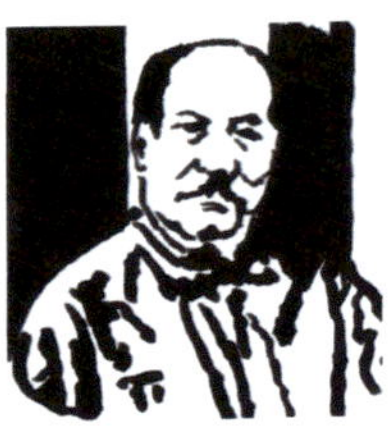

Barnett Newman 1905-1970

William de Kooning, rapid energetic broad colourful brushstrokes with no attempt at true representation.

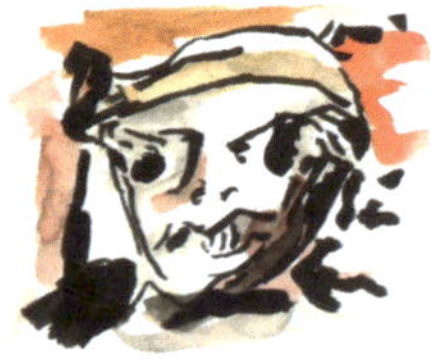

William de Kooning 1904-1997

*

Pop Art

Ferdinand Léger (1881-1955) could be considered a progenitor of Pop Art with works such as his 1939 '*Portrait*'.

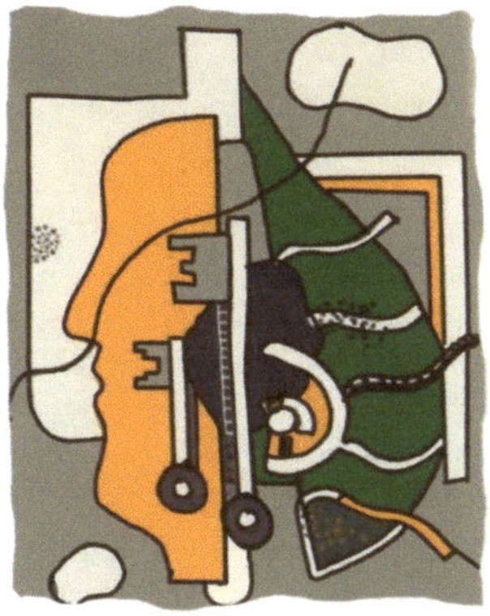

In Britain and America, artists were inspired by popular culture. Of particular note was the artist, Roy Lichenstein.

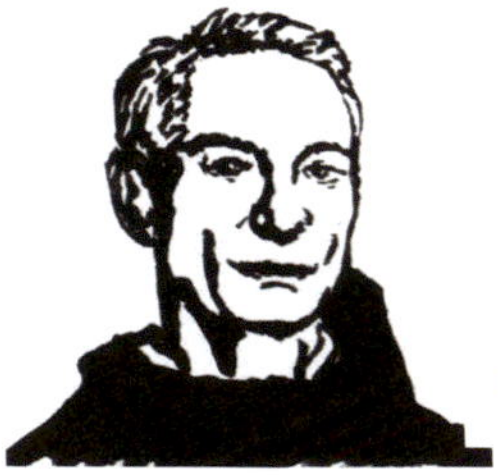

"This is my response to my son who in 1961 challenged me to paint Mickey Mouse. Pop Art."

Roy Lichenstein 1923-1997

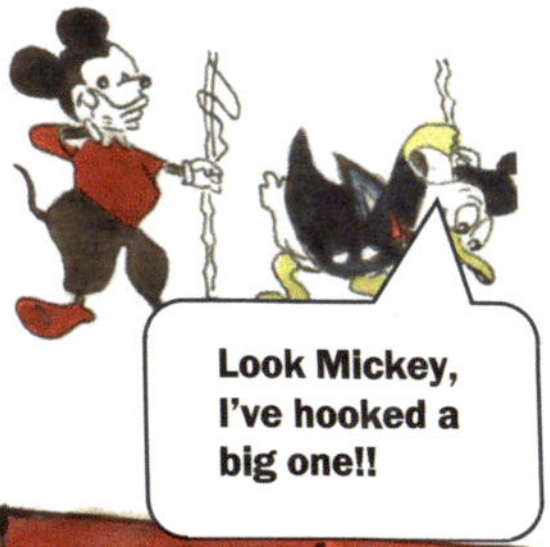

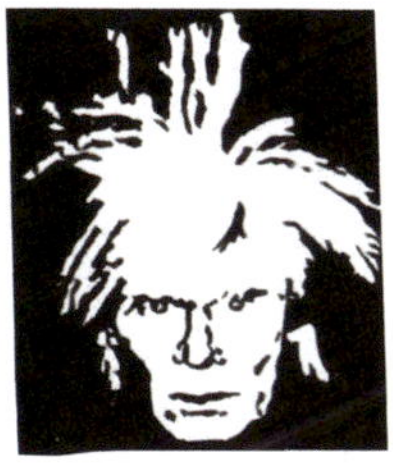

In 1964, Andy Warhol painted his *Brillo Box* series. Subject matter: Consumerism and ready-mades as an art form. This illustration on the right typifies his approach.

Andy Warhol 1928-1987

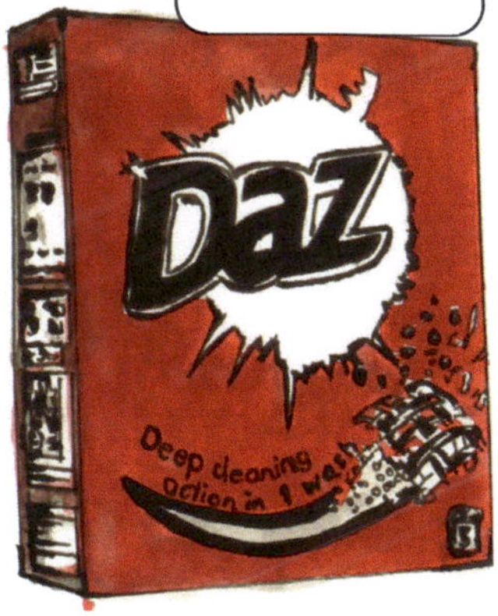

Illustration after the style of Warhol's *Brillo Boxes*

"I see 'ready-made' products as social equalisers. Both the rich and poor by Coca Cola and wealthy and poor households use Brillo pads and detergent".

David Hockney

Sunny California? The disappearing diver – a comment on the transience of life or this lifestyle?

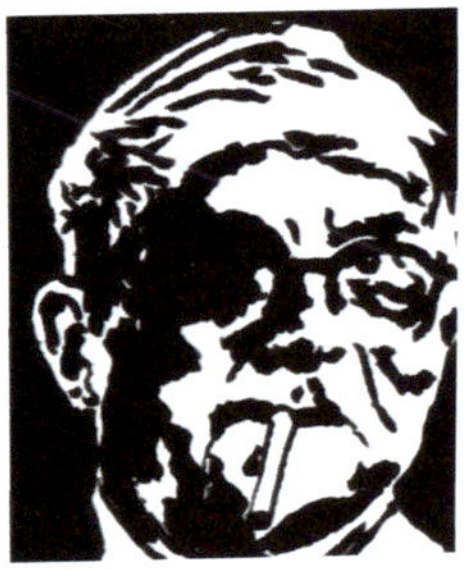

David Hockney b.1937

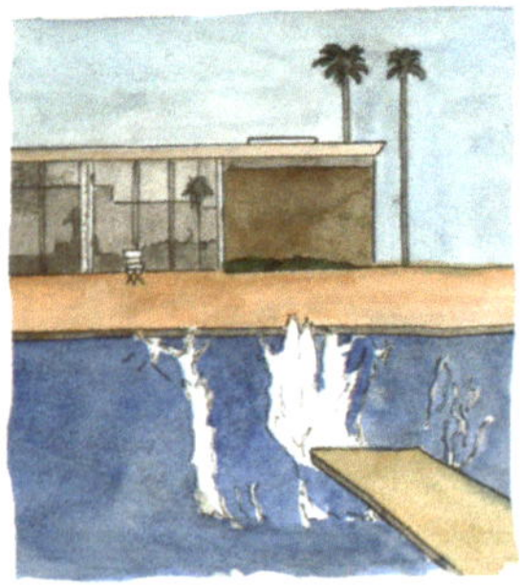

***A Bigger Splash* 1968**

*

Post Modernism

We have now moved on from Modernism to Post-Modernism. And the definition of Post Modernism? It's an enigmatic concept of our times. Essentially, it's a sceptical interpretation of culture, the arts, literature through to architecture and economics. Deconstructive and post-structural late 20th Century thought.

Look at Damien Hirst's *The Physical Impossibility of Death in the Mind of Someone Living* alongside Tracey Emin's *Everyone I have ever slept with 1963-1995*, consider televisual kitsch alongside the London National Theatre's or the New York Met's live theatre broadcasts.

Post-Modernism: from the 1960s onwards, for example, Warhol, Lichtenstein, Beuys, Hirst, Emin and Perry. Neo-Conceptualism, Minimalism, Sensationalism, Deconstructivism, mass media, Internationalism and Street Art.

Sensationalism

At London's Royal Academy in 1997, the exhibition 'Sensation' was staged, and it was the Young British Artists (YBA) including Damien Hirst (sharks and cows in formaldehyde), Tracey Emin (who slept in my tent) and Chris Ofili (elephant dung) Marcus Harvey (Myra Hindley) who stole centre stage and created the most advanced 'sensation in art' in recent years.

It was part of the movement Conceptual Art. You've got to work at it. The meaning, the story, the concept is for you to determine. It's hard work but rewarding if you can identify with where the artist is coming from. Or indeed make your own mind up. Look into yourself. What is that piece of art saying to you, about you, the world, the universe, life itself?

There are no rules, no traditions, no constraints. It's for you to decide.

Concepts, ideas rather than items. Materials to conduit concepts.

Damien Hirst produced a whole range of these 'spot' paintings in the 1980s and 1990s. What do you think the subject matter is all about? It's conceptual art: ideas, emotions, thoughts. Think about the effect it has on you.

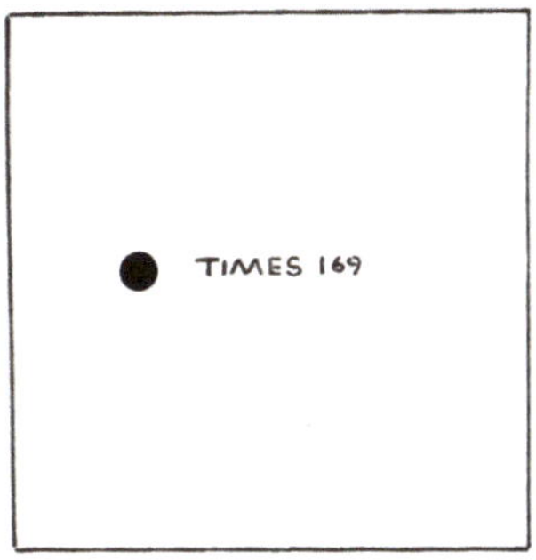

Illustration in the style of Damien Hirst

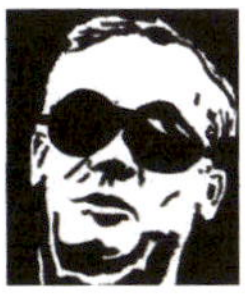

Damien Hirst b.1965

The new avant-garde – Conceptual Art. A blank canvas: the subject matter – completely open. But question: how many conceptual art avant-garde works do you see that are actually paintings?

*

Street Art

Brought to international attention in particular by the artists Banksy and New York City artists such as Futura 2000. Street Art is now a world-wide phenomenon. Largely started the New York City in the early 1970s as a protest response to the Vietnam War and the poverty in the mainly black communities, street art started as graffiti with artists such as TAKI 183, Cornbread, Daze, Dondi White and Tracey 168, amongst many others.

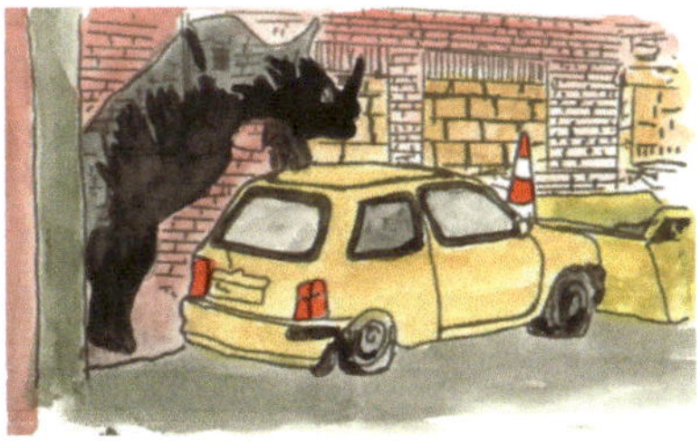

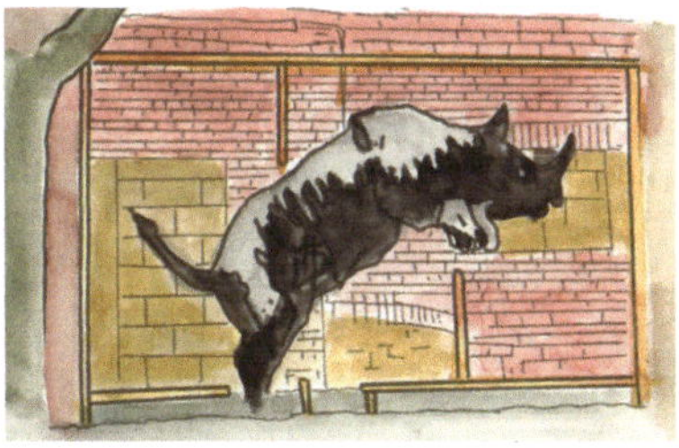

Banksy *Rhino* street art, London 2024 – original and after car removed and perspex screen installed.

It is thought that Banksy drew inspiration from the French street artist Blek le Rat Xavier Prou, who following arrests for his work, switched to using stencils for quick get-aways. Blek le Rat is particularly known for his images of rats.

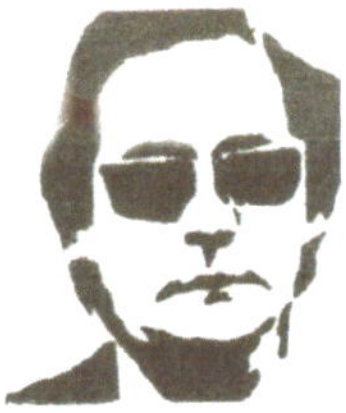

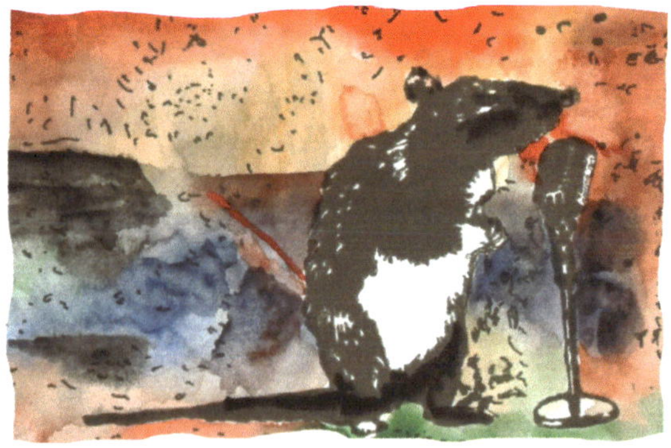

The DJ Kool Herc, Jamaican Clive Campbell born in 1955. Initially a tagger (graffiti). At his sister's party he used his unique style of DJing, and kids flocked to the party because of him. He used 2 turntables looping together the most danceable music.

He became popular and famous and gave birth to the Hip Hop and DJ culture all synonymous with Street Art. Hip Hop soon became a dominant cultural movement in the world.

Not to be confused now with the original graffiti, street artists take immense pride in their works and in some cities across the world it is actively encouraged.

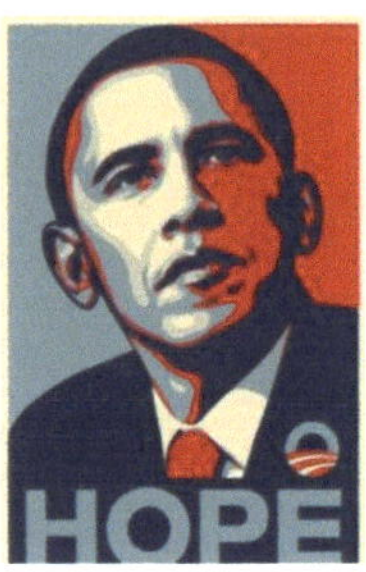

Shepard Fairey created the poster that helped Barack Obama win the Presidential election in 2009.

However, unfortunately for him, his image of Kamala Harris did not win her the Presidency in 2024. That as we know, fell to Donald Trump.

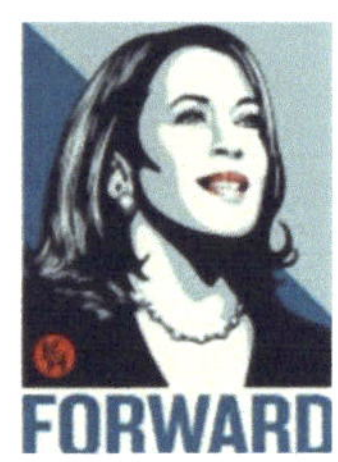

*

Finally, we come to **Internationalism.**

21st Century art is particularly associated with the globalised world. The world has shrunk, and the art world knows no boundaries. Galleries, festivals, fairs and artists are international.

One particular player associated with Internationalism is the conceptual artist Ai Weiwei and he was brought to fame in the western world not only for his iconic bird's nest architecture in Beijing, but his protests against the Chinese regime and his subsequent imprisonment.

He caused a sensation with his exhibition in London's Royal Academy in 2015 and also at London's Tate Modern.

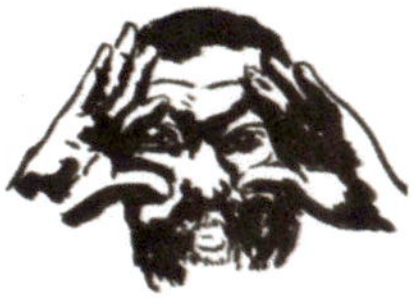

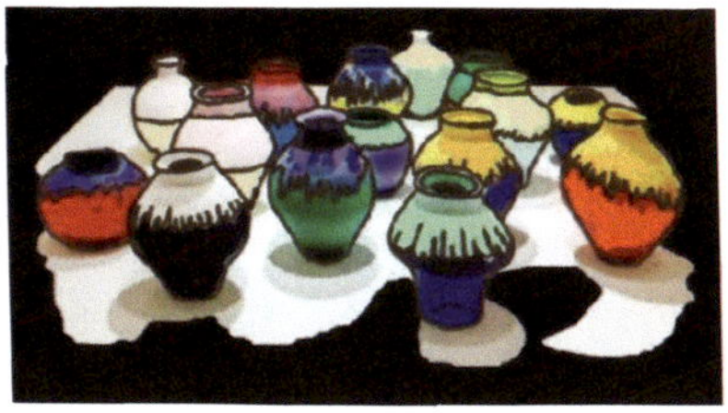

*

And that concludes our whistle-stop journey through the evolution of pictures, the two-dimensional visual image. We've covered the main themes of western art since the beginning when people used charcoal to paint animals on their cave walls to spray cans on walls.

This exploration and explanation is to give some background to that picture you are having a conversation with, in that gallery in the perspective of being a component of the story of western art and the philosophy of dialecticism, or as a 'stand-alone'.

Where did it come from? How did it arrive where it is now? What is its pedigree? What influenced it and how did it influence what came after?

How did it all evolve to what we see before us?

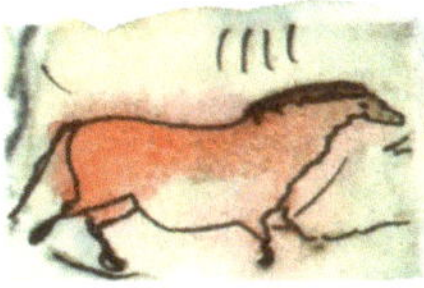

20,000 years of the evolution of pictures. Cave art to street art.

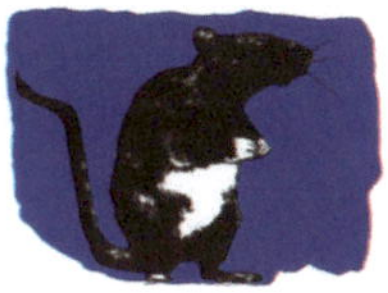

A fascinating story is the tale of the rescue of thousands of works of art by the World War II Monuments Men.

Following the D-Day invasion of Normandy, the Monuments Men's task was to help protect monuments from the retreating and invading forces.

This role eventually changed to retrieving stolen art looted by the Nazis.

On one occasion, one of the Monuments Men attempted to persuade a local commander to be aware of the culture within a town they were about to liberate.

The Monuments Man was challenged by the commanding officer along the lines of 'what do you think this war is all about?' To which the response was:

'This is a great part of what we're fighting for, the protection and recovery of a 1000 years of European culture from the dark ages of the Nazis and the complete removal of our humanity and heritage.'

And there we have the saga of the evolution of western art and the importance it holds for our very way of life and values.

Quite a story, quite a journey.

Storyline

Can you spot the plot? A storyline? Are we at the beginning, middle or end of a tale? What happened beforehand and what's happening now? What'll happen next do you wonder?

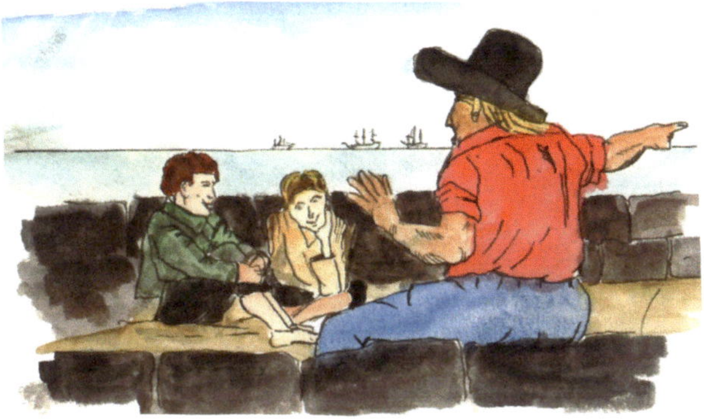

As in life there may be no neat beginning or ending, things may be just rolling along. Maybe enjoy weaving the plot from what you see in the picture, for yourself.

Let's start with these three examples. William Holman Hunt, Edward Hopper and Norman Rockwell, do not go away. They are always there and whilst the purist art critics are not there for Norman Rockwell, the public certainly are.

And so, thank you...

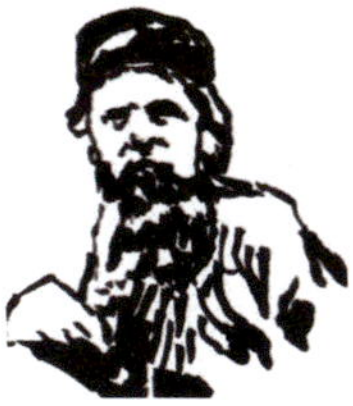

William Holman Hunt
1827-1910

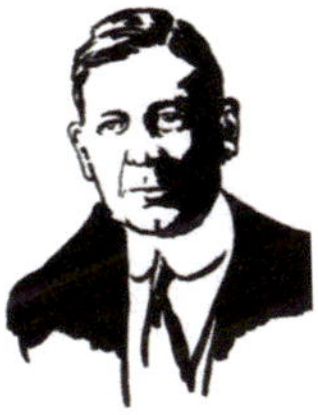

Edward Hopper
1882-1967

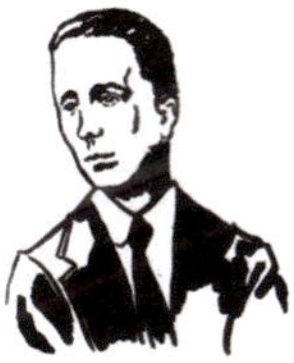

Norman Rockwell
1894-1978

... for bringing us your stories as we'll see over the next few pages.

William Holman Hunt, a British PRB artist, painted *The Awakening Conscience* in 1853.

Critics at the time slated it as being **'drawn from a very dark and repulsive side of domestic life'**. But others, including the influential figure of John Ruskin, defended it as having a serious message grappling with the thorny issue of prostitution.

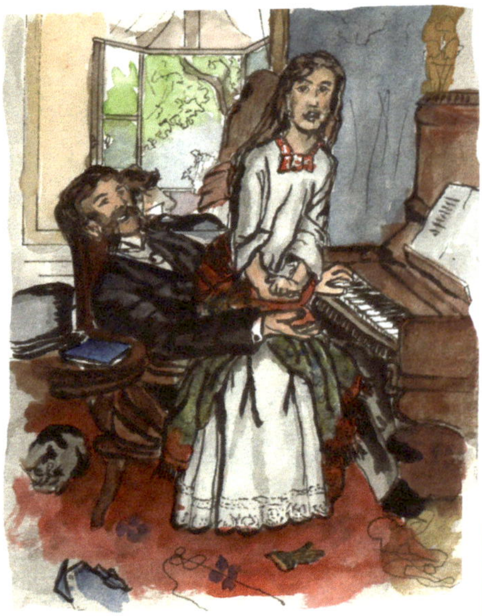

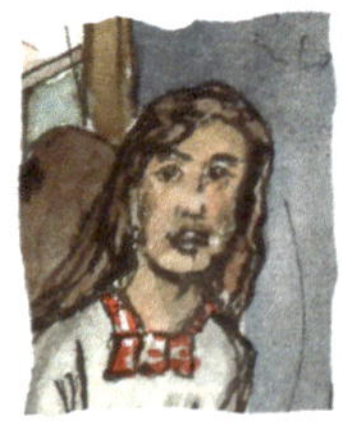

"Oh woe. What has become of me? Who is this groping man? But I'm trapped? How else can I eat and pay the rent? What will become of me?"

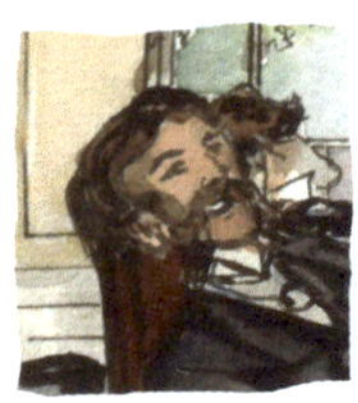

"Oh, come now. don't get off my lap I'm so enjoying playing this piano. I'm just here for a goodly time don't you know. You'll be ok, there'll be other men after me."

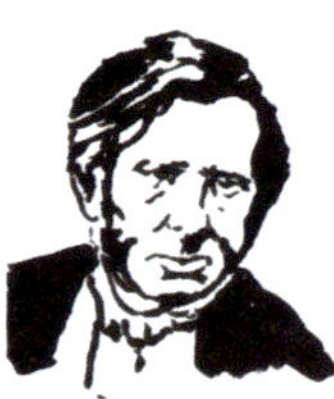

"Greetings. I'm John Ruskin. I was a most influential artist and art critic. I may have been a bit of a prude, but I was insensibly angry about the plight of women in society and domestically. Who is this man? What is the girl's story? How has she ended up like this? What future does she have? Will she be incarcerated for her downfall as with the other 3386 London prostitutes in 1853?
Wait a minute though. Mr Holman Hunt has called his work *The Awakening Conscience*. Surely, she'll go on to better things. But how? The position of many women alone is quite untenable in Victorian society."

Is there another storyline that could be woven here?

*

As we will be concentrating on later, it can be illuminating to look at paintings from the perspective of the contemporary viewer, so from the point of view of an American in 1942.

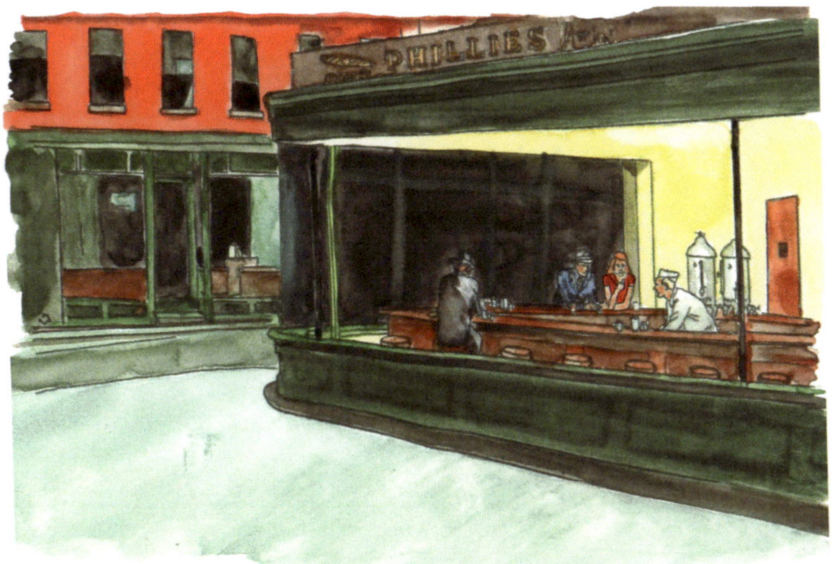

Edward Hopper's *The Nighthawks* 1942

What was happening in 1942? Pearl Harbor was attacked in 1941, so the USA was now drawn into the World War II. 32nd US President Franklin D Roosevelt was in charge. US motor manufacturers switched their priority to war machines. Daylight Savings War Time goes into effect. Nazi U-boat sink an American cargo ship at the mouth of the Mississippi River. Gasoline rationing introduced. In New York – no more baseball night games. Bing Crosby's *White Christmas* and *Silent Night* recorded. The British wartime movie *Mrs Miniver* makes a dramatic impression on America's attitude to the war in Europe. USA & USSR sign Lend-Lease. *Bambi* is released. It has been raining a lot. And on and on...and this is just up to the fall in America.

What do you think were the prevailing attitudes at the time? The politics and the economic situation? Do you think any of these influenced Hopper?

The answer is almost certainly 'yes'.

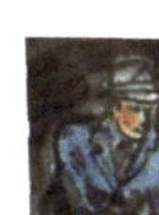

"Look at my fellow players in this picture. Are we looking at loneliness or companionship? How do you think me and the others are making a living – or are we not? Remember the above: huge increase in industrial manufacturing and with show-business – business as usual.

I might even be here because the baseball has been cancelled."

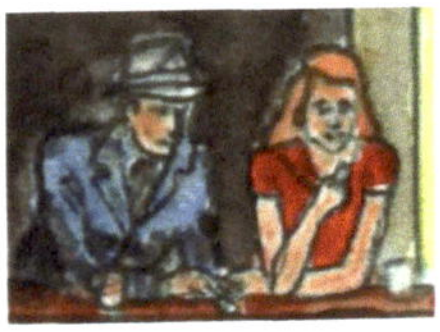

"Do you think there's any serious relationships here? Where will my customers be going on to? Where have they come from?"

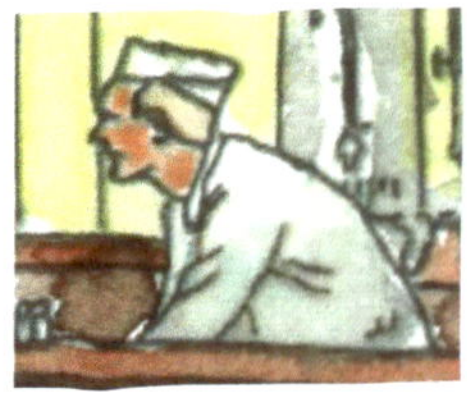

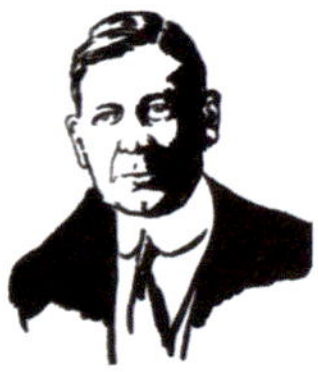

"What time of night is it? Late hours or wee small hours?
Are my players drinking tea, coffee or what?
Look at my location: a typical diner.
I set this picture in Greenwich Village NYC nearby where I lived. Have I created a sense of *alienation* and isolation or companionship

A good story line, isn't it"

Let's now look at the American artist Norman Rockwell.

Rockwell illustrated for the *Saturday Evening Post* for many years and his work epitomises the ideal of the American Dream.

This work is called: *The Runaway* and was featured in *The Saturday Evening Post* in September 1958.

What do you think the story is here?

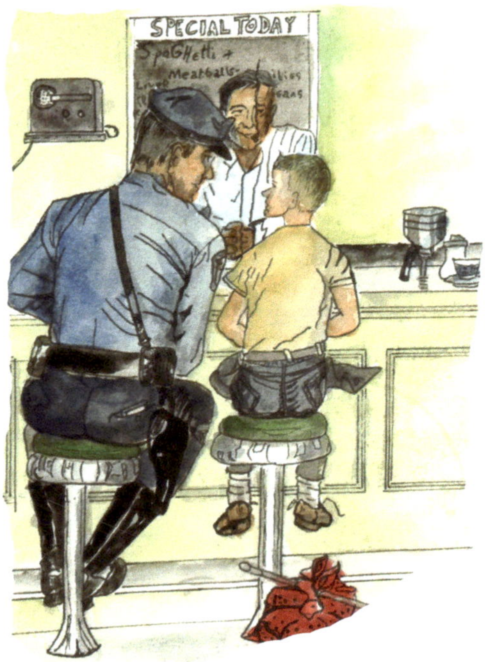

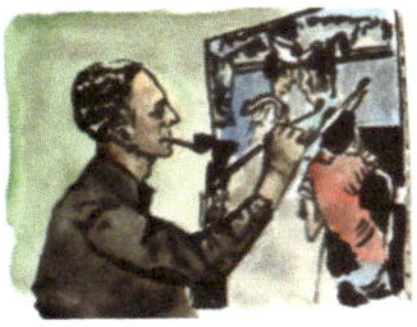

"I painted this for readers to enjoy the warmth and comfort of seeing a little boy who has run away from home, being looked after by his elders and indeed what was then protective, consensual police authority, in a typical American diner.

Where do you think the little boy was running away from? His home? An institution? What do you think his circumstances are all about? Is he just following a spirit of adventure?"

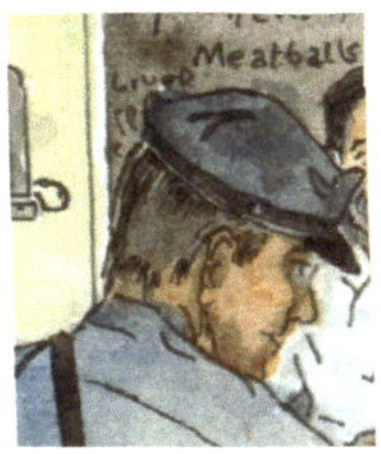

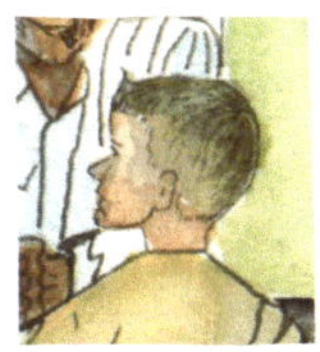

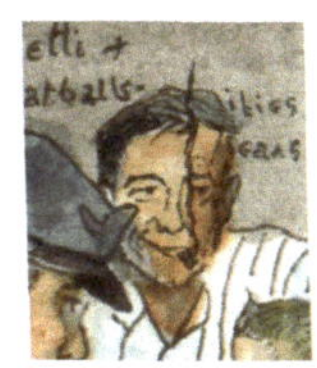

What do you think the officer is saying to him? Look at his face, it's firm yet understanding and friendly. Look at the way the officer leans towards the boy and looks kindly down at him.

A perfect communication posture between the boy and the officer.

And look at the diner owner. We'll assume he's the owner. Look at his kindly, paternal and understanding face, and the way he completes the close communication poses in this scene.

A good storyline excellently illustrated but with no clear dialogue or definitions and it's left to you to read into it what you wish.

And that's the deeper enjoyment of paintings with a storyline, so much for you to enjoy if you spend just a few minutes contemplating.

Look at the way Rockwell has structured his painting. We've mentioned the players' pose and posture but notice how they form a 'golden triangle'.

Also look at the form: the vertical and horizontal lines in particular. Comforting solidity and structure. Look at the everyday objects: the radio and cup and sugar dispenser. Reassurance of the domestic known.

And now Sir John Everett Millais and his 1891 work *Glen Birnam.*

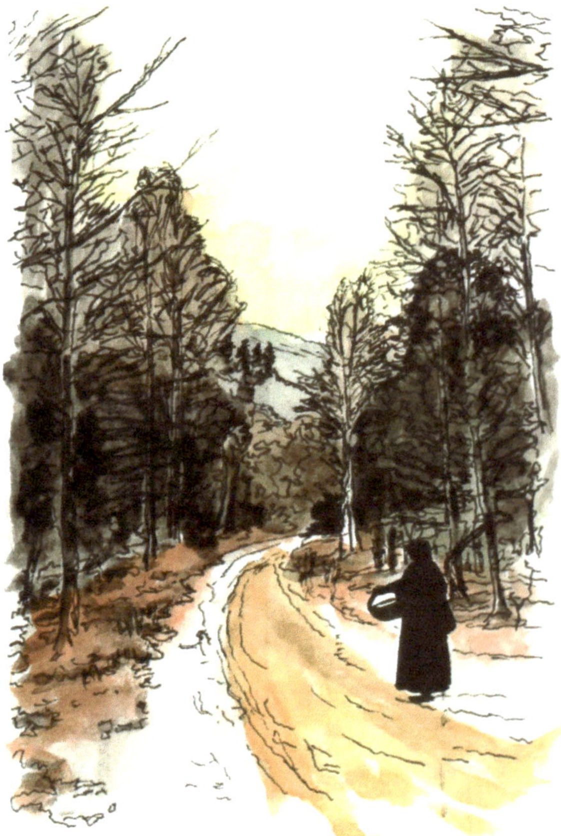

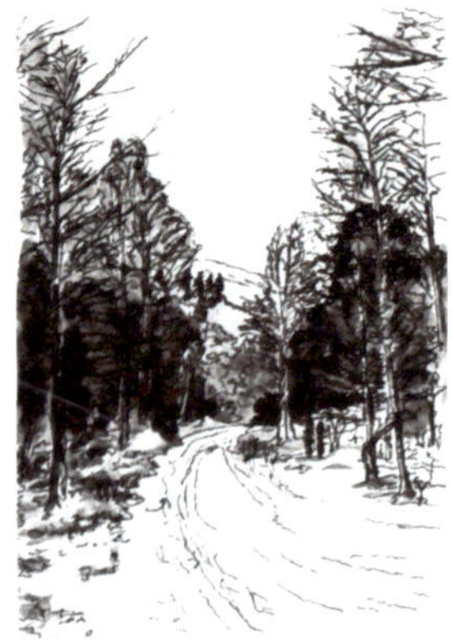

Consider the picture as though it was finished without the figure. Don't you think the figure adds so much evocative narrative appeal, and the more enigmatic the better?

*

Delving a little deeper into the picture, there is naturally the full story of the work to enjoy. Not only the picture's content as we've seen, but also the artist's and the work's historical and social background.

A good example to illustrate this is Johannes Vermeer's *The Art of Painting.*

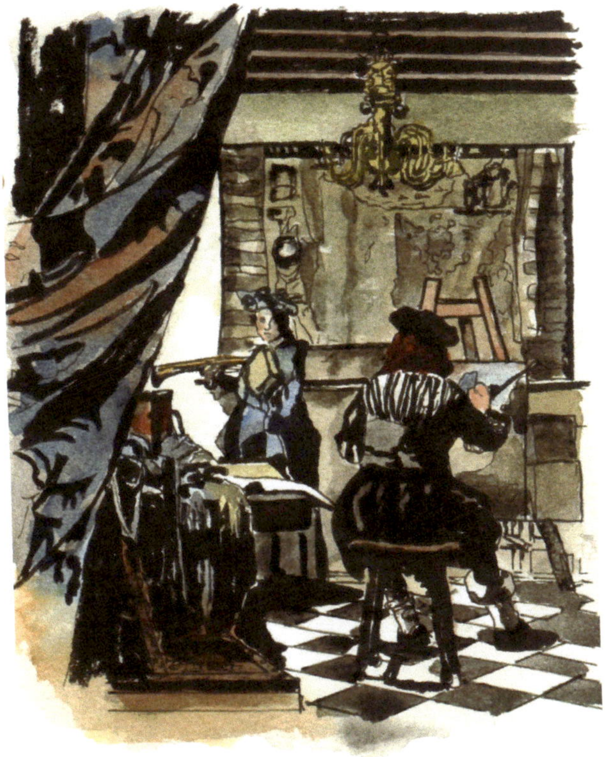

Johannes Vermeer was born in 1632 and died in 1675. He lived and worked in the Dutch towns of Delft and The Hague.

In 1653 he married a Catholic woman, Catharina Bolnes. They had 15 children, four of whom were buried before being baptized.

The Art of Painting was created between 1665 and 1668. Opinions on its exact date differ.

The work shows a painter sitting before an easel painting a woman posing before a map and a window. The interior of the room is beautifully illuminated with Vermeer's mastering of the power of light.

At the time the Dutch had recently secured independence from Spain after 80 years of struggle leading to the Treaty of Westphalia. The Netherlands United Provinces governance became decentralized and religious tolerance was strong.

This is the Dutch Golden Age. With the north and west Netherlands being now a Calvinist Protestant country there was no religious imposition on artists to comply with their dictates. Hence, the Golden Age saw freedom of expression and a wealth of newly formed genre and personal painting. Ordinary people in everyday situations. In the south and east the country remained under the Catholic Church.

The Dutch East India Company was formed in 1602 and was one of the first joint-stock companies in the world. The Dutch were trading across the known world. Hence the emerging middle and merchant classes were rich and on the rise.

Trading hubs were Amsterdam and Rotterdam, and trade was especially centred on spices, ceramics and textiles from Asia and the New World.

Merchants became the new commissioners of art. Dutch homes were not large. Artists painted canvasses of the size to be accommodated in these homes.

Vermeer's contemporaries were Frans Hals and Rembrandt van Rijn.

Looking at the content of *The Art of Painting*, the elegantly dressed artist is thought to be Vermeer although there is no direct evidence of this. The female dressed in blue with floral headdress is possibly his daughter. The map on the wall is showing the newly formed 17 United Provinces and is a proud display of the trading nature of the country.

The painting is an allegory. It is telling a story that invites interpretation.

The female figure is thought to depict Clio the muse as is evidenced by her symbolic laurel headdress and holding a trumpet. Clio is one of nine muses from Greek mythology. A muse of history. Muses were thought to be goddesses inspiring the arts and sciences. Hence Clio here is also holding a book thus a reference to the recording and study of history to help to ensure the history of past civilizations' achievements and experiences are not forgotten thereby helping future generations.

Vermeer has painted this work with his typical meticulous technique and innovative use of colour. The use of light and shade as well as the display of perspective is outstanding.

Even though he was hard up at the time of this work, he did not sell the painting. However, upon his death his wife sold it to pay off debts in 1677. It has remained much of a mystery exactly to whom. It emerges again in 1813, when it was purchased for 50 florins by the Bohemian-Austrian Count Rudolf Czernin and was placed on public display in the Czernin Museum in Vienna.

During World War II it was looted by the Nazis and stored in the Altaussee salt mines before being rescued by the Monuments Men and presented back to the Austrian Government.

The work is now on public display in the Kunsthistorisches Museum, Vienna.

And that in brief is the story of Vermeer's *The Art of Painting*.

Can a greater depth of enjoyment be secured knowing a little more about a picture albeit in brief outline?

Deeper, richer storylines. Empathising with human experiences of fear, joy, wonder, threat, relationships and excitement. It can be a wonderful and fulfilling experience with many pictures to contemplate what is going on and what stories you can weave for yourself.

It really doesn't matter whether your stories match those of the artist. You may not even know what the artist's original story was all about.

You are having your own personal conversation with that picture across the years, and of course with the artist who painted it.

Now here's a tale in a nutshell, that has been woven over the centuries. It certainly demonstrates how a plot can be weaved from paintings whether truly historical or fabricated. This story is such a powerful one that it could be the very dilution of the essence of the established church's theological dominance and involves many artists, paintings and an enormous amount of alternative theory, literature and the very structure of western society. Also, if it is to be believed, could undermine a belief system that structures many people's lives.

Recall Dan Brown's best seller book and the subsequent film *The Da Vinci Code* where in Leonardo da Vinci's *Last Supper*, the figure leaning away from Jesus Christ's right side is Mary Magdalene and not the Apostle John? This book and subsequent film was inspired by *The Holy Blood and The Holy Grail* by Michael Baigent, Richard Leigh and Henry Lincoln.

The salient part in question of Leonardo's *Last Supper* is thought to have been itself inspired by Fra Angelico's *Last Supper* and alternative biblical theories that are still there in the background and supposedly suppressed by the Catholic Church. Note the 'V' in the hairline. A symbol of the 'Sacred Female' and consequently, the figure is certainly a female.

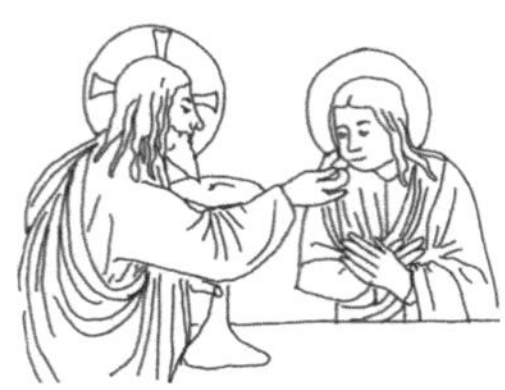

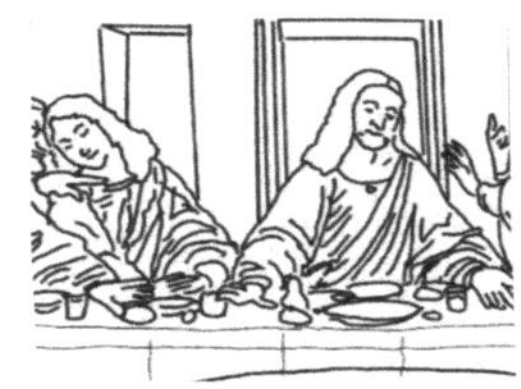

Detail Fra Angelica's *Last Supper* 1440 Detail from Leonardo's Last Supper 1495-8

The Roman Church's version of the saga is that Mary Magdaline, dressed in red with red hair, therefore shown as a scarlet woman, whilst Jesus' mother Mary by dictate from St Thomas Aquinas, is always shown in blue. Mary Magdaline, is described as an allegedly sinful yet wealthy woman from the town of Magdala, a fishing town on the western shore of the Sea of Galilee in Roman Judea. Mary bathed Jesus' feet with her tears and wiped them with her flaming red hair and then anointed them with a concoction of herbs. Later she, together with Jesus' great uncle, Joseph of Arimathea, accompanied his great nephew on the way to the crucifixion and was there at the end. On Easter morning, Mary was the first person meeting Jesus following his resurrection and many paintings such as Antonio da Correggio's, depict this event '*Noli me tangere*' or 'touch me not' c 1523.

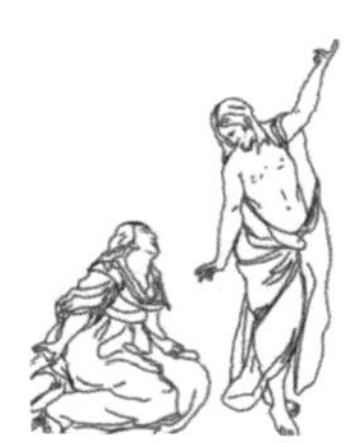

The version that the Church considers heresy is that Jesus married Mary Magdaline at the feast of Cana, the event where he changed water into wine, and they bore a child whose line went on to found the French Merovingian royal dynasty. Academic opinion dismisses the notion that it is Mary Magdaline in both Last Suppers. The Church did not want a human woman to be the bearer of Christ's progeny, so misogynistically, a female must be denied otherwise the divine virgin birth would feature no more.

Jesus, according to this alternative story, did not die on the cross but was given on the sponge not just vinegar but a form of opiate that made him appear dead. Longinus, the Roman soldier who stabbed him with a spear, was in fact relieving the pressure on his lungs. Longinus went on to become a Christian bishop. Christ was taken down from the cross and hidden in Jospeh's tomb and there he was administered with aloe vera and other medicines at the time and recovered enough to be found missing from his tomb on Easter Sunday and then met with Mary Magdaline where we have the *'Noli me tangere'* incident. Jesus therefore survived the crucifixion in human bodily form.

Meanwhile, as the tale unfolds, Joseph of Arimathea, as a merchant visited Cornwall where he traded in tin and Jesus as a child is alleged to have accompanied him on one of these trips. Subsequently, upon the Roman purge of the early church in Jerusalem, Joseph came to the British shores where he planted what is now known as a 'holy thorn', in Glastonbury. However, it must be said that this is all very much shrouded in the undocumented mists of time. The Romans arrived in 43 CE and the Druids were supressed, but within the mists there is a theory that in the 2nd Century CE the Culdees carried on possibly in the southwest of England, although this is undocumented but certainly in Ireland, where they may have evolved from originally and Scotland. Tenuous to say the least but intriguing, nevertheless.

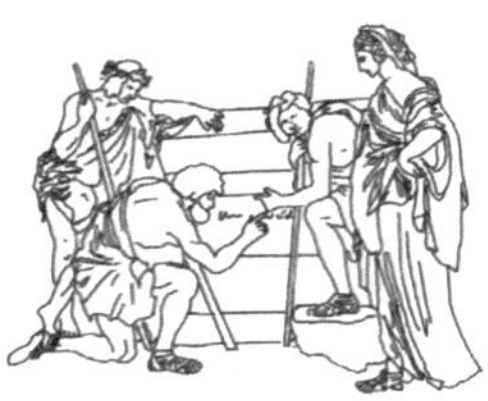

Where did Fra Angelica and Leonardo gain their inspiration for John in fact being Mary Magdaline or Nicolas Poussin's (1594-1665) enigmatic work *Et in Arcadia ego* or anagrammatically as *I tego arcana Dei* or as transliterated *I hold the secrets of God*? It was their membership of a secret society.

Even the scientist Issac Newton was supposed to be a Grand Master of this secret society that was started by Geoffrey of Boullion, the first Christian king of Jerusalem, around 1099. The Priory of Sion, the holder of secret knowledge and documents gained from ancient monasteries and the Crusaders returning from the Holy Land. It was a particular gospel within the Gnostic texts, discovered in 1945, that was purported to have been authored by Mary Magdalene, that gave an alternative to the canonical Biblical story.

If you wish to believe it's fact, The Priory of Sion was dreamt up by a Frenchman Pierre Plantard de Saint-Clair, later exposed as a con artist, but who wanted to have himself linked to the Merovingian royal line of centuries before. Following this line of thought, the whole tale of Mary Magdaline in Leonardo's *Last Supper*, Christ coming to Britain, The Gnostic Gospel and the rest of the story is all a hoax. Or is it?

All this has inspired images of Jesus and Mary Magdalene from Jan van Eyck's *Ghent Altarpiece*, Leonardo's *Last Supper*, through to Dan Brown's *The Da Vinci Code.* This story simply shows the absolute power of art, the overwhelming influence artists and their pictures can have on our way of life and belief systems, whether or not those artists were knowingly complicit in what they were giving clues about or whether it's pure fabrication, that is the official version of the Passion or the alternative version.

Pictures relating tales from many perspectives and enticing you the viewer to allow your imagination to be inspired.

*

Relationships

This next section is closely associated with subject matter and story line. Here we are looking at relationships.

With the figures in the painting the viewer can ponder on their relationship. Are they looking at each other or not? Are they touching or not? What about the movement and positioning of each character portrayed?

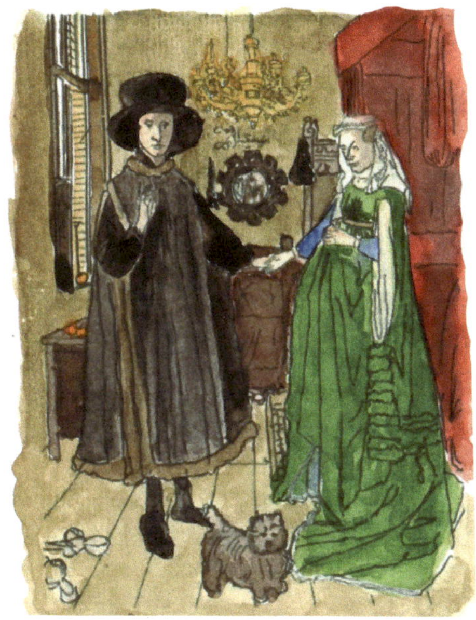

Let's start off with *The Arnolfini Wedding* by Jan van Eyck painted in oil on oak panel. Note the date: 1434, the Dutch Early Renaissance: very early indeed for such a subject rather than religious matter as we've seen.

Notice the eye and physical contact. More subtly, look at the poise and postures, the location and proximity to each other. Look at their respective sizes and their location in the perspective of the picture.

We know they're married as according to scholars, this can be confirmed by the wife's hair being up. Unmarried women wore their hair down at this time.

We've got gender roles here too. The woman by the bed and deeper inside the room – domesticity, whereas the man is by the window. He'll be out there in the world working on his business enterprises.

He's holding his hand up in a symbol of authority and he's looking directly at us, she is looking at him, maybe from a position of equality. The joining of hands, the joining of two families. The nuptial agreement.

Sumptuous clothes and refined features indicating high status. The dog perhaps symbolising faithfulness between the couple?

Was this work painted as part of a contract? A confirmation? A sealing?

Look at the other items of symbolism: the mirror on the wall, the various items of domestic ownership draped on the walls. The bed. The sofa.

Look at the perspective achieved. The use of lighting to create depth and cosiness.

A unique work for its time and ever since.

Let's now move on 60 or so years and journey south to Italy where religious paintings were still the order of the day, albeit as we've explored, many now being more humanist in nature.

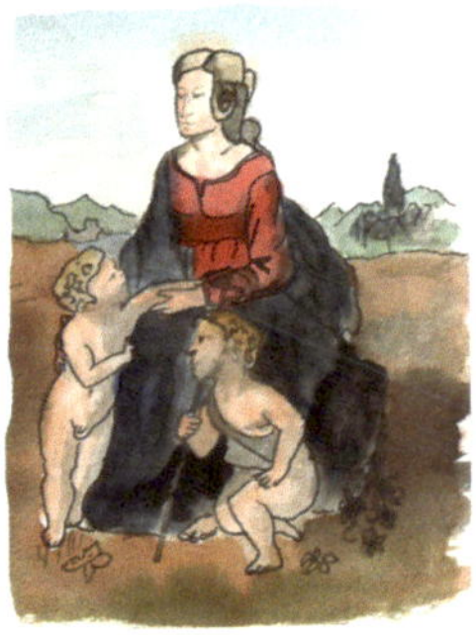

Sketched here is a work by Raphael. The Louvre's title is in French *La belle jardinière.* Mary, Jesus and his cousin John, later to become the Baptist.

Forget for a while the religious iconography, look at the relationship. The way they're looking at each other. Mother adoringly at Jesus, Jesus lovingly at his mother with John looking up at his inspiration in Jesus.

The mother child relationship. Probably captured most supremely with Leonardo's *Cartoon* in the London National Gallery and simply sketched here as finely as possible to capture the subtleties of light, poise and features sufficiently to read into the picture. Of note is Leonardo's use of the technique called sfumato, the deliberate softening of the figures' outlines for enhanced effect.

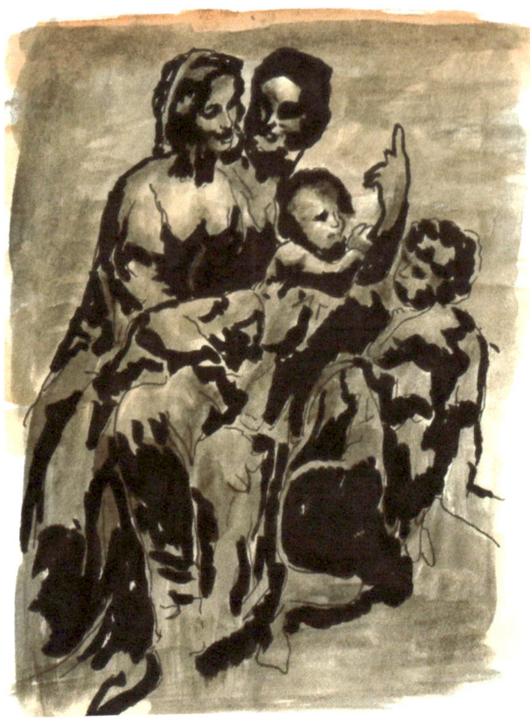

Look at how Jesus is pulling away from his mother whilst she reluctantly lets him go to his destiny. And we all know what that was to be. He will, as we all do, die and Mary knows this. Mary has brought life and death into the world.

He is growing up and pulling away and is blessing John. Mary knows she must let him go as mothers do but with her arms and hands, she is emotionally holding on to him.

He is looking away to his future, with her eyes he is the only centre of her world. Mary's mother Anne looks on in support, but there is nothing she can do to prevent the inevitable, as an older woman she knows the pain and grief of the empty nest.

Look at the composition: the direction of the heads, the gazes, the knees, the bodies twisting, and the relationship between all the physiques. All perfectly and beautifully executed.

If you allow yourself to be moved emotionally into this image, it may have the power to bring a tear to your eye if you dwell long enough on its meaning.

*

We now move on a few centuries, to France in 1875 and a work by Edgar Degas' *L' Absinth* currently in the Musée d'Orsay in Paris.

The female is Ellen Andrée, an actress, and the male is Marcellin Desboutin, a painter, printmaker and a bon-viveur. The café where they are taking their refreshment is the Café de la Nouvelle-Athènes in Paris.

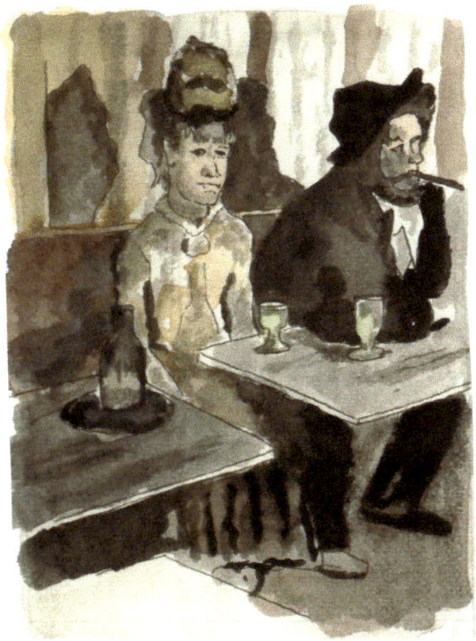

When shown in Paris and London in the late 19th Century it caused a storm of controversy. Low life. Alcoholism. The green addictive and brain damagingly devil, absinthe. A Bohemian lifestyle.

Now look at the relationships. Are the players a unit? Have they just met or are we looking at something long term? Platonic or more intimate? What is the storyline?

With the population of Paris growing fast there was concern about the increasing isolation of its citizens. But surely these two are together? What do you think? Ponder on the relationship between the principal characters before you.

Movement

Let's now consider the portrayal of movement in the picture.

So far most of what we've looked at is static: still posed figures and landscapes. Now for movement.

"Greetings from Cornwall. I'm Alfred Wallis and I retired from the sea and started painting at the grand age of 67. I was discovered in 1928 by the artist Ben Nicholson who moved to St Ives. My work is 'naïve': it's simple with no perspective and no scale. In respect of movement – of course there's movement – look at the sails on my *Blue Boat* and the flowing sea."

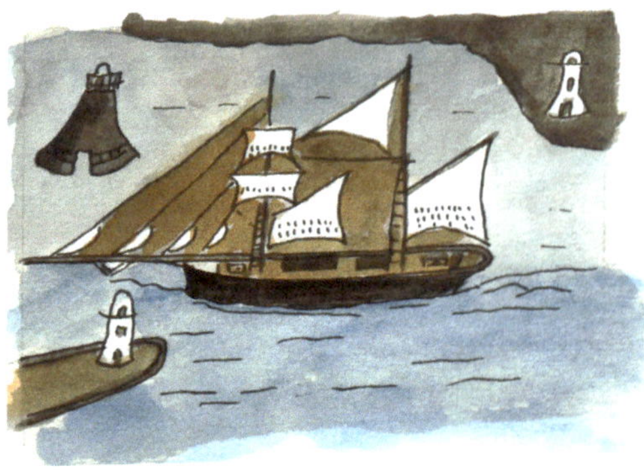

We are considering here how artists have tried to depict movement onto a two-dimensional static surface.

A canvas: static, rigid, vertical and horizontal with no depth, a simple flat surface. So how on earth can genuine movement be a part of painting?

"I'm Jean-Honoré Fragonard. My work *The Swing* painted in 1767 really shows movement as this detail admirably illustrates."

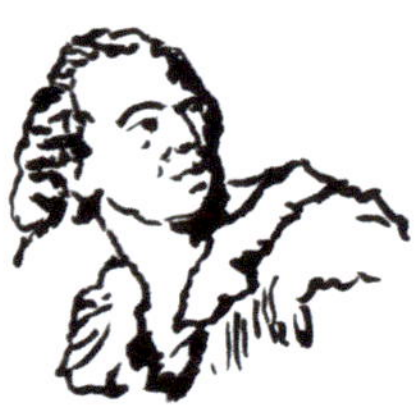

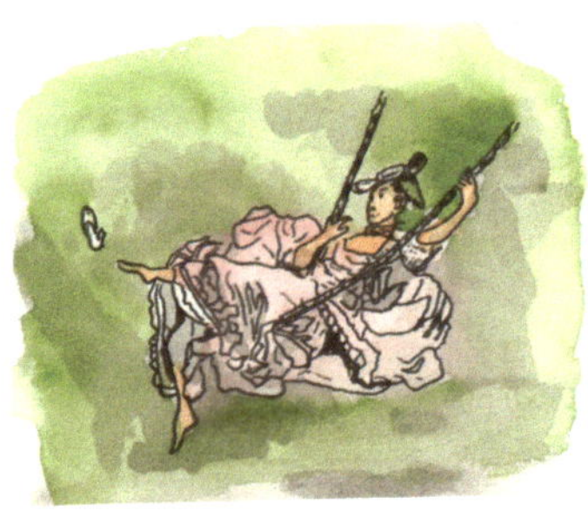

Well, it does, and it doesn't. As Jean-Honoré admits, movement is 'depicted' but it's not actual movement, it cannot possibly be on a static surface.

Others have displayed movement but alluding to it almost as a photographic still or a snapshot of a scene. Let's look at a few examples and see how successful the allusion not illusion, is.

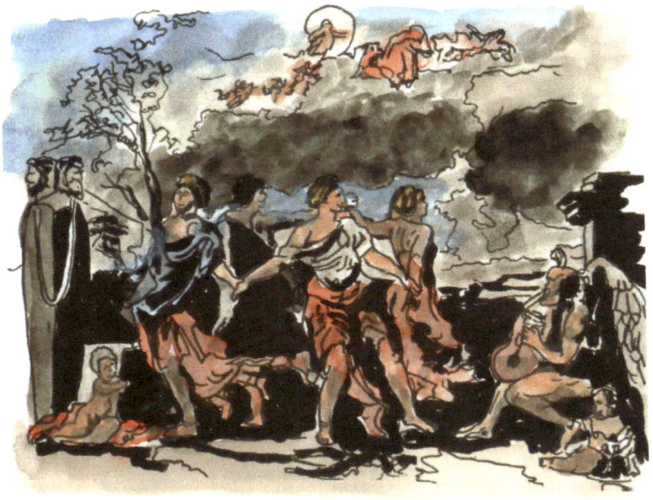

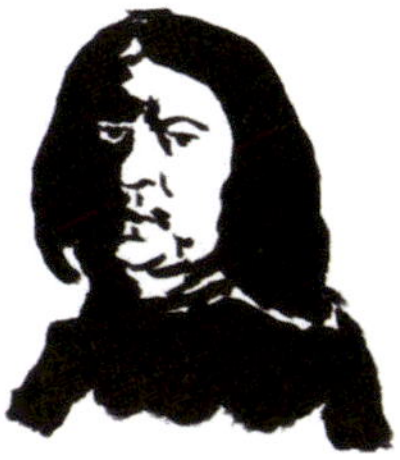

Nicolas Poussin
1594-1665

Dance to the Music of Time
1640

Ferdinand Victor Eugène Delacroix (1798 - 1863) was an artist who was regarded as the leader of the French Romantic School.

Consider the extensive movement here in his most famous 1830 work *Liberty Leading the People.*

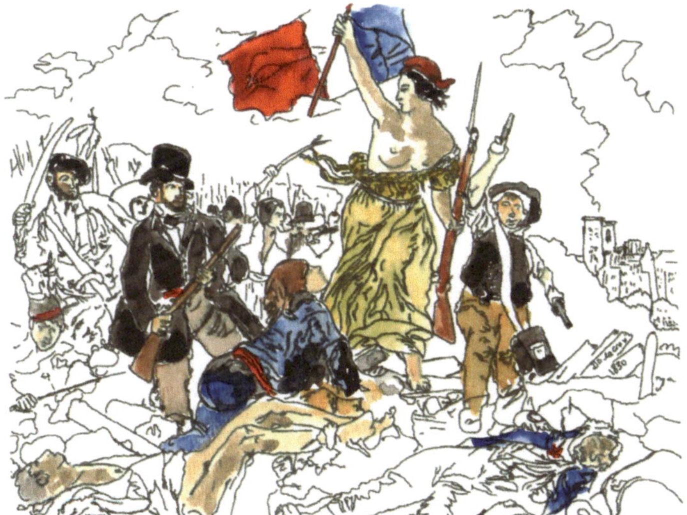

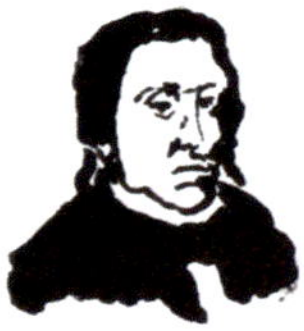

"Edgar Degas here. Look at how much movement I've captured."

Ballerina 1874

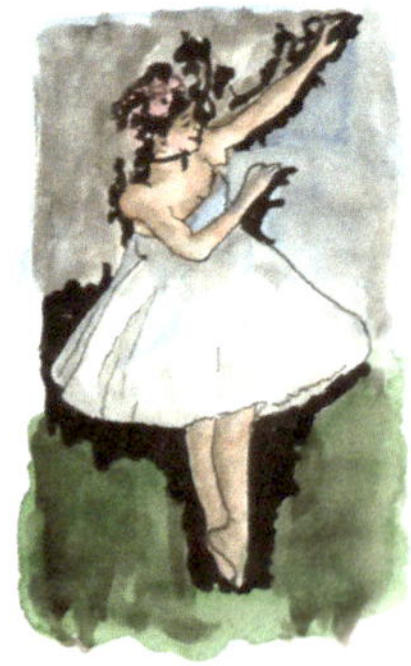

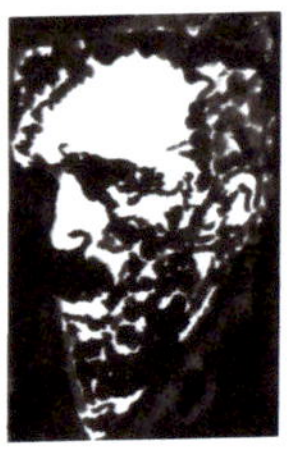

"Look at my trees and the movement with the clouds, wind and trees."

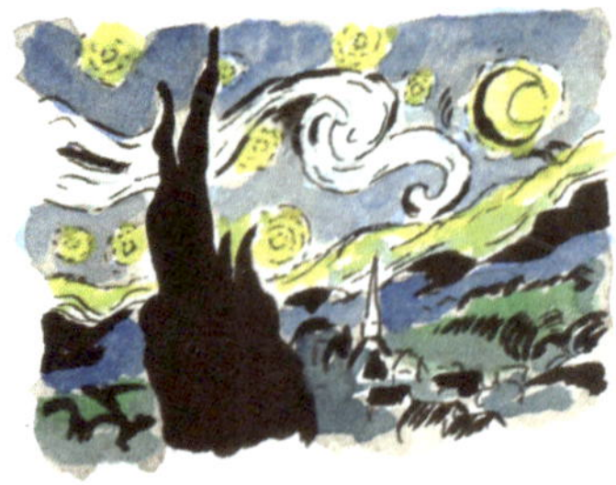

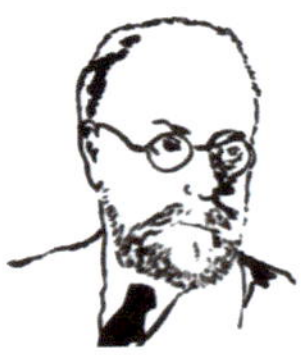

"I'm Henri Matisse and in 1910 I painted this work *La Danse.* I did indeed try and capture an allusion, but of course not an illusion."

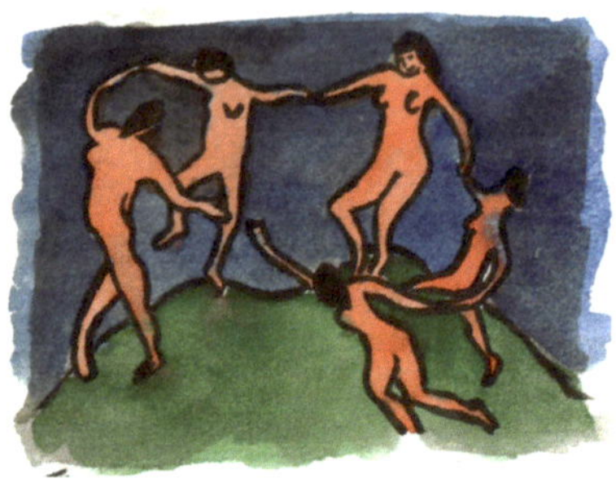

Paul Nash: " My 1941 work, *The Battle of Britain* gives an allusion to movement: the planes, the smoke streams and clouds. I painted this from high on the Sussex Downs. Lots of movement but on my static canvas. "

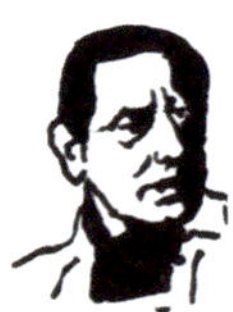

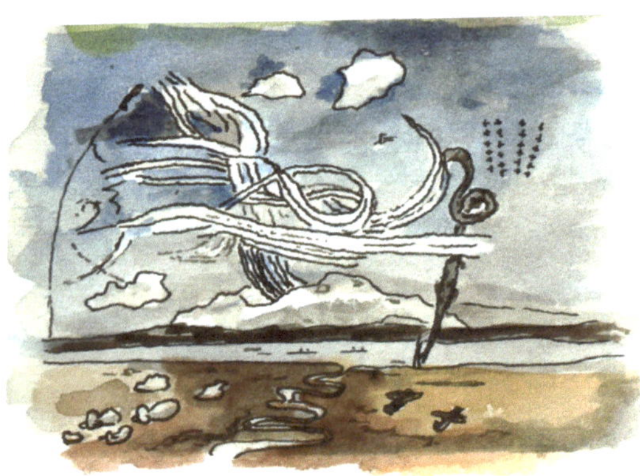

Now look at a work that went a little further in attempting an illusion and not simply a depiction of movement.

Remember that we're now talking about the era of the emergence of cinema: the moving pictures. Apparently, these scenes influenced Marcel Duchamp to create his 1912 work *Nude Descending a Staircase.*

Early cinematic moving images. The world would not be seen in the same way again.

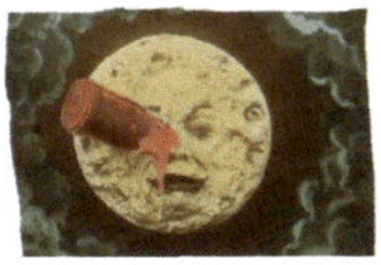

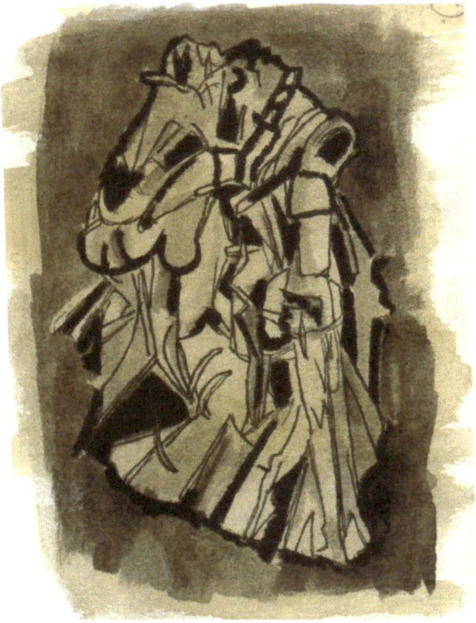

By studying this work carefully, you'll be able to just about pick out the figure moving down from left to right. Duchamp has frequently overlaid the figure with more figures similar to a slow movie. He's trying to give an illusion but of course is still restricted to the static canvas.

So, when you look at a painting, is there movement and how has the artist attempted to depict it or alluded to it? How successfully has the artist acknowledged the rigid static two dimensionality of the canvas?

Later on, we are going to look deeper at the relationship of the artist to the constraints of their canvas and you the viewer.

Weather, time and location

Look at the painting and ask yourself: what is the weather and the time of day?

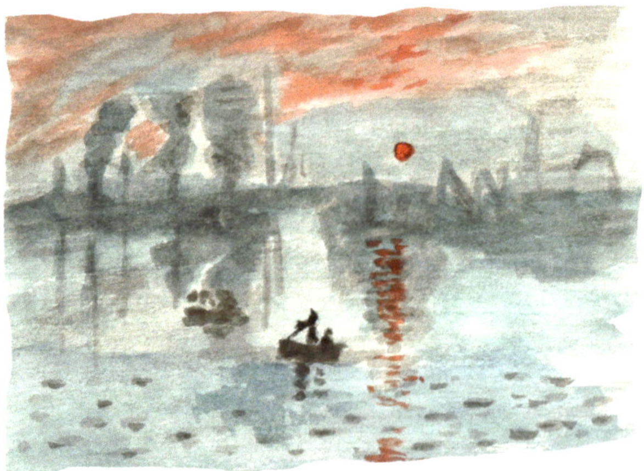

Impression, Sunrise 1872

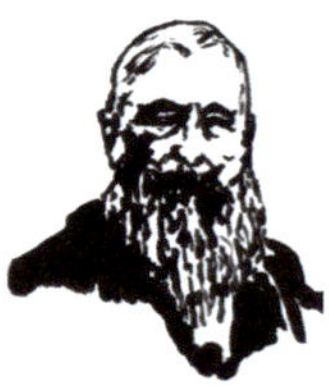

Claude Monet

"I'm delighted you've chosen me to illustrate this topic. I went to great lengths to capture the impression of weather and time.

I painted this in Le Harve first thing on a sunny morning and as we've seen, it helped lead to the movement Impressionism."

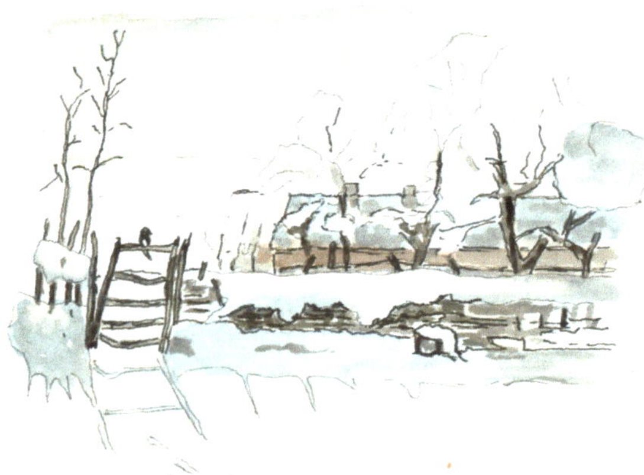

How many paintings can you think of that are showing it raining? Not many, I guess.

Now let's look at another Monet. This is his *La Pie* or *Magpie* – see it sitting on the fence?

This painting captures a bright winter's late afternoon. Look at the shadows, look at the snow-capped fence, trees and building. There's no signs of life here except the magpie and the footprints in the snow.

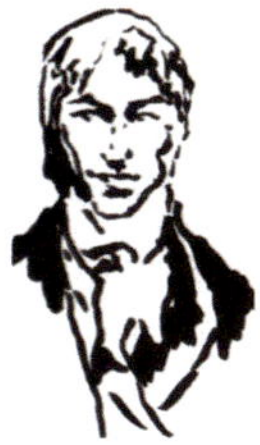

JMW Turner

"With my *The Fighting Temeraire* I wanted to capture the calm sea during the end of a summer's evening. The grace and curves of the old ship going to the breaker's yard set against the close of a day, the close of an era – to be overtaken by the smoke belching tug. Romanticism, the passing of days heralding the Industrial Revolution. In respect of the location, the Temeraire is being towed across the Thames towards the breakers yard in Rotherhithe, London."

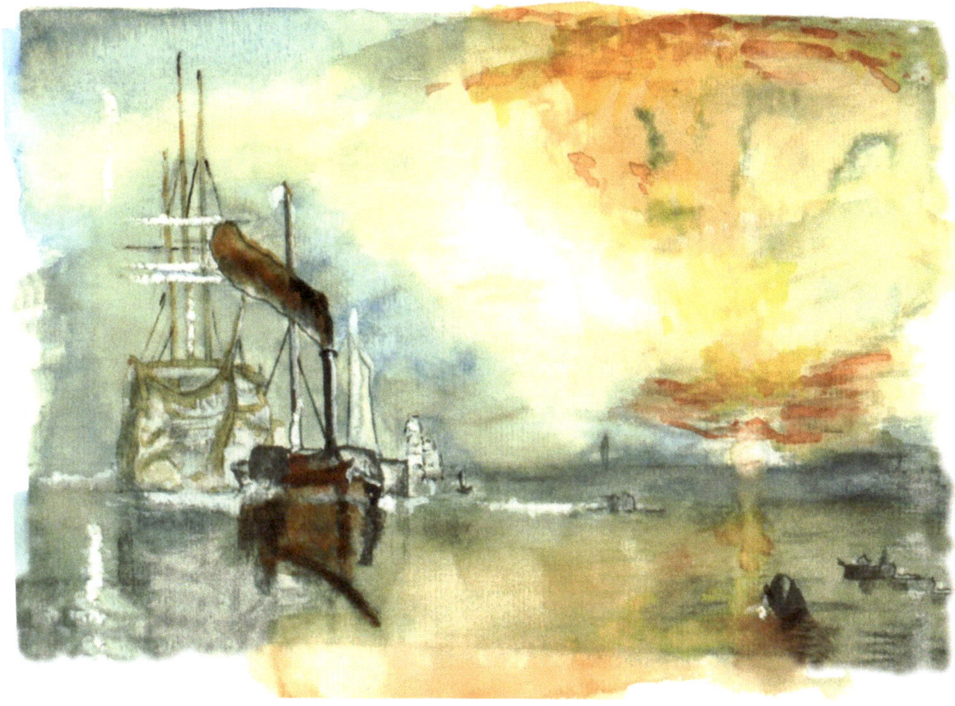

Most artists who chose to accurately depict the weather seemed to prefer sunny days or at least neutral weather. The weather is of course an environmental consideration, and artists were more concerned with their principal subject matter rather than the weather.

Can you think of any exceptions? A good one is John Constable. Look at his storm clouds. They indeed are subject matter in their own right and Constable used these to symbolise the turbulent times, as with Turner, the onset of the Industrial Revolution. *The Haywain* is set in Flatford Mill in Constable's home county of Suffolk England.

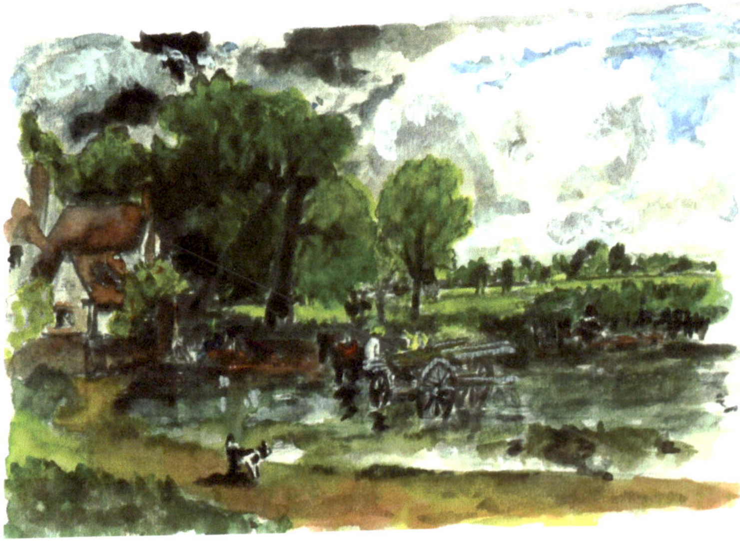

Most pictures, obviously landscapes, urban settings and with many indoor spaces, the location is evident. Many works even state the location in their title like Cezanne's *Mont St Victoire*. Vincent Van Gogh painted Arles, the German Expressionists, Berlin, Gainsborough's *Mr and Mrs Andrews* is set in rural England.

Here is an example of beautiful weather and a stunning location by an especially skilful and talented British artist, Dame Laura Knight. It's called *The Cornish Coast* and was painted in 1917 at the height of World War I.

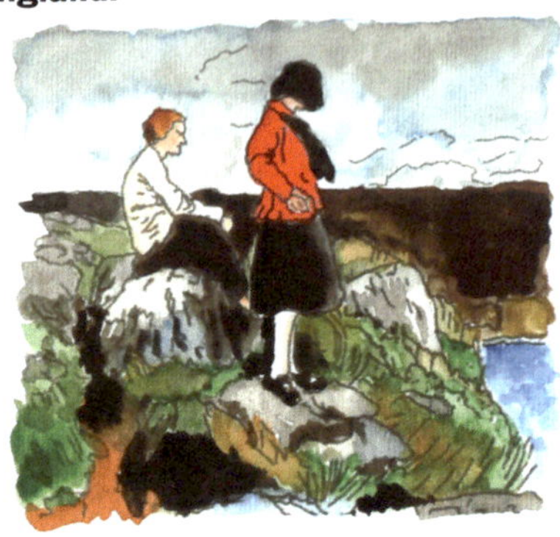

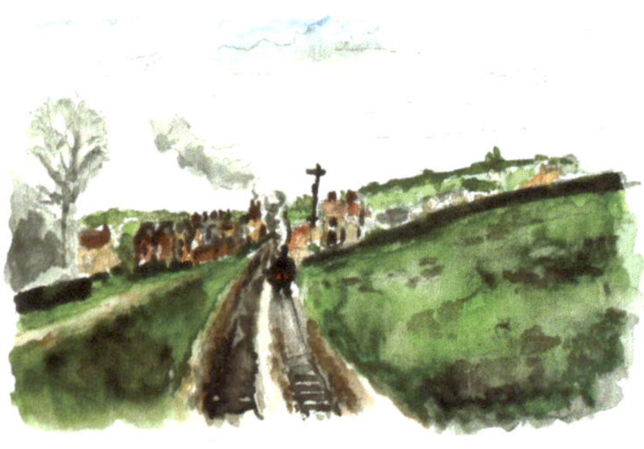

Camille Pissarro, one of the founders of the Impressionist movement, spent some time in England and we can recognise where he lived and worked by this picture and indeed how he titled the work.

Camille Pissarro 1830-1903 *Lordship Lane Station Dulwich*
1871

Looking at a picture's weather, time and location can tell us a lot about the artist's ways of working and what was important to them in respect of subject matter. The art movement too can be revealed by the way the artist's style has treated aspects of weather and location.

The Picture's Background

There are many paintings that contain important background images and details for instance the clock on the wall, the various objects on shelves and tables, the castaway pair of shoes on the floor or various depictions of items of symbolism.

Nothing has been placed in a picture by accident. It is all deliberate.

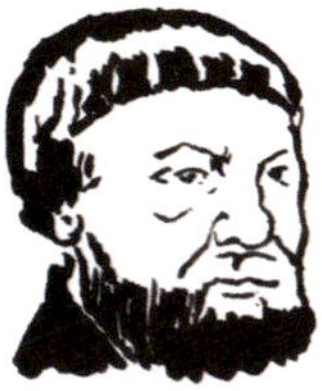

"I'm Hans Holbein. Look at My painting called *The Ambassadors*. A couple of lads visiting the Court of Henry VIII in 1533. On the left is a landowner called Jean de Dinteville and on the right is a cleric called Georges de Selve, who is a bishop."

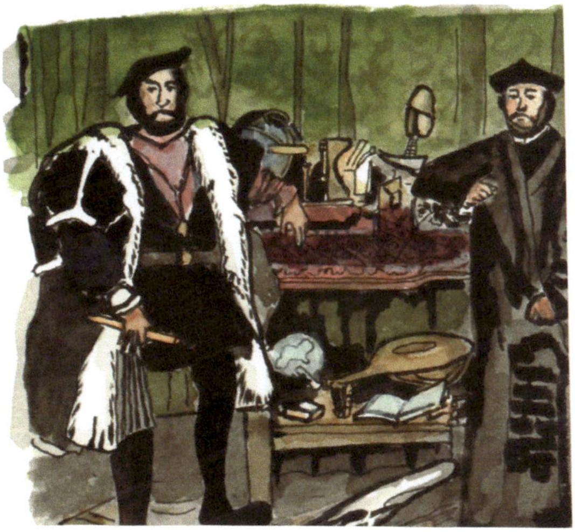

Remember the religious strife at the time. The Protestant reformation: Martin Luther, Henry VIII: the old ways of the church versus the new ways of science and discovery and humanism or indeed the unification of secular capitalism and the modern church before the Counter-Reformation. So, what has Holbein placed between these two? See if you can pick out the universal equinox dial, the sun dial and the globe. Also, there's the arithmetic book and mobile sundial and an astronomical instrument. We also have a measuring instrument and some musical instruments together with a Lutheran hymnal psalm book, a stretched skull and finally an Anatolian carpet. Can you spot them all?

Finally, what do you make of the crucifix at the very top left of the picture? Look at the date. It is set in England. What happened in the 1530s?

The component parts are unified – they all contribute to the subject matter. They are all important items of learning, science and discovery. Each is interdependent upon one another and the primary subject matter which is of course the ambassadors themselves. In addition, these parts are harmonious in that they represent important features of progress, education and understanding of the time.

Many works of the Renaissance contain important codified objects that contribute symbolically to the painting. Viewers could look out for such objects and say for instance "Oh that's so and so. I know that because she is holding a thingamajig as she always does". Let's look at a few examples.

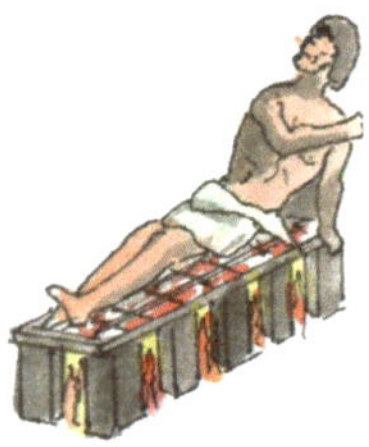

St Lawrence on the grill

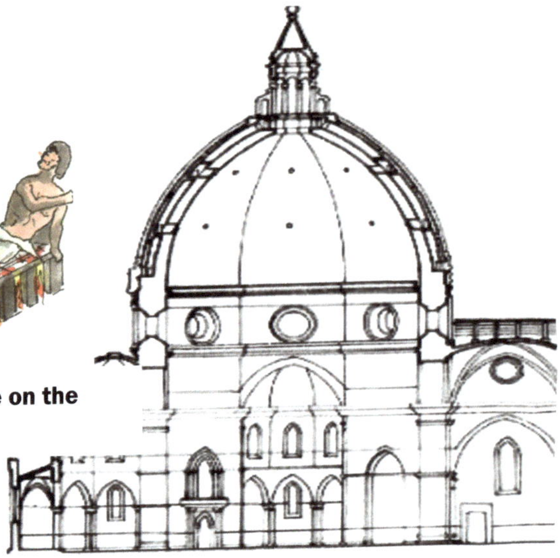

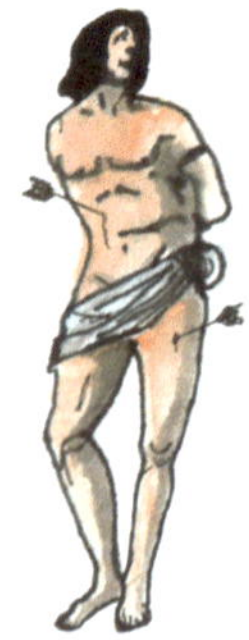

St Sebastian and the arrows he was shot with

St Catherine and her wheel that she was going to be broken on.

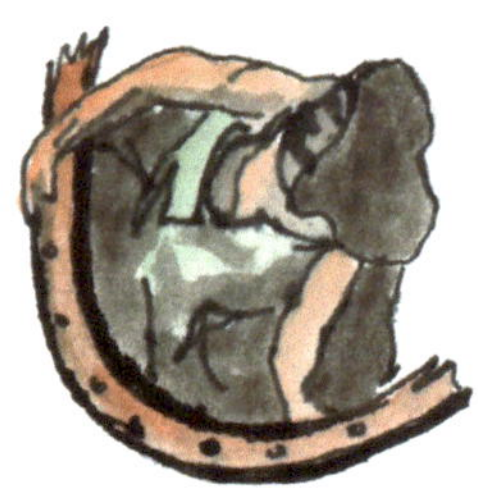

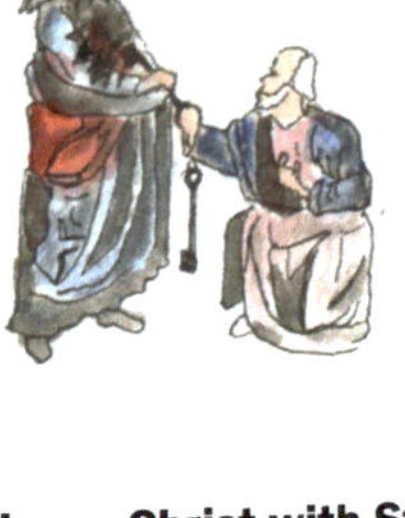

Jesus Christ with St Peter and his keys to heaven

"All rather gruesome"

Extract from *Christ Carrying the Cross*

Hieronymus Bosch 1516

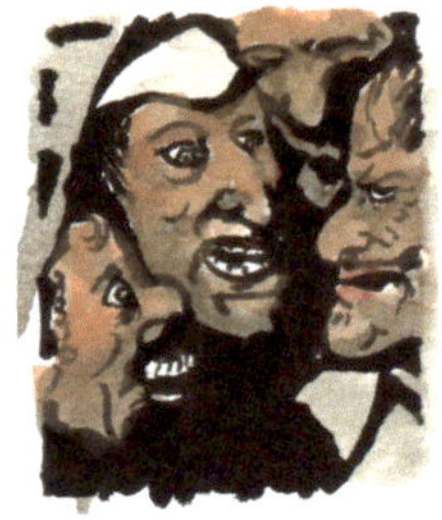

The power of art to convey messages and meanings. Look at Bronzino's 1546 *Venus and Cupid*. It's High Renaissance: Italian Mannerist as we've seen. For many, art had reached its perfection in the Renaissance, Mannerism was a reaction.

Bronzino has added a lot of additional detail as component parts adding to the depth of his message – the pleasures, agonies and ecstasies of love. What greater human emotion could you wish for as with Correggio, Raphael and Titian's depictions of love and lust.

Again, see if you can spot the images.

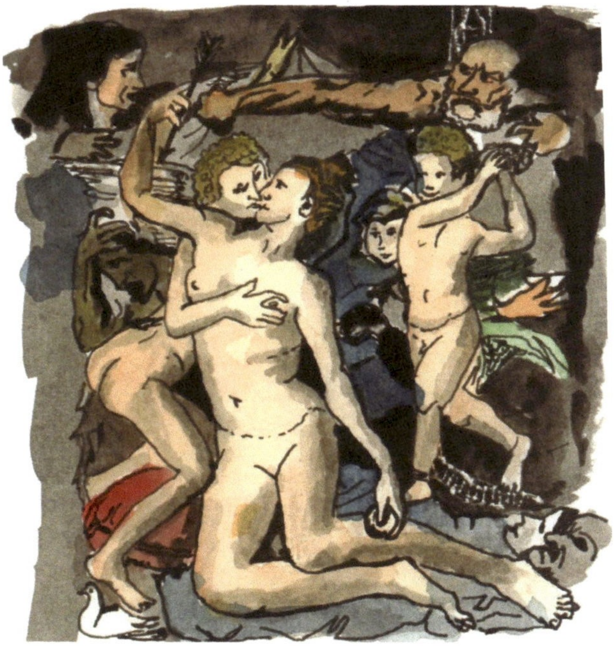

From the top left going down: Uncertainty pulling the curtain back, Cupid and his arrow, the face of rage and despair, that physical loving feeling, cushions to enjoy love on and the dove of peace.

Top right and reading down: Old Father Time, rose petals, serpent of jealousy, masks of illusion and a pomegranate as a symbol of love and lust.

If this was just a picture of Venus and Cupid, it would be nowhere near as powerful without the aspects of the emotion that Bronzino has dramatically and symbolically included.

*

Paul Gauguin led a fascinating life. After working on the Panama Canal, he married a Danish girl, and they had 5 children. They moved from France to Copenhagen where Gauguin became a tarpaulin salesman, but he couldn't speak Danish. So that did not work. He became a stockbroker, but that did not work. So, he became an artist.

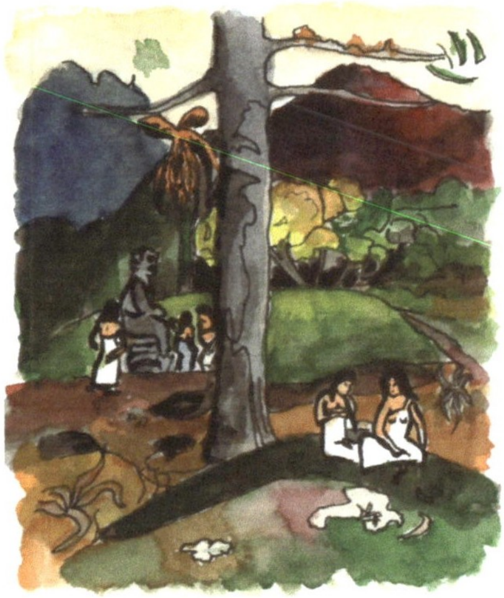

In 1885 he left his wife and children and moved to Paris to enjoy the art community there.

Following his move to Arles in 1888 to join his friend Vincent Van Gogh he journeyed to the South Seas where he sought and found the free primitive hedonistic lifestyle that suited him.

With his 1892 *Mata Mua* the two women on the right are playing and listening to a musical pipe, the group on the left are dancing around a pagan image, all against the backdrop of the rich vegetation of the unspoilt island in the South Seas.

The pagan image is of a female oceanic deity Hina or the Moon. In Tahiti this deity was held responsible for women and their affairs and work, the characteristics of their sex and their capacity to emphasize and deceive.

It is about celebrating women as well as ritual celebration, the place of music and dance in the culture, worshipping through bodily movement. The mountain behind is the home of the old gods still dominating the living.

Let's now look at this 1931 work by Edward Hopper called *Hotel Room*.

There is a deep psychological depth at play here. The young woman is depicted sitting alone or is she just resting from the crowd? Hopper's work is constructed as though we are looking into the room through a peep hole.

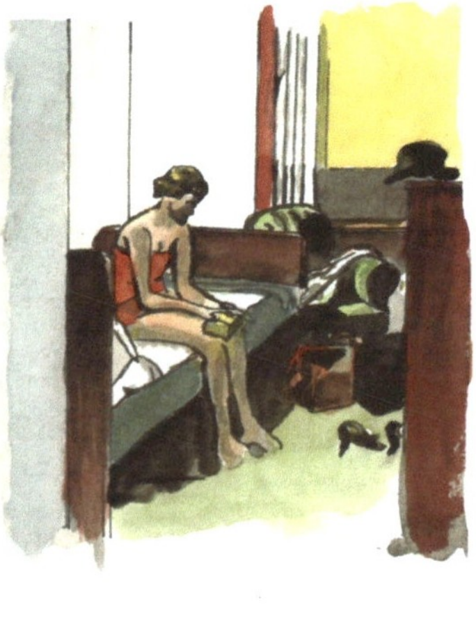

How do we know that it's warm daytime and the sun is shining outside? The strong shadows and her state of undress. Or of course it could be nighttime with street lighting and advertising neon spilling into the room. Therein holds the storyline to weave.

Questions: what is she reading, a novel, a bus timetable or the Bible? Why is she alone? Is she resting and if so, from what? Running away from what or who? Just arrived? From where? Waiting, for what or who?

Why do you think Hopper decided to paint her almost anonymously? You cannot make out any particularly distinguishing facial features. Is there something here about the vulnerability of young women in the city?

Look at the unpacked suitcases on the floor, the cast away shoes, the discarded clothes on the chair. Consider also the heavy verticals and horizontals contributing structure and solidity to an uncertain narrative.

*

From looking at component parts let's now look at the picture's background where it is obviously an essential part of the primary subject matter, a part of the narrative.

A good example of this is Thomas Gainsborough's *Mr and Mrs Andrews* where the background landscape is also the subject matter that is Mr and Mrs Andrews' status, ownership and position in society. A bourgeoise art but Gainsborough of course was responding to the market demands of the time.

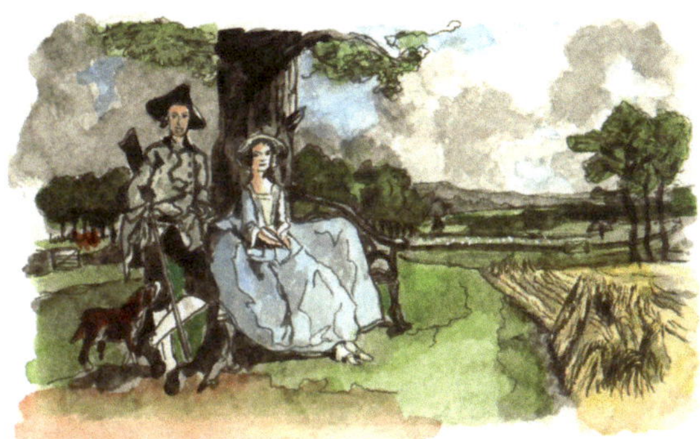

"I'm sick of portraits and wish very much to take my voil-da-gam and walk off to some sweet village, where I can paint landskips and enjoy the fag end of life in quietness and ease. But these fine ladies and their tea drinking, dancing, husband hunting etc. etc. will rob me out of the last ten, and I fear miss getting husbands too." So said Gainsborough.

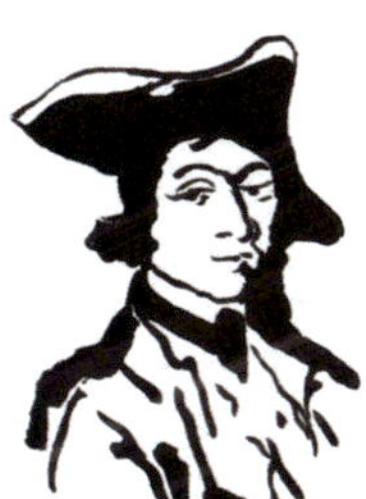

"The story here is in the background: the Andrews' estate. My painting is a unique combination of landscape and a double, informal portrait. Robert and Francis invited me to paint this shortly after their wedding in 1750."

Thomas Gainsborough 1727–1788

Many paintings depicting a particular storyline contain important background material – not just component parts. These contribute to the events that are taking place in the foreground and complete the narrative

In *Grey Day* by George Grosz, in the foreground is obviously the rich fat architect, whilst immediately behind him the wounded soldier whose wartime sacrifice is now negated, and he is cast away in favour of the new world. 'Component parts' could be the two figures against the background structures of the new post war industrialisation.

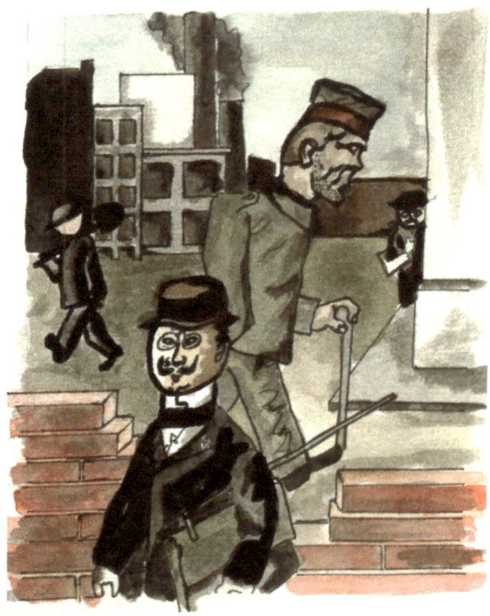

Brushstrokes and the application of paint

Look now at whether the painting could be considered as, to quote Heinrich Wölfflin, an important Swiss art historian, in his book first published in 1915, *Principles of Art History* ... 'painterly' or 'linear'?

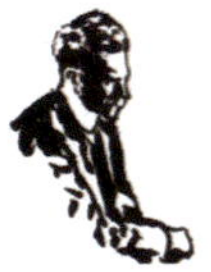

Heinrich Wölfflin 1864 – 1945

Was the painting painted in a fine brush style or is it difficult to spot the brushstrokes? This would be where the artist portrayed his or her subject matter almost as could be described as a photogenic style: no texture to be seen, the final image smooth and completely flat.

The converse would be the artist who painted with obvious brushstrokes. The viewer can easily see the direction of the strokes and maybe even the type of brush used or the use of a palette knife. Painterly: a lush almost tactile paint rich work with perhaps for example non-precise figure edging; a melding and mellowing of all subjects in the canvas. Heavy layers of paint, impasto.

In contrast to the linear approach where the artist has depicted the work with obvious lines, draughts-manly or plasticity even. More of a drawn approach rather than lush rich paintwork.

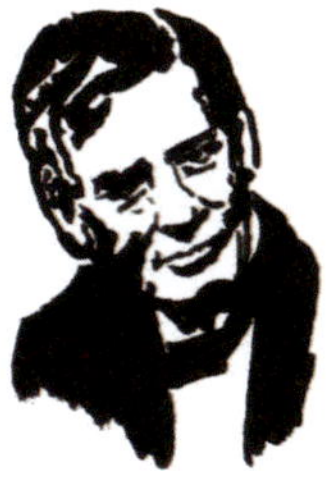

Walter Richard Sickert 1860 – 1942

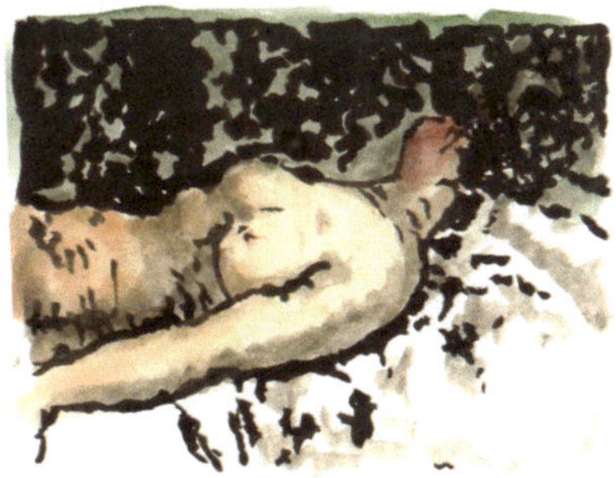

Detail from *What Shall we do for the Rent?* ~1909

You can certainly see the loose brush strokes in this work by Walter Sickert. Painterly.

And most dramatically is the painterly work of the late Frank Auerbach.

Look also at this extract from Georges Seurat's (1859 – 1891) *La Parade de Cirque* (1889). This is known as pointillism, almost as we would know today as pixels. You can see how the work has been made up of thousands of points of paint, applied by the tip of his brush. This could be defined as painterly.

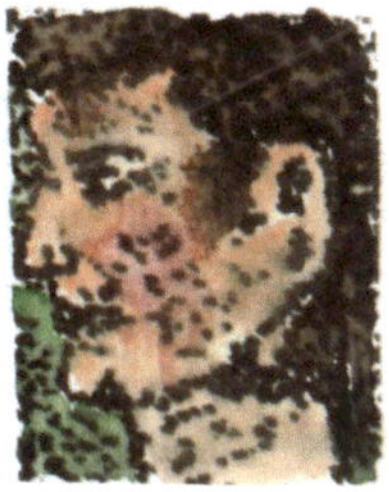

Jackson Pollock's drips falling accidentally at random or as he maintained: the drops were his own deliberately created pattern. Painterly.

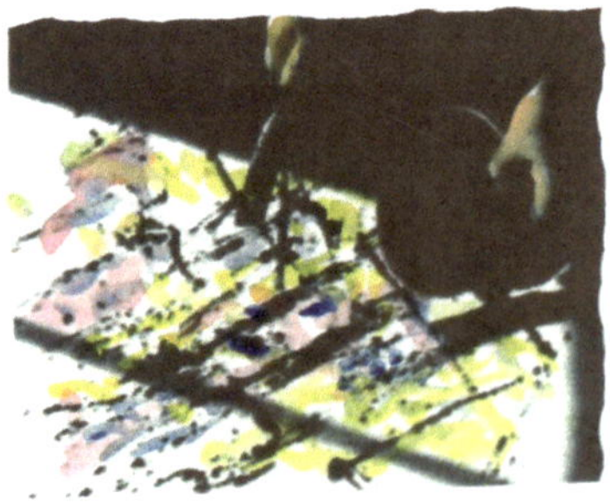

Or Mark Rothko's (1903 – 1970) extremely broad strokes.

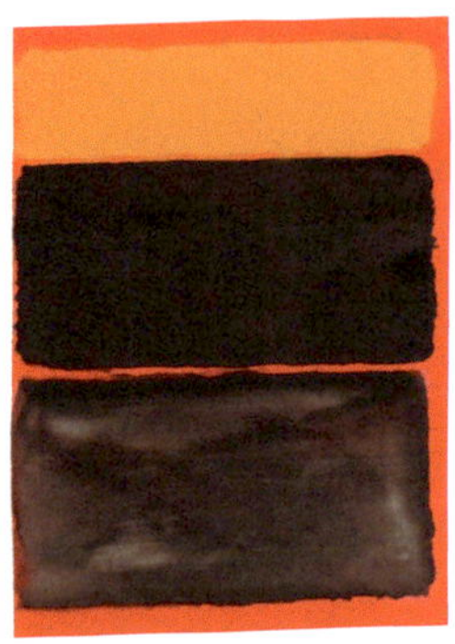

Think of brushes: broad and square bristles, fan brushes, palette knives and even stipple brushes – opening up the work, capturing light and spontaneity. Fine bristles – for fine lines and details.

The application of paint – fine or heavy?

Is painterly the right way to describe the works of Vassily Kandinsky for instance, or his contemporary Soviet Russian avant-garde Malevich?

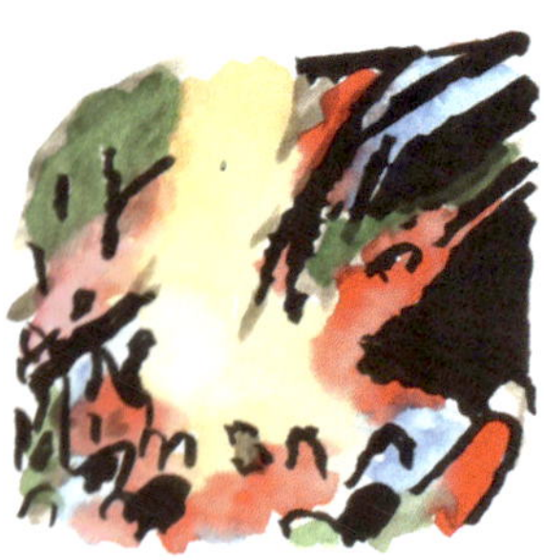

Wassily Kandinsky

Malevich *Black Square*

Also worth a mention is Jackson Pollock's fellow Abstract Expressionist Willem de Kooning as his works can appear unrefined, messy and slapdash.

As do many German Expressionists for instance together as a network but not as a movement under the title Blaue Reiter. Artists such as Wassily Kandinsky and Ernst Kirchner of the Blaue Reiter Group.

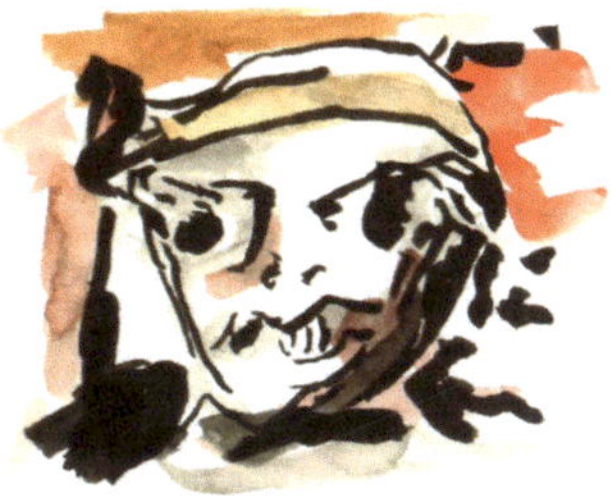

Extract from William de Kooning, *Woman V*, 1953

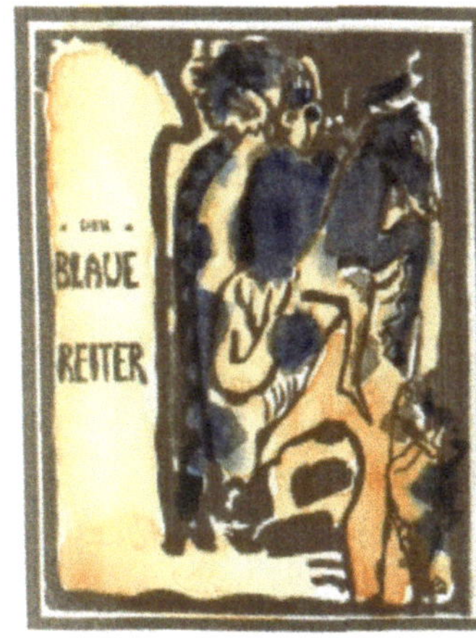

Ask the questions: "what is the artist trying to achieve?" "What is their rationale and criteria for success?" "Why did they choose to paint in the manner and style as they did?"

"In 1878 I sued John Ruskin for saying that my painting '*Nocturne*', was like "asking two hundred guineas for flinging a pot of paint in the public's face" I don't think he liked my expressive brush-strokes. I won the case but was only awarded one farthing for my troubles"

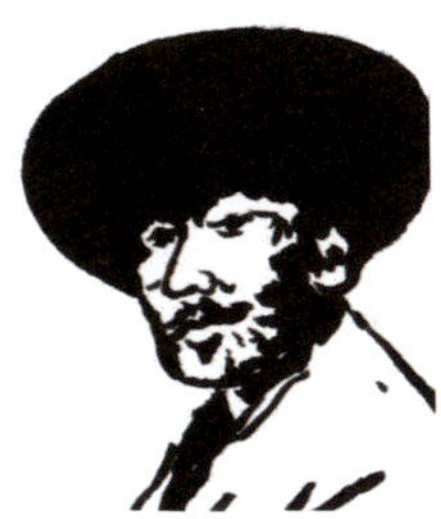

James McNeill Whistler 1834 - 1903

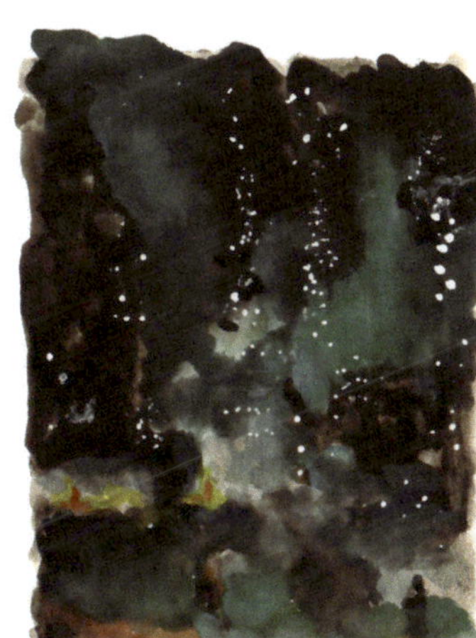

Nocturne in Black and Gold: The Falling Rocket 1875

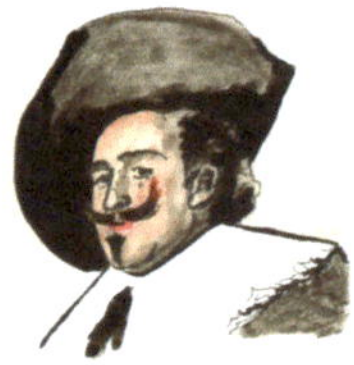

The Laughing Cavalier
1642
Painterly

Frans Hals 1582 - 1666

Stanley Spencer *The Resurrection of the Soldiers* 1929

Linear

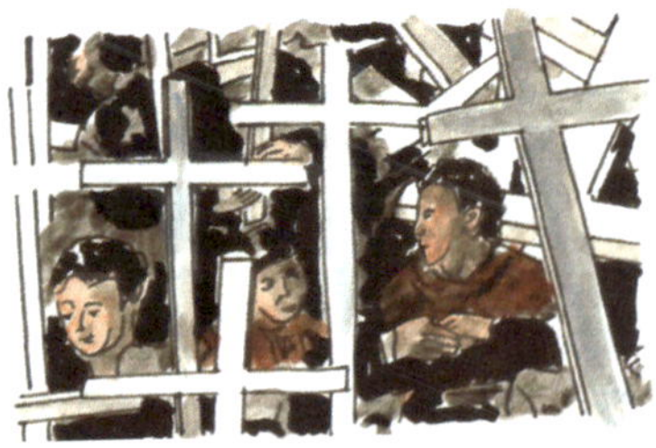

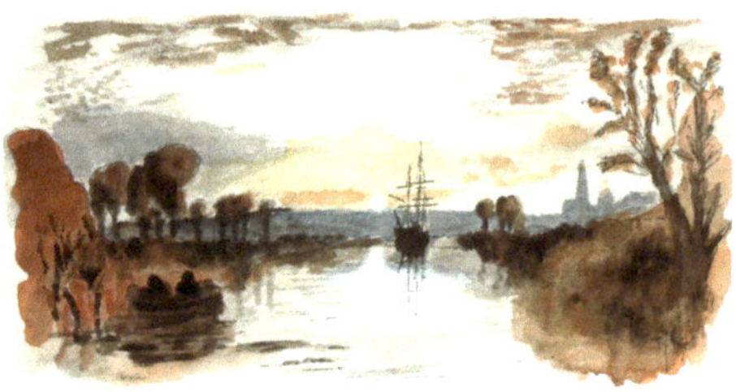

JMW Turner
Painterly

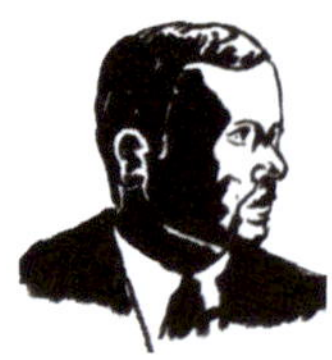

Joan Miró i Ferrà
1893–1983

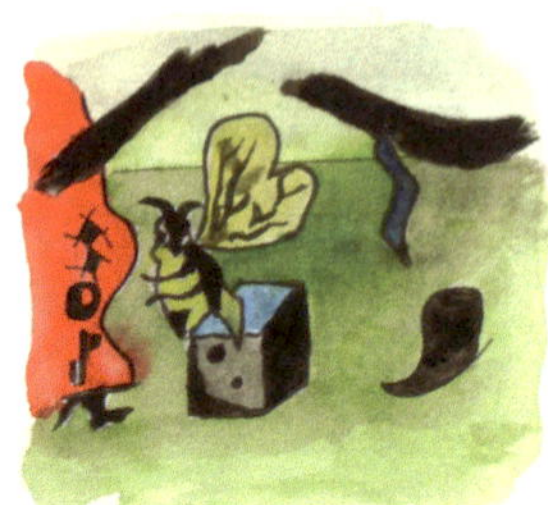

Schematic of *Carnival of Harlequin*
Linear

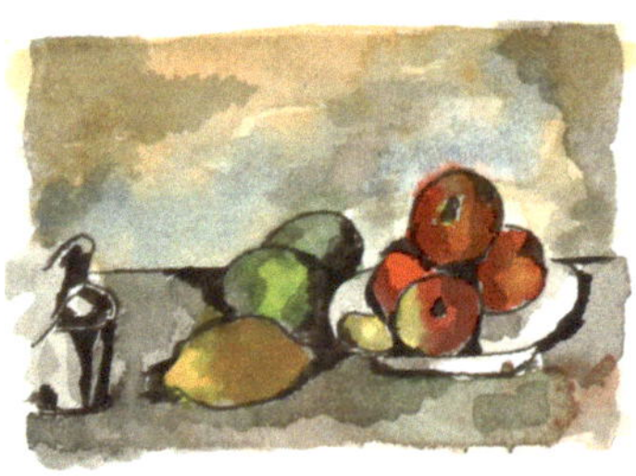

Cezanne *Still Life with Apples,* 1890
Painterly

"But how would you describe me Herr Wölfflin - painterly or linear?"

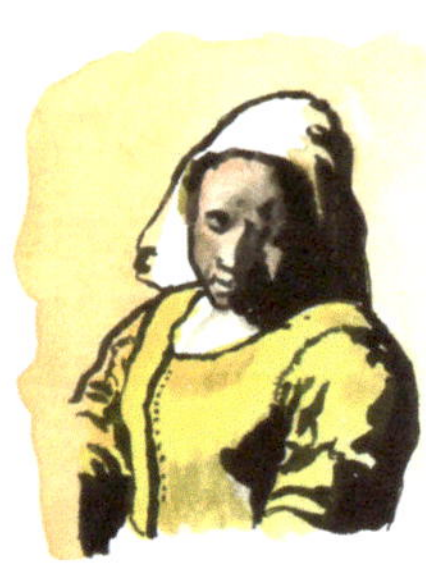

Detail from Johannes Vermeer's *The Milk Maid* 1658

Sometimes it is difficult to be precise between painterly and linear. Look for lines or lush paintwork being prominent.

Studio or outdoors

Where did the artist choose to paint their works. Indoors or outdoors - En plein-air...outside? Generally speaking, until the age of the Romanticists and later the Impressionists, artists completed their work within the confines and comfort of their studios.

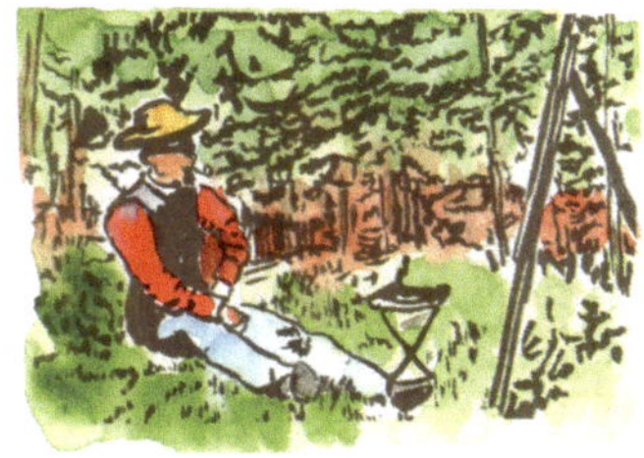

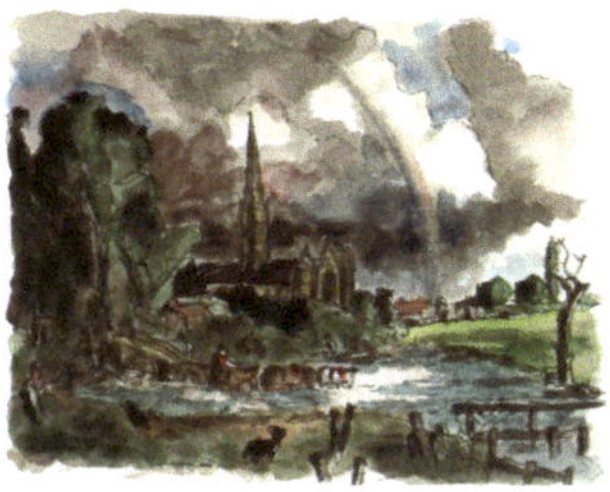

"But I took my sketchpad and actually visited my locations in order to obtain a real feel for my landscapes, and I completed in my studio. You try and paint six-foot square canvas in the open air!"

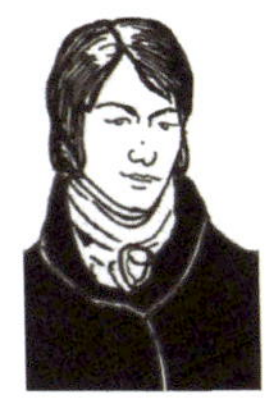

John Constable

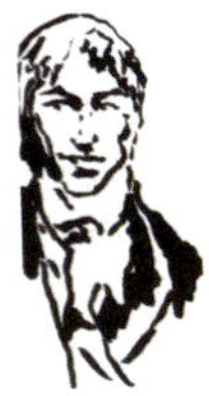

"And I like the story of me being lashed to the mast of a boat so that I could witness for myself what a storm at sea looked and felt like. But again, of course you couldn't expect me to paint my picture from that mast."

JMW Turner

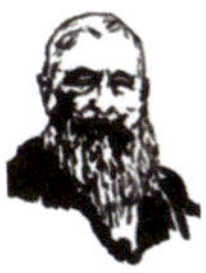

"But I actually painted in the open air, en plein-air."

Claude Monet

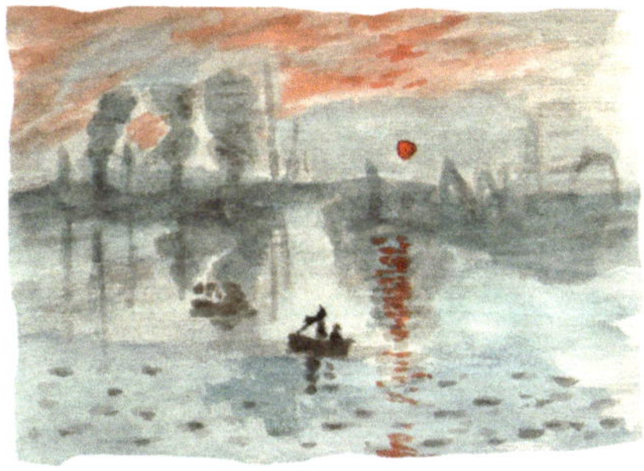

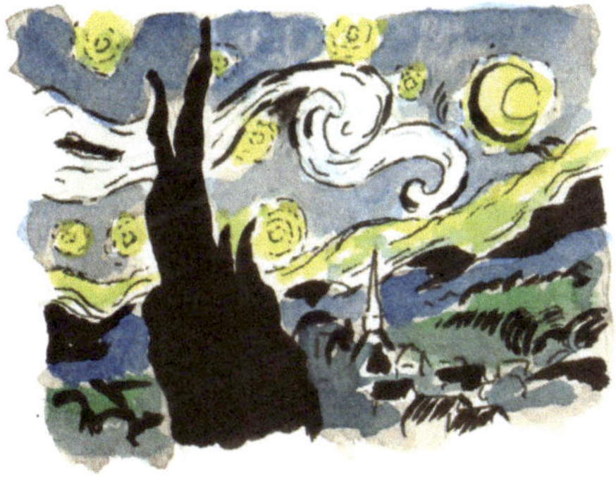

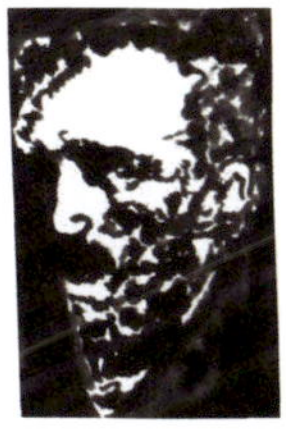

"So did I. Although *The Starry Night* was painted in my room in the asylum"

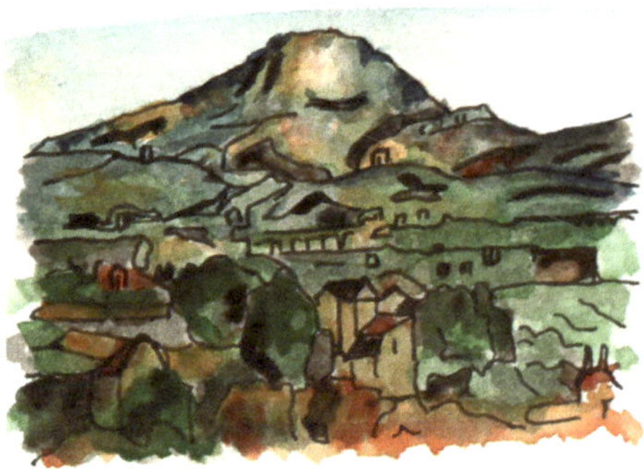

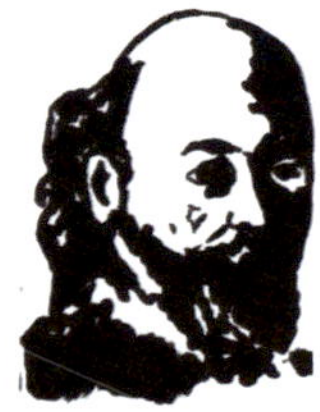

Paul Cézanne

"Outdoors for me in the sunny hills of Provence"

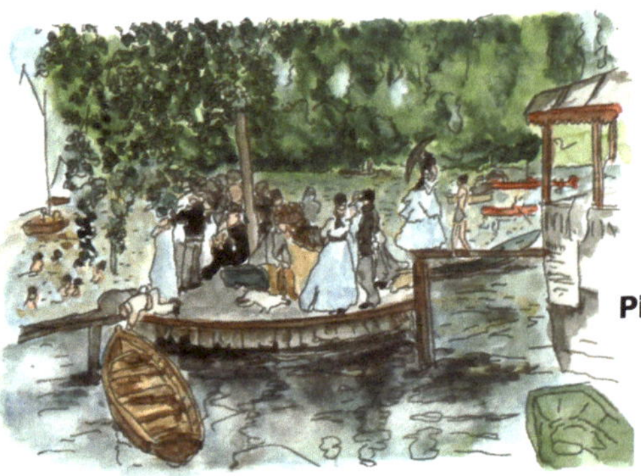

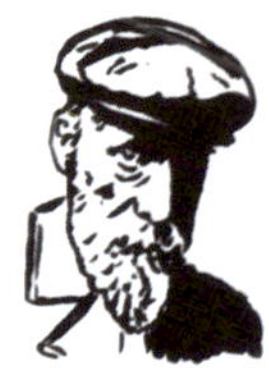

Pierre-August Renoir

"Sitting by the river with my paints and canvas on a warm afternoon. Bliss"

Advances in technology came into play with artists in the 19th Century being able to take advantage of the new invention of oils being ready mixed and available in tubes for easy packing and transporting to the open air.

Form and composition

Essentially there are three particular criteria that determine an artist's arrangement of figurative parts: the iconographic traditions, the need to emphasise certain items and the artist's own imagination.

Leading the eye and drawing us in, journeying us through the picture, arriving at the destination on the picture that the artist intended.

*

First of all: To the fore or to the background? Open or closed form?

Is the subject matter depicted to the fore of the canvas towards the middle of the scene or at the back of the picture? Does the picture open up to you or does it seem to be closed within itself?

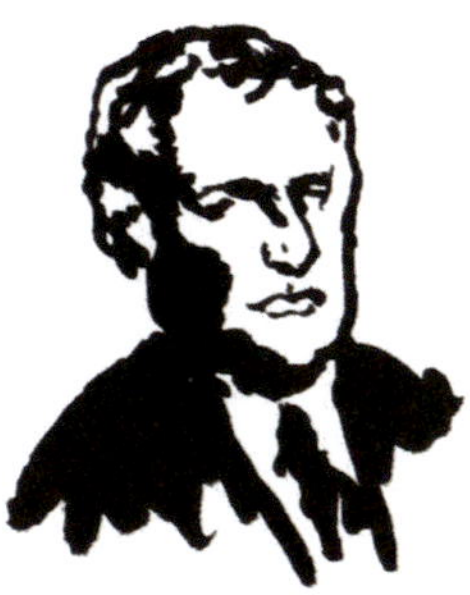

"I'm Edvard Munch and I painted a series of these images *The Scream of Nature.* Look how I've positioned my central figure. Look how I've brought the image straight into your space with the pier and the cut off of the figure below the frame."

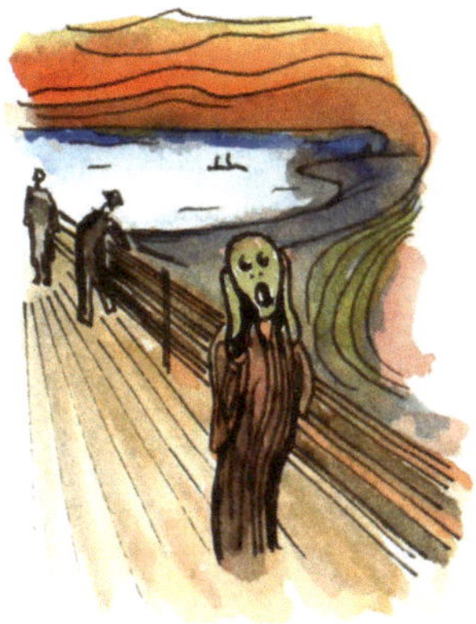

In the *Scream* a very deep perspective is achieved with the landscape in the background and the small figures on the pier.

The pier itself travelling from the rear to the front and off the canvas, drawing us in as part of the scene.

We are stood before the screamer.

How else could Edvard Munch have positioned his figure?

Receding

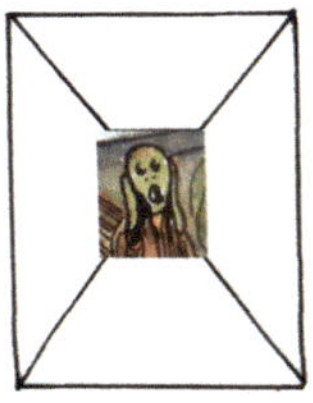

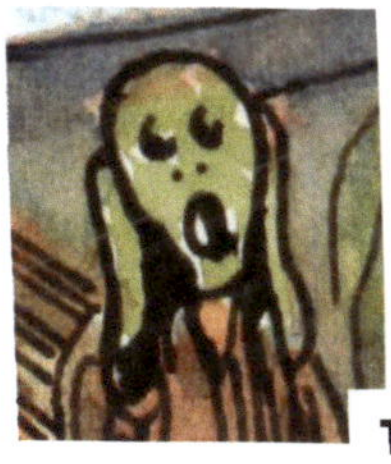

To the fore

A look at Grant Wood's

American Gothic 1930. As it is...

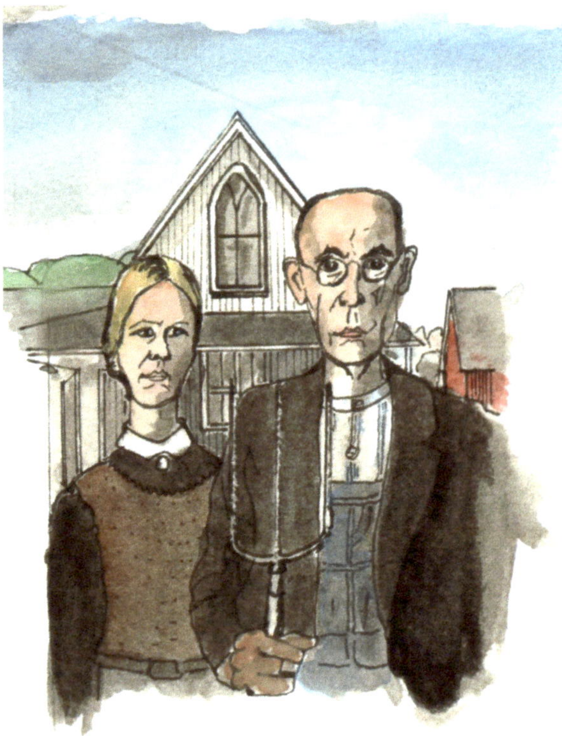

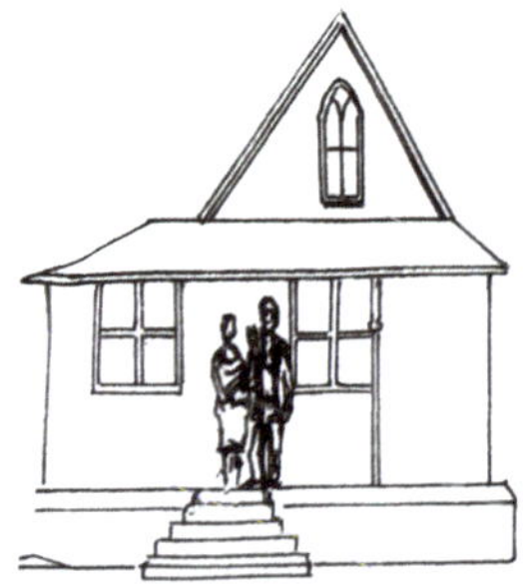

... and as it could have been composed.

What difference does it make to how you see the painting? How involved are you? Feel your emotions, are you drawn in? Do you feel a sense of belonging or foreboding? Does the work close you off?

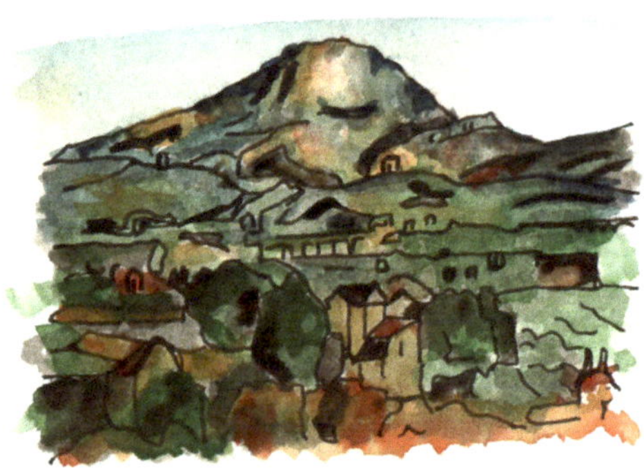

Looking again at our familiar *Mont St Victoire* it is far distant; there's no immediate foreground inviting you in. Do you feel involved? It's a distant landscape. But you could feel as though you're standing on the hillside along with Cézanne.

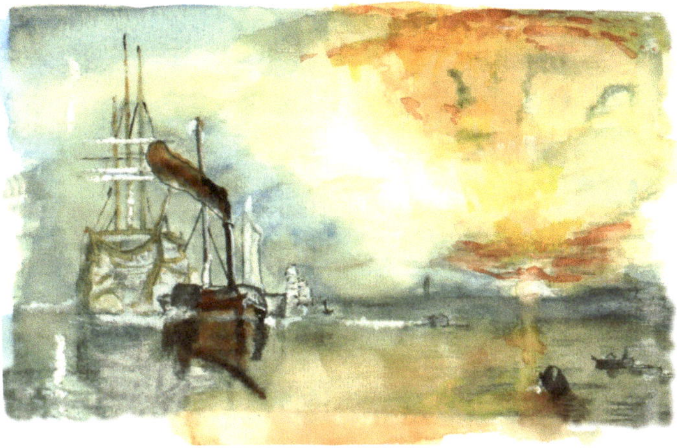

The Temeraire and the tugboat, whilst away in the background are coming towards you the viewer. The sea itself has been composed in such a way that it is opening up from the front of the canvas and narrowing towards the rear to again draw you in. Turner has made such a composition to help you to imagine the sea as opening arms to give you a feeling of intimacy with the story, empathising with the fear and excitement of human vulnerability. Turner particularly used this approach with his stormy seascapes.

To the fore or to the background? Open or closed? What has the artist done? What effect does it have on the picture and particularly on you?

Now let's consider 'open and closed form'

Heinrich Wölfflin, pointed out that generally speaking the Renaissance saw closed form with everything in the painting pointing back into within itself, totally self-contained with close symmetry.

Whilst the open form, by and large from the Baroque onwards, saw the painting extending beyond itself and purposely looking limitless.

Let's look at a couple of examples to try and get a feel for what Wölfflin meant.

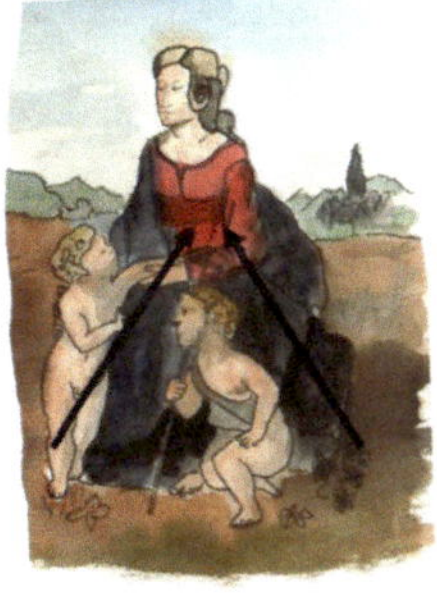

Closing into the picture.

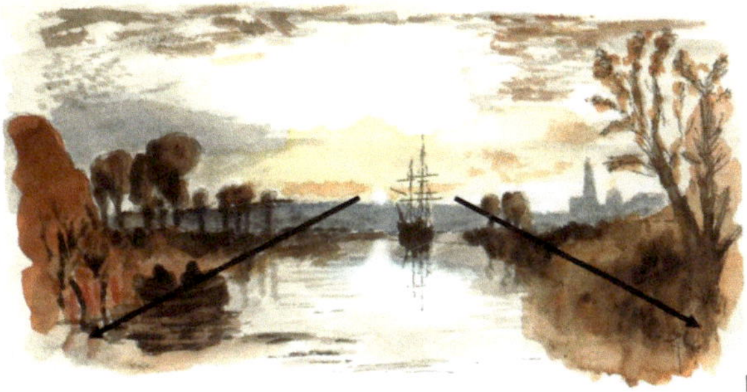

Opening up. Coming out of the picture.

The Raphael is self-contained whereas the Turner extends beyond the canvas.

Golden triangle or section. The Fibonacci Formula

Let's now give some thought to how structurally most pictures work and how they fulfil their role and purpose for you the viewer. Without us being in front and looking at that picture it would have no point or purpose whatsoever. A little like the Universe being out there but without us, so what? The picture has of course been made for us to look at. That's obvious. But how and why does it work?

What we are now going to consider are compositional techniques that play to our needs and desires as humans. The bottom line is that fundamentally, we as humans have an innate sense and need for harmony and balance and artists can use this innate sense by creating harmony or deliberate disharmony. Making us content, satisfied and comfortable or uncomfortable with what we see before us.

It is all based on us as humans existing wholly and intrinsically within the heart of nature, and nature's natural inclination for balance, harmony, symmetry, proportioning and ratioing. Eggs, seashells, flowers and even our own ears for example. Even the distance from the soles of your feet to your navel is relative to the rest of your body by approximately 1.618 i.e. the golden ratio.

Our brains are wired in such a way that makes images more pleasing to the eye when they follow the golden ratio whether a balanced rectangle or triangle.

Phi. By utilising nature's proportional symmetry an artist can achieve the aesthetic quality we as humans respond so positively to. So, if we applied measurements to the most successful works, by and large framing of the composition would be along the lines of 3:2 or 5:3 rectangles.

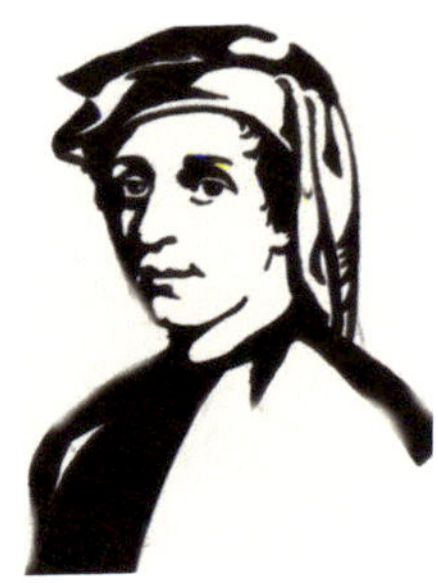

And that brings us neatly to the Fibonacci sequence.

This number sequence is named after the Italian mathematician Leonardo of Pisa, later known as Fibonacci.

In his 1202 book *Liber Abaci*, Fibonacci introduced the sequence to western European mathematics.

It implies that the ratio of two consecutive Fibonacci numbers tends to the golden ratio as *the numbers* increase. 1,1, 2, 3, 5, 8, 13, 21, 33.

The Fibonacci Sequence

1,1,2,3,5,8,13,21,34,55,89,144,233,377...

1+1=2	13+21=34
1+2=3	21+34=55
2+3=5	34+55=89
3+5=8	55+89=144
5+8=13	89+144=233
8+13=21	144+233=377

Fibonacci sequences appear in biological settings such as branching in trees, arrangement of leaves on a stem, the fruitlets of a pineapple, the flowering of artichoke, an uncurling fern, shells and the arrangement of a pine cone and daisies and the family tree of honeybees. Even waves.

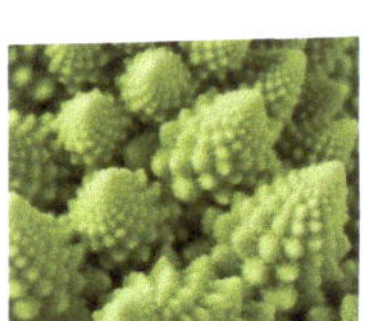
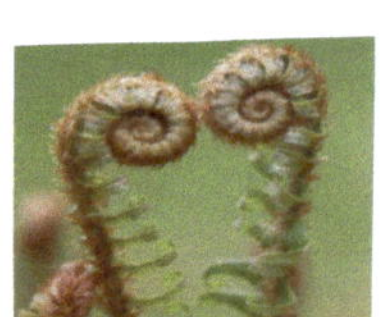
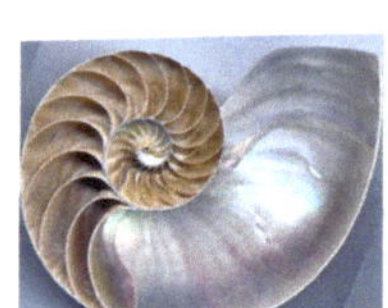
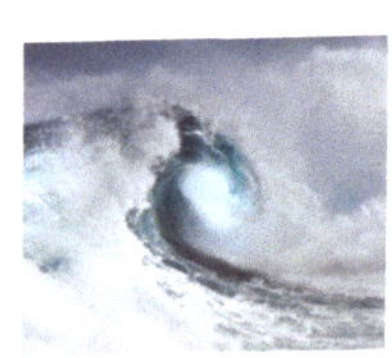

Fibonacci numbers equal the golden ratio and from this the golden spiral:

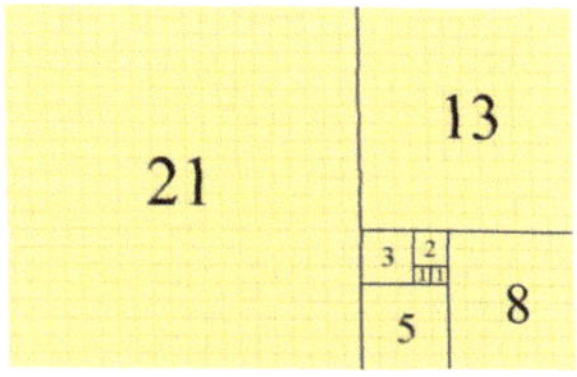

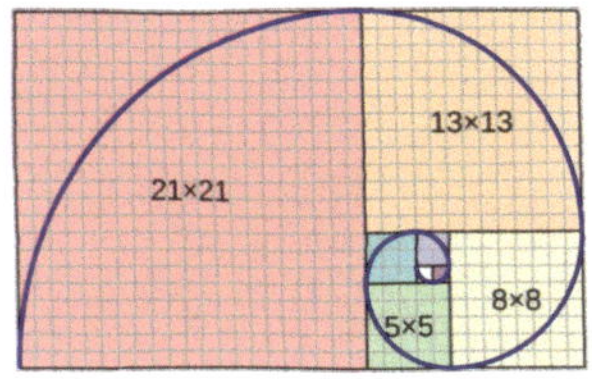

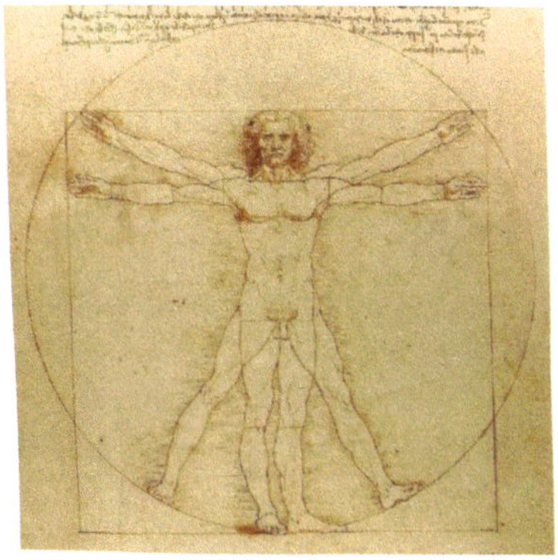

We are fundamentally constructed of these eurythmic symphonies of form woven into the very fabric of our existence, as seen in Leonardo's *Vitruvian Man,* to connect and resonate with the patterns of nature within which us as humans fundamentally fit.

With many works of art, you can apply the Fibonacci spiral and golden ratio and appreciate how artists have composed their pictures to give to the viewer a pleasing sense of balance and harmony or the obverse.

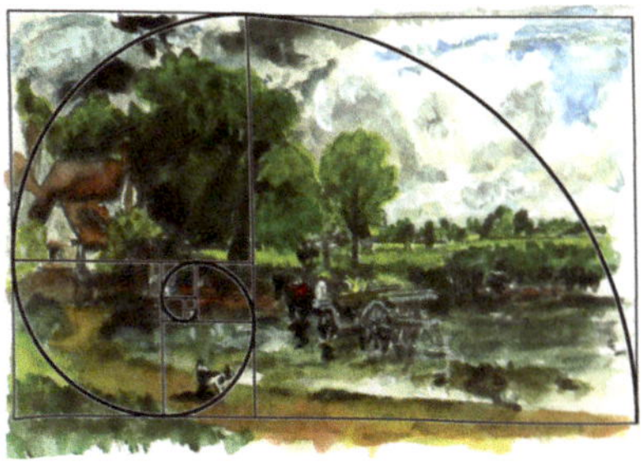

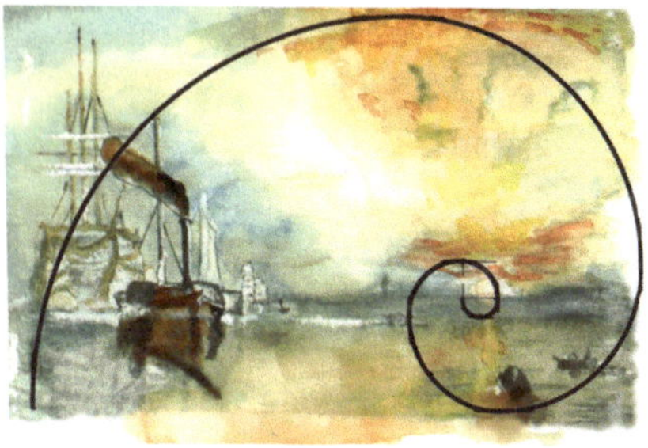

In addition, we like structure and a solidity. In technology, engineering and physics terms this is usually the triangle.

The golden triangle rule is a rule of thumb in visual composition for photographs or paintings, especially those which have elements that follow diagonal lines. And therefore essentially, with many works you can place a triangle over the central featu and see how the triangular solidity has been performed by the artist making works, work.

Let's superimpose a triangle on some pictures we are familiar with.

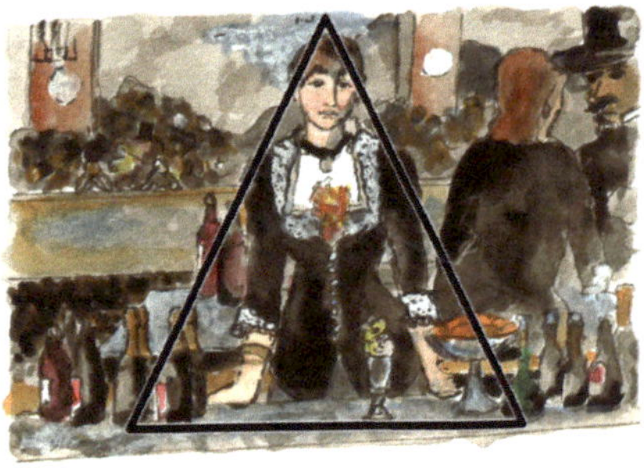

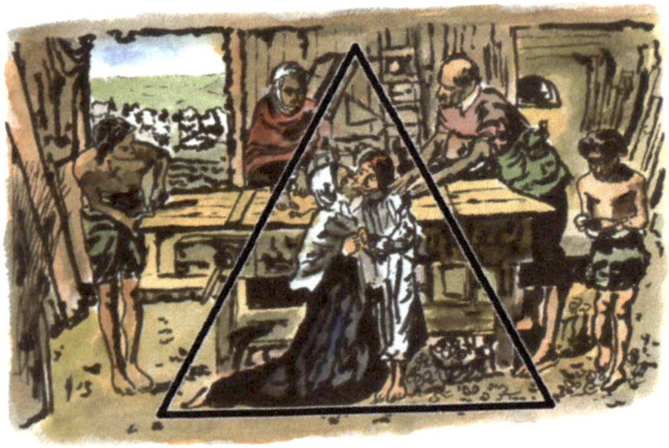

The principal subject matter is more or less contained within a triangular space, a golden section.

We respond to the shape and surface and mass of things. The Fibonacci spiral and the golden triangle and section are important means whereby artists can give us a pleasurable sensation whilst the lack of pleasing forms can lead to indifference, or even positive discomfort.

The spiral and section can guide our viewing eyes, giving or denying harmony, proportion and balance. Equilibrium created or challenged. Framing and establishing a focus and formulating a compelling image.

Visual tension can be an outcome creating an engaging experience as for example with *The Fighting Temeraire*. Compare this work and John Constable's landscapes with the disharmony and awkwardness of Ernst Kirchner and the Expressionists. What were these artists attempting to achieve, to tell us, to involve us in?

Where the Fibonacci spiral is particularly used a strong sense of aesthetic appeal is revealed with subjects becoming naturally attractive to our eye. A sense of beauty derived from geometric proportioning. The spiral connects art with mathematics, technology, biology and physics, bringing to the picture interdisciplinary links between sciences and the arts.

Follow the spiral and you will be led into and within the picture according to the artist's intention, drawing you deeper into the scene. Remember how the Fibonacci spiral reflects true proportions and patterns in nature of which we are intrinsically a part of. Consequently, anything that conflicts with this harmonisation, conflicts with our natural well-being, and artists of certain movements very well knew this.
The spiral is therefore a most important and powerful tool for the artist to employ, deny or distort. Enriching your experience before that picture.

Horizontal and vertical planes

Let's now consider the painting's horizontal and vertical planes – its strata parallel to picture plane. Its geometry.

Look at the picture and work out what the plane of the composition is. Is the subject matter along a horizontal or vertical plane? For example, a portrait is usually depicted up and down that is vertical whereas the landscape is usually depicted left and right that is, an horizontal plane.

Let's look at some predominantly horizontal pictures

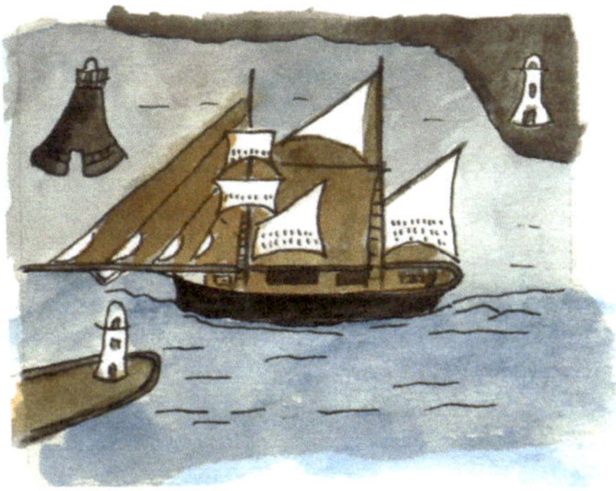

Alfred Wallis *Blue Boat*

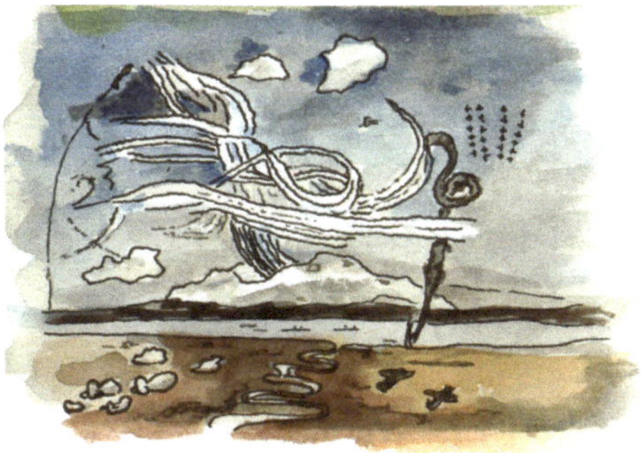

Paul Nash *Battle of Britain*

And an example of both vertical and horizontal.

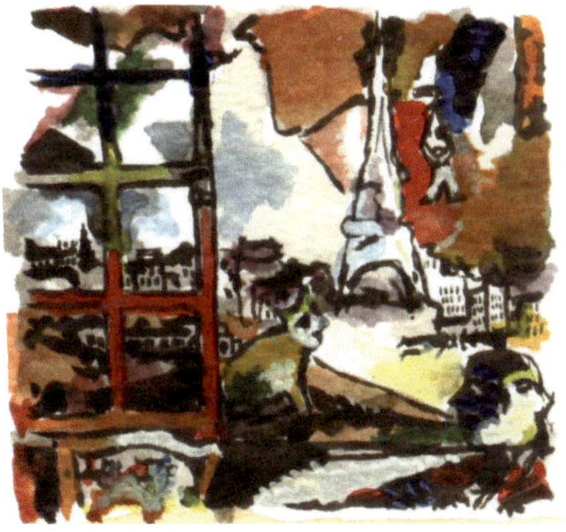

Mark Chagall. *Dream Class Parte Deux.* 1913

And for more examples of both vertical and horizontal

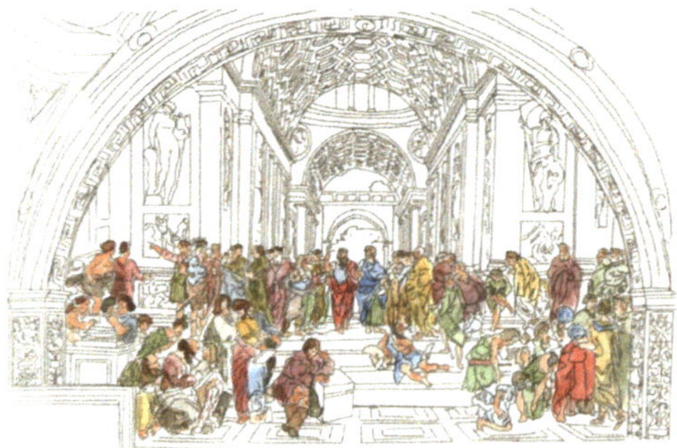

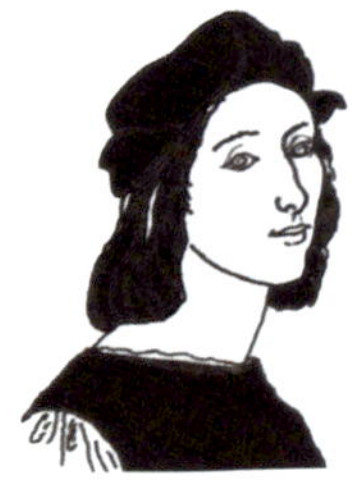

"In my *School of Athens*. I painted lots of verticals and horizontals.

Raphael

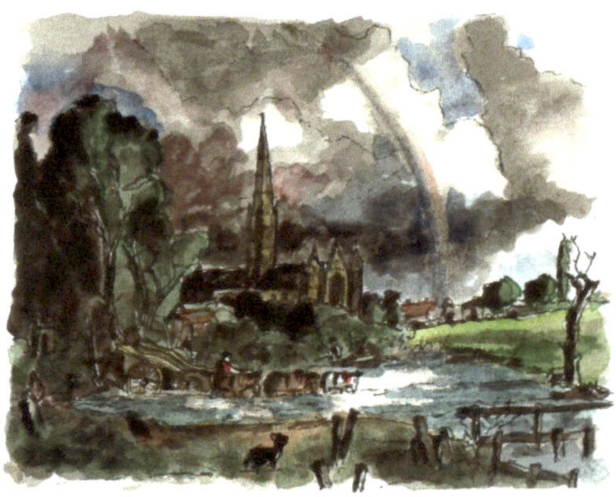

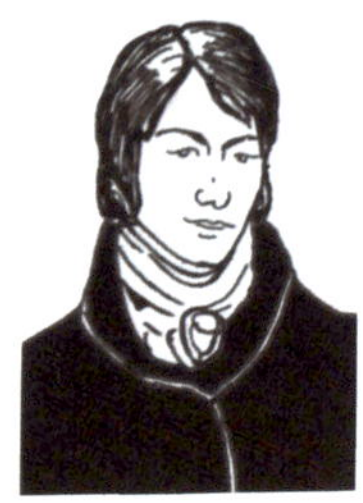

Constable

"In my *Salisbury Cathedral* you can see that I've used horizontals with the landscape and verticals with the trees and cathedral. The river is horizontal with a slight diagonal. Do you feel drawn into this picture? Do you feel the flow of the river?"

And some illustrations of vertical

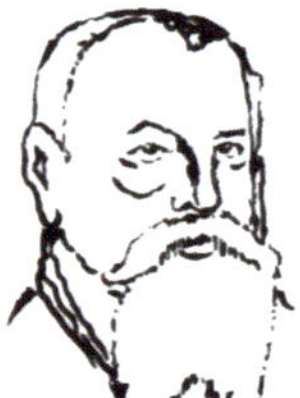

Lucas Cranach

"I painted my *Venus* on a wood panel in 1509. A most advanced study for the time do you not think? I concentrated on her elongated vertical form to give the feel of regality."

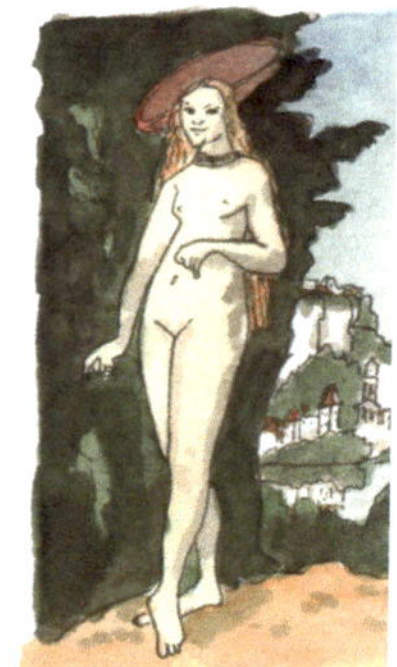

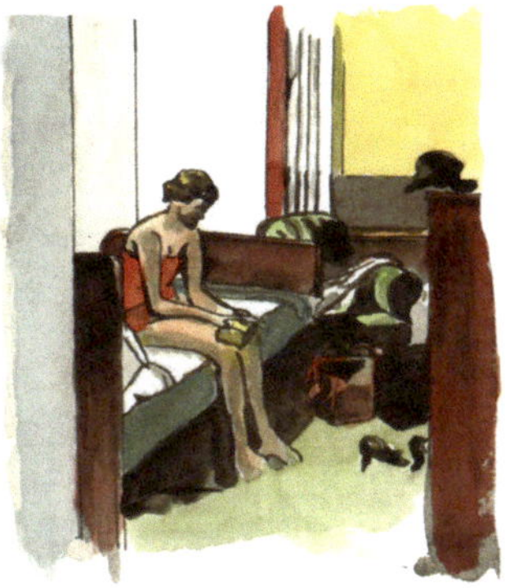

Edward Hopper's *Hotel Room* 1931. Predominantly vertical with diagonal bed drawing you into the room.

"Look how vertical my dominant tree is in my *Mata Mua*. There's the horizontal too. Consider the subject matter. Consider how erect the tree is and the women resting on the horizontal. How do you interpret this?"

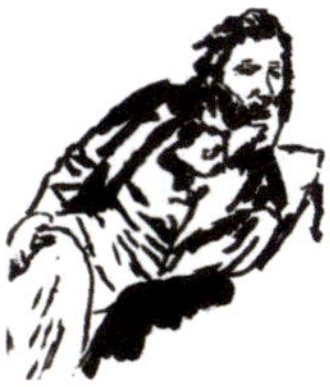

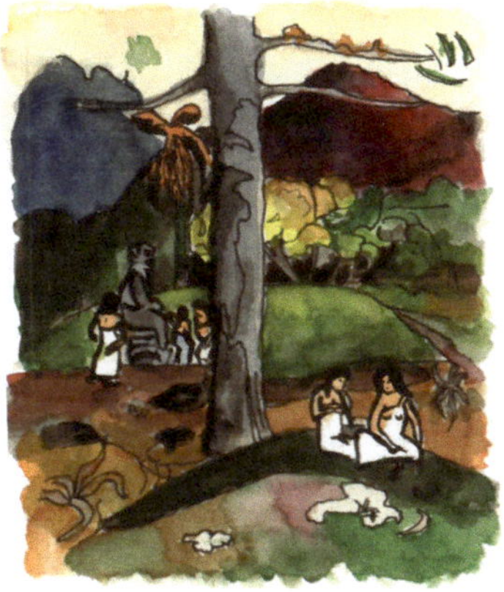

Perspective

When looking at a picture is the artist attempting to create space and perspective represented as two dimension or three dimensions. In other words, does the painting attempt at an illusion of space or does it acknowledge that the surface it is painted on is actually flat?

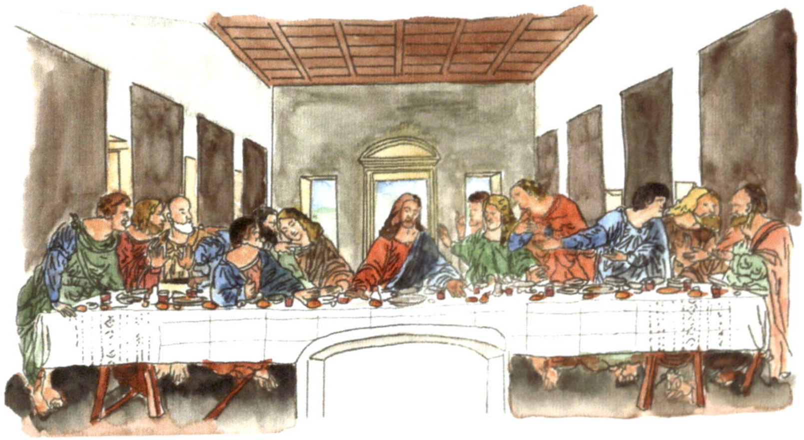

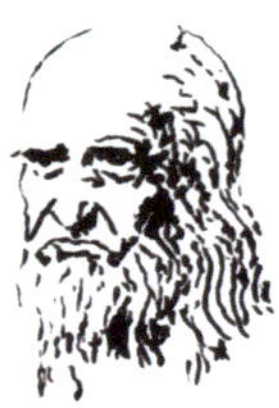

"Here I have gone to considerable lengths to create a three-dimensional illusion on a two dimensional surface thereby projecting my work from the flat wall on which the picture was painted to give the appearance of the *Last Supper* room projecting far into the landscape beyond it from where you are stood on the dining room floor. Have I succeeded in creating space?

"I'm inviting the dining monks on a journey through time and perspective. To challenge their viewpoints, to encourage their imagination. To question their perceptions of reality"

The theory of 'one point' linear perspective first came into vogue in the early Renaissance with people like the Italians Leon Battista Alberti who first published a description of perspective, Lorenzo Ghiberti, Filippo Brunelleschi of the Florence Duomo fame, and Piero della Francesca taking the fore.

These people rediscovered the groundbreaking pivotal moment of the lost ideals of the classical mathematical perspective.

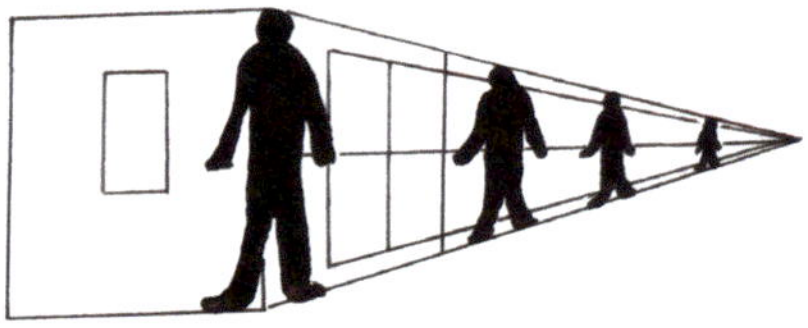

Linear perspective is where objects, buildings and people are shown in relative size to the distance they are from the viewer that is the nearer the larger, the further away, the smaller.

This illusion is heightened by receding lines merging into a vanishing point in the distance. So, all the floor, building lines and sizes of things and people recede, until they vanish.

One day in Florence, Masaccio was walking with his friends Filippo di ser Brunellesco di Lippo Lapi, known as Filippo Brunelleschi (1377-1446) and Donato di Niccolò di Betto Bardi, known as Donatello (1386-1466) and Leon Battista Alberti (1404-1472) and joined in with their discussion of the theory of perspective. From this Masaccio achieved a new form of art stylization using the technique incorporating linear perspective.

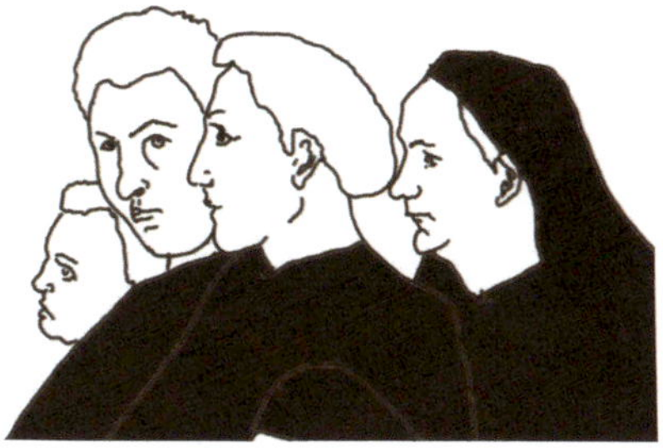

Masolino, Masaccio, Alberti and Brunelleschi from Masaccio's work in the Brancacci Chapel, Florence.

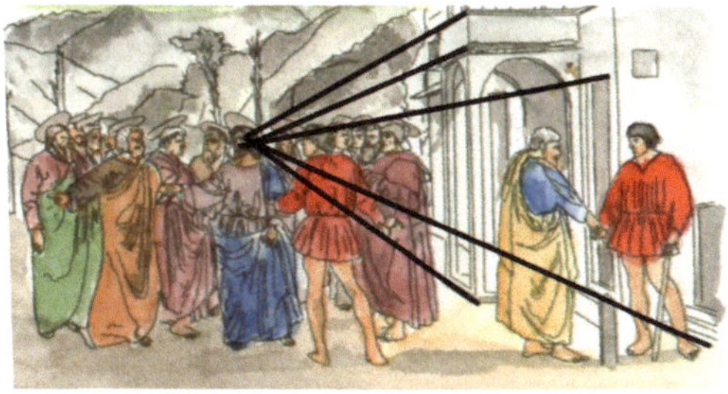

Masaccio, *Brancacci Chapel* 1425

"Look how my vanishing point is at Jesus Christ's head."

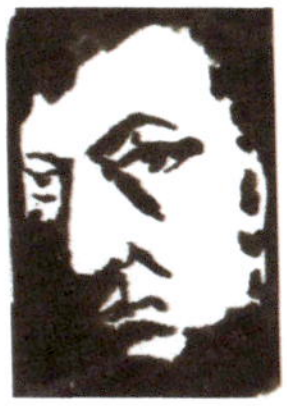

Masaccio

Jan van Eyck didn't employ linear but isometric perspective and certainly multiple points of view as is evidenced in his *Ghent Altarpiece*. And Michelangelo called working on perspective a **'complete waste of time'** as can be seen for instance in his Sistine Ceiling.

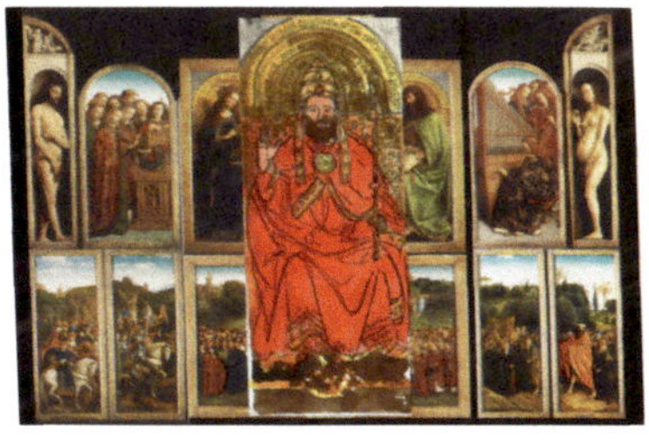

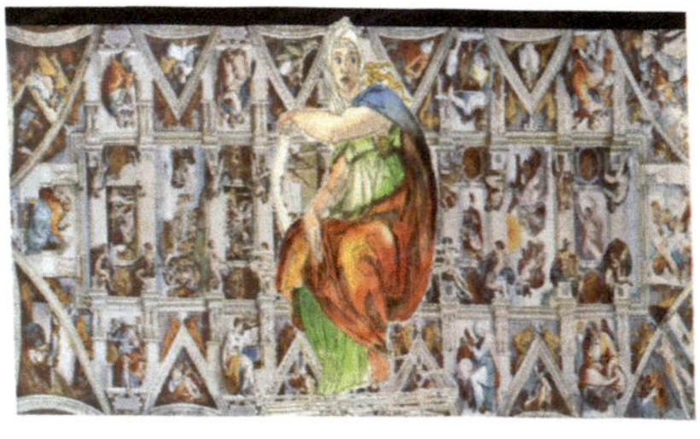

Isometric perspective: as seen in paintings before the linear vanishing point become the vogue. The question is, is isometric perspective a more real way of seeing things given our constantly shifting points from which we view and everything remaining in parallel?

Look at the work of Giotto and how the parallel perspective was achieved. Was Giotto attempting to be 'perspective real' as we actually perceive things or simply itemising his images?

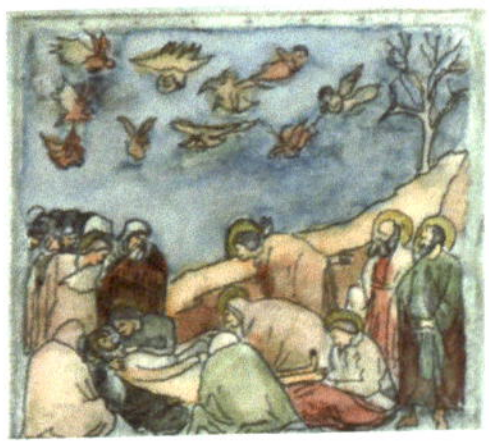

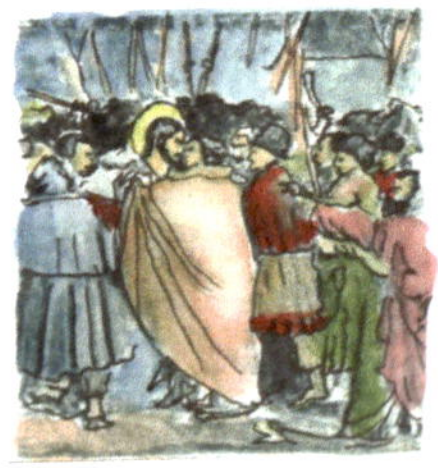

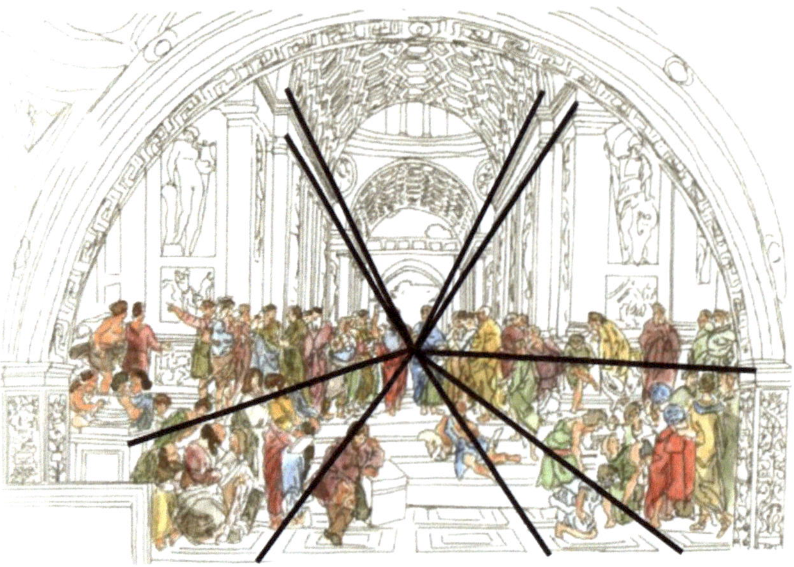

"The vanishing point in my *School of Athens* is between the two philosophers Socrates and Aristotle. I was attempting a three dimensional spatial illusion onto a two dimension surface."

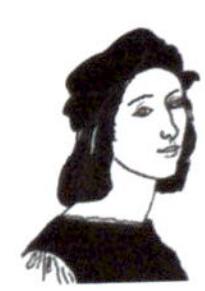

Does linear and isometric perspective separate us from the subject matter? Does it push us away, distancing us? Or are we drawn in by it? If there was no perspective, would we be there with the subject? And what about aerial perspective?

Aerial perspective is created by the use of colour, tone and saturation – strong colours to the fore, softer 'weaker' colours to the rear. Friedrich's *The Stages of Life*, 1835, is a great example.

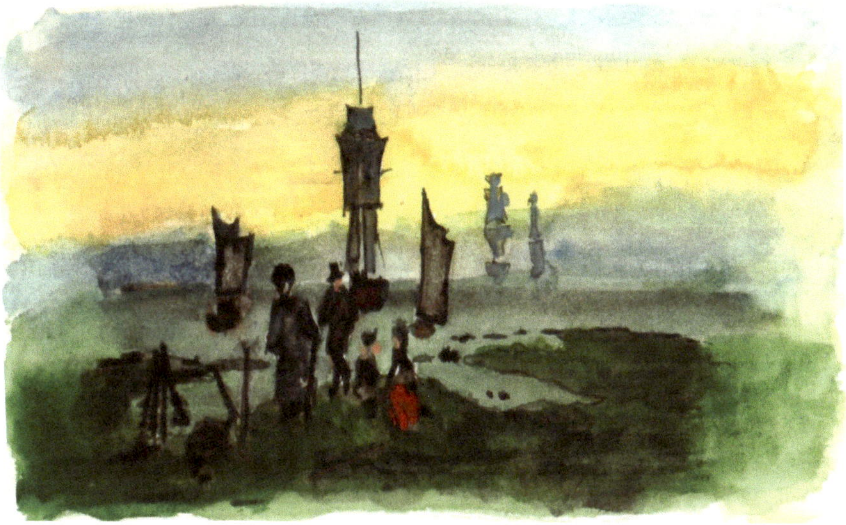

Casper David Friedrich *The Stages of Life* 1835

Think of paintings of landscapes where the artist has created an aerial perspective, the foreground is bold and prominent, whilst as the scene recedes, blues and more pastel like colours are used.

Like Claude Lorraine for instance.

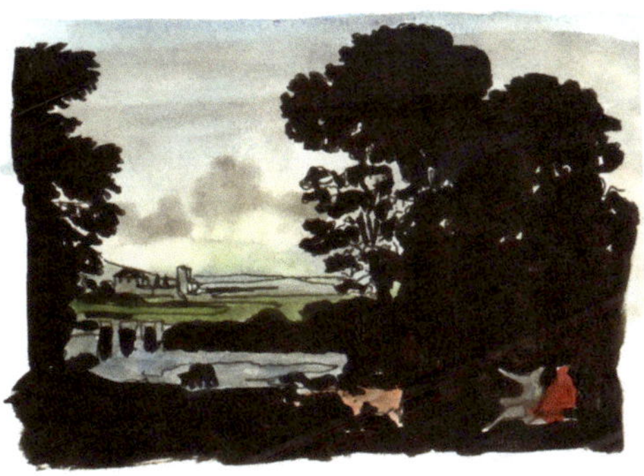

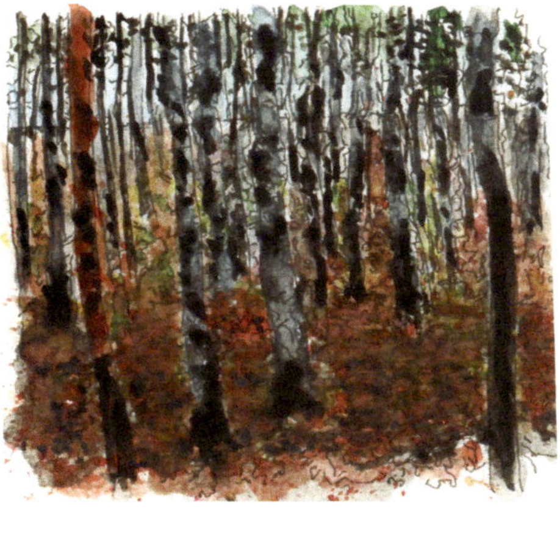

Also think of the role of colour in this respect – generally red, orange and yellow – bring forward. Blues and greys push back.

With works such as Gustav Klimt's, look to see the broader strokes at the front and the smaller towards the rear. Exactly as you see in real life. And as we saw in the diagram and here we see in reality. Things get smaller the further away they are and conversely bigger the nearer they are to you.

Gustav Klimt *Birch Forest 1* 1902

"Hey. Clyfford Still here. Compare Leonardo's last supper with my abstract expressionist work where a pure canvas of paint is depicted with no attempt at a three - dimensional illusion."

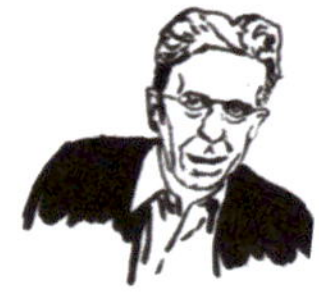

1953. 1953

"And don't forget me. My pioneering two-dimensional work was overshadowed by the Soviets and post WW2 American hegemony using Abstract Expressionism as a political tool. The 'freedom in America to express yourself as you wish'. Ha – I had that in what was then Russian Ukraine although I was eventually muzzled – until now!"

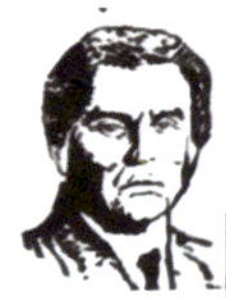

Black Square 1915

Consider Johannes Vermeer's 1662 *The Music Lesson* where he has deliberately depicted the room in a linear three-dimensional perspective, look at the tiles on the floor, compared with Renoir's 1918 *Le Café Concert* where the artist has avoided reference to linear and to an extent, aerial perspective.

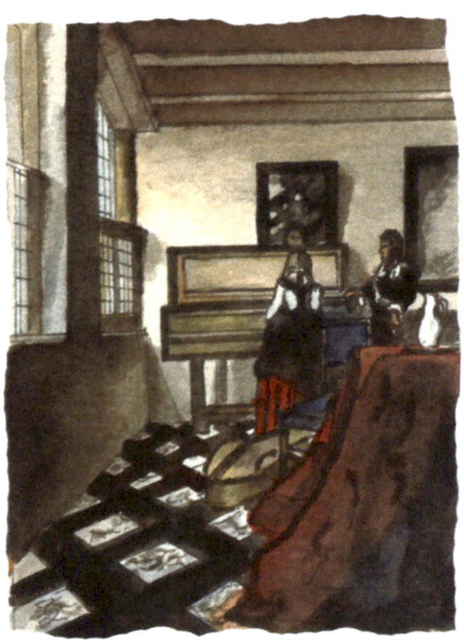

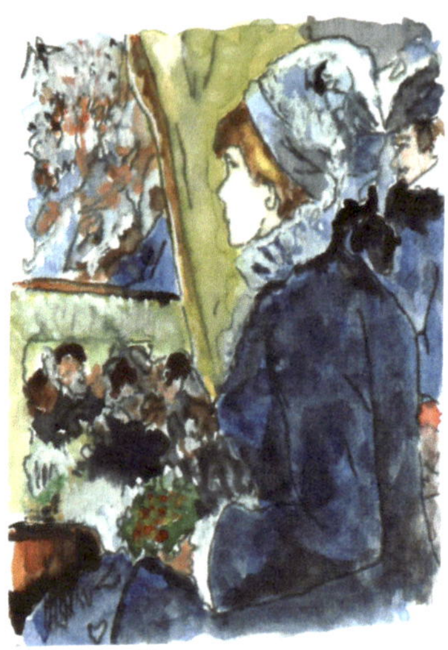

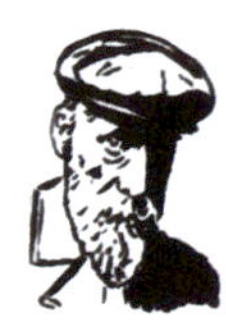

"I'm simply acknowledging that I've got a flat surface. NOT a trompe - l'oeil This is an impression, not a representation of structural integrity"

And let's not forget the huge influence of Utagawa Hiroshige on European art at this time: note – no geometric perspective – no vanishing point, no aerial perspective. Hirosage's work was collected by and influenced Monet, Manet, Van Gogh, Whistler and Degas.

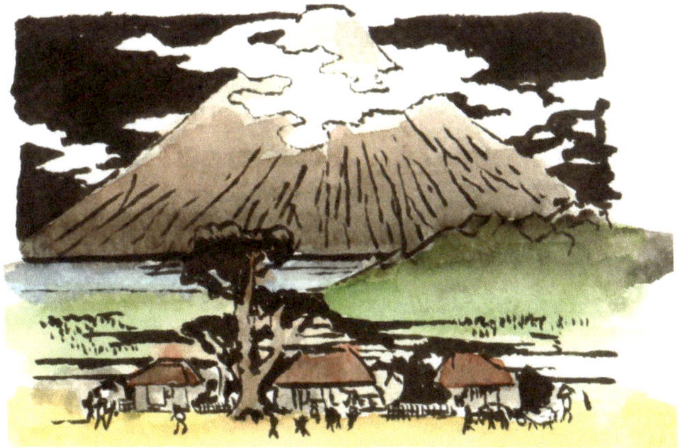

From the 53 Stations of the Tôkaiô Road Series. ***Views of Mount Fuji at Hara* 1840s/50s**

Édouard Manet's *The Railway* 1873, sited at the Gare St-Lazare, Paris at first appearance seems to be deep in its perspective, but when you look carefully, there is actually no real absolute depth.

The model is one of Manet's favourites, Victorine Meurent who you've seen before as *Olympia* and the nude figure on the grass in *Le Déjeuner sur l'herbe.*

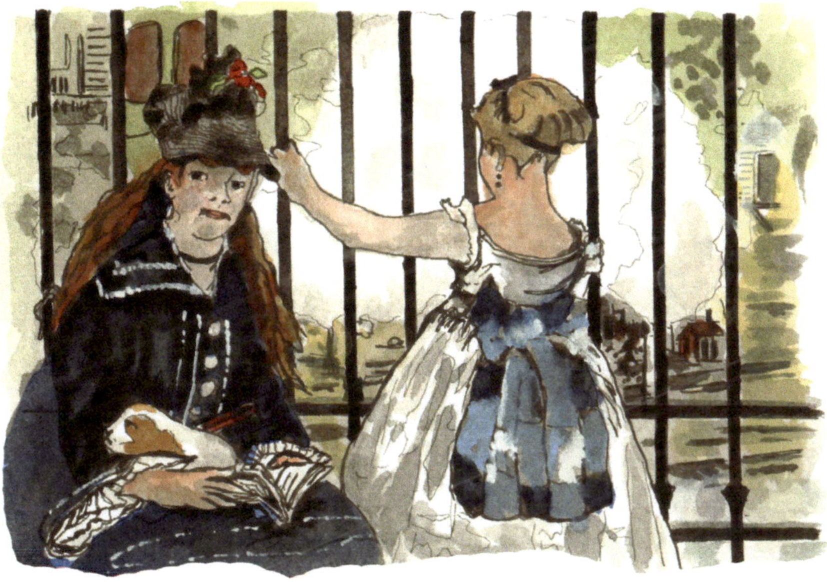

The whole image is flat. There are strong verticals and horizontals, but no aerial or linear depth. The space between the fore figures and the background is non-existent.

Manet has acknowledged and challenged you to accept that he has simply painted onto a flat surface with no pretence at perspective.

The canvas is real, but the image is an image, you can't get into the picture and move about in it. You are physically distant from being within the scene, but you are involved. You are there as the viewer.

It's a two-dimensional canvas of limited size. Manet's figures and railings extend beyond the canvas. You can't bend your head into the picture to see the train the smoke is coming from or see the model Victorine's feet or where the railings end. You can't see what Victorine or the child are looking at. You can't peer around the child's head to see the colour of her eyes or indeed get her to turn around. Of course you can't, it's simply layers of paint on a canvas. Flat.

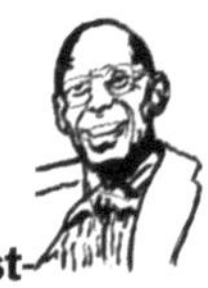

Michel Foucault, a French philosopher specialising in post-structuralism and postmodern philosophy in his lectures in Tunisia in 1971, stated: **"With Manet, painting brutally ceases to be a normative space which assigns to the author and viewer their respective places in the service of a general idea and freezes their status, and becomes a space in relation to which the viewer must place their self, reminded of his or her mobility and his or her ontological disinclination before a flat object, deprived of depth."**

And this is all about the role of the gaze.

The role of the gaze

"Art has the power to inspire and uplift, to bring beauty and joy into our lives, even in the darkest of times." Sir Ernst Hans Josef Gombrich.

Look at what is going on in a painting. Is the story, the action directly involving you or is it all happening irrespective of you the audience being present before the picture?

Has the artist attempted to embrace you or kept you at a distance? As we've explored, could it all be happening regardless of your presence or are you an essential part of the artist's intention with your psychology?

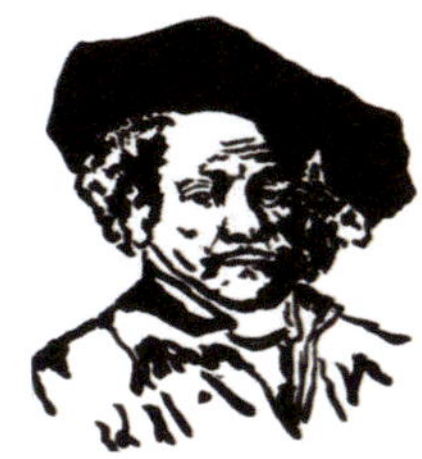

Look at many of Rembrandt's self-portraits. In most the artist is looking at the viewer directly. The viewer is invited into the picture with the artist. It's almost as though Rembrandt is directly communicating with you.

Contrast this with Édouard Manet's *A Bar at the Folies Bergère* where the waitress is gazing away from the viewer. You've no reflection in the mirror behind her. You are deliberately not involved in the picture. But you are. Without you it would be purposeless. You are stood in front of it, not in it, as a viewer.

There is an absence of direct communication between the bartender and the viewer. How do you feel about your relationship with the bartender? How do you feel about her thoughts and feelings regarding her position as a bartender? This is Paris in the 1880s. The man on the right is a vital component in the mirror looking directly at the bartender.

You are essential to the picture's existence, but you are not actually a part of it.

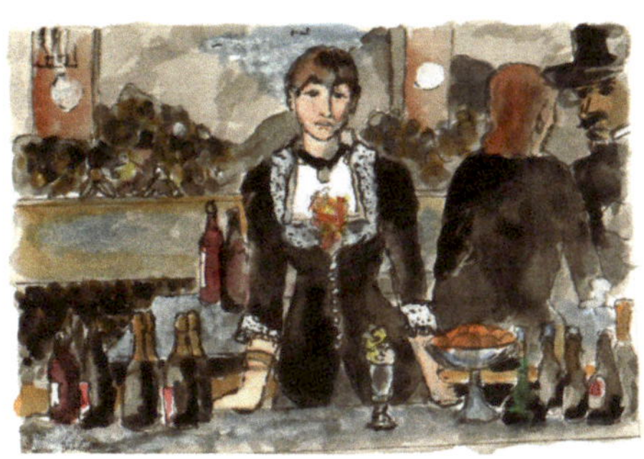

Manet: **"However, I'm involving you in the picture - without you - there would be no point - but I obviously can't physically draw you in.**

"Remember, I'm rejecting the academic dictates of the Paris Salon that emphasise 'good art' as being 'pure' in terms of perspective illusions: creation of depth, aerial curvaceousness on mythological nudes as well as the refined finish so demanded by them.

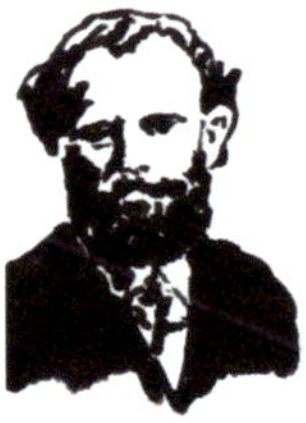

"I've created a modern approach to art and by challenging you to acknowledge the two dimensionality of my works, I'm involving you too in the modern movement.

"It's all very simple really: you see before you a canvas with paint on it, challenging you to reconsider what you might believe good art is: illusion, depth of field, perspective."

Manet is not trying to get you to suspend your disbelief compared to Leonardo's '*Last Supper*' where he's creating a visual illusion to get you to think the room extends beyond the wall, which you know, doesn't.

Manet is acknowledging that you know the image doesn't extend beyond the canvas, and so don't be taken in by the 19th Century Salon concept of 'good art' and thus let art serve other purposes: the beginnings of Modern Art. Not just attractive pictures, but delving into your emotions, feelings and psychology.

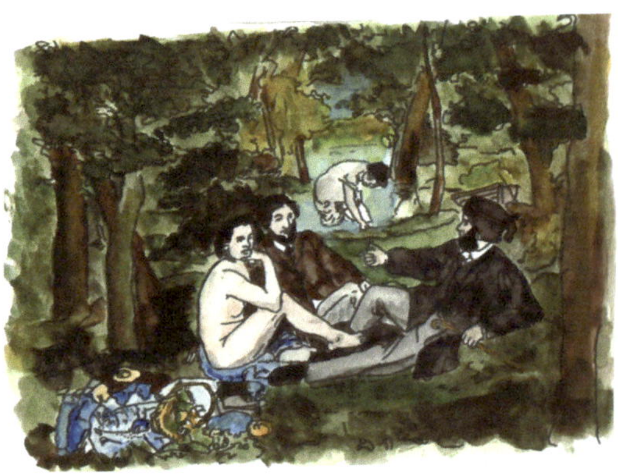

Look once again at *Déjeuner*. Manet's work is such an important development in the history or art.

Look carefully, the woman is staring at you directly. You are involved, but again you are not. You are not physically part of the picture. You can't be. Manet has created your invisibility.

The work's physical reality is a two-dimensional flat surface canvas. And that is what is so striking.

The 'picture-object' is pure materiality. A coloured surface. You the viewer are made to be an autonomous subject with no means to get into the picture. But you are involved because of the psychological impact the voyeuristic impulse within you creates when you stare at the naked woman.

That stare, your stare psychologically if you like, lighting her up. You are conscious of your presence and position within a such larger psychological system. You and your consciousness are making the picture.

Manet: **"that is why I've been attributed with creating the role of the modern viewer."**

Marcel Duchamp: **"It's the viewers who make the pictures."**

How included or excluded are we with the painting? Think about yourself as the viewer and what your gaze is doing for you? Are you intruding? Are you looking afar as for instance at a battle scene or a landscape?

What was the artist's intention with how he or she painted the picture with communicating: how are they involving you or not? Remember the closed and open form?

Think about the physicality and materiality of the paint on a flat canvas. Think about this in the context of a portrait where the sitter is looking directly at you. Are you involved? Are they communicating with you?

Can layers of paint on a flat surface actually be in contact with you?

Furthermore, take for example a primary subject figure gazing away from you. What are they looking at? We are not party to the subject of their gaze, we are excluded. They may be looking at nothing at all on the other hand they may be gazing at something which is of paramount importance to them, that has happened to them, that is about to happen to them. We do not know.

The painting stands independent of our involvement. And the subject matter is just a layer of paint after all.

The role of the viewer. The gaze of the spectator. Artists walking the line between illusion and reality.

What is the picture's gaze doing or not doing? What is the role of your gaze? What was the artist's intention?

Let's look again at John Everett Millais'

Glen Birnam

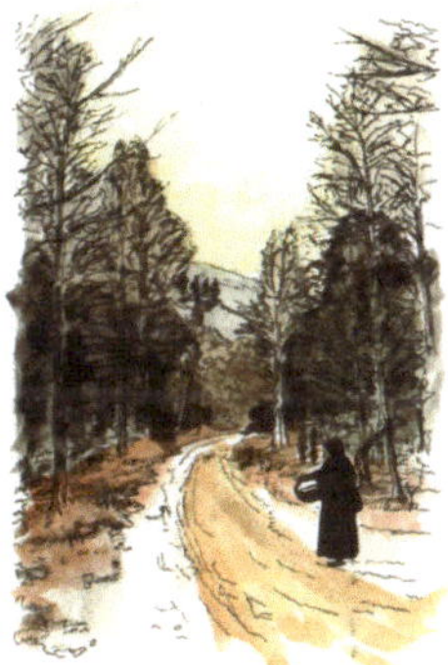

Previously we looked at the difference between the picture with a figure and without a figure. With a figure, the narrative has been dramatically added.

The landscape has been beautifully presented; the figure encourages you to become part of the painting by inviting you to interpret what's going on.

Thinking again of the Abstract Expressionism movement, look at Clyfford Still's *1953* where you are forced to interpret what you are looking at in order to complete the story.

Of course, your interpretation will probably differ from the person next to you and that is the subject of the next section.

*

The Germans have a word for it *'Einfühlung'*. Most people of any sensibility cannot stand before a picture and not experience a feeling. And that could simply be whether they like the picture or not.

A picture can be perceived as a living breathing entity showing human being's soul and life. It can perform magic by bringing that subject, a portrait, a landscape, even an apple in a still life, into our very presence. Royality, Jesus Christ, nobles, peasants and workers are brought one yard before us, into our territory, our lives.

A work of art we say can move us. This is an emotional response and with what we like to see, produces an instantaneous nature of aesthetic appreciation, the most successful being *Einfühlung.* Empathy, not sympathy, but a feeling of 'into'. Our sympathy for any, let's say, afflicted is reenacting in ourselves the feelings of others. When looking at art, we can project ourselves into the picture and our feelings are then the result of what we find there.

For example, when looking at Hirosage's *Wave* we can feel sympathy for the figures in the boats in the dangerous waters and by allowing ourselves to move into that picture, we can gain a feeling of empathy, we are feeling into that picture.

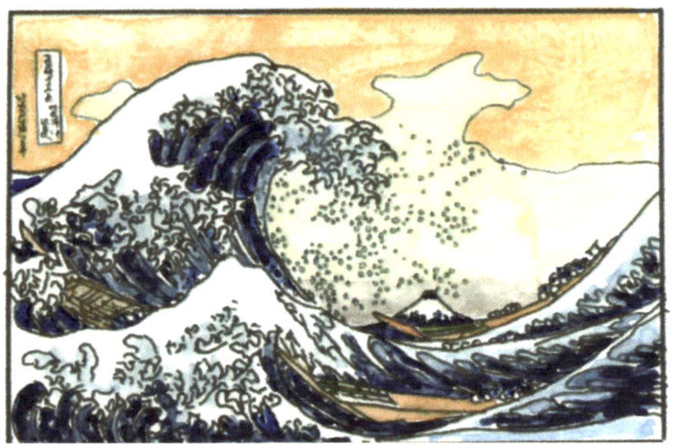

We have sympathy for the peril they are in, we can empathise by joining with them to share the emotions they are experiencing.

JMW Turner's *The Slave Ship* painted in 1840, is a supreme example of this. Here we have a true story of a slave ship caught in a typhoon and jettisoning sick and dying slaves to drown in order to stay afloat.

Set against a beautifully dramatic sunset, the horror of the subject matter reflects nature's indifference to human suffering and cruelty and looking at this picture and allowing ourselves some empathy, we can be emotionally deeply involved.

Referring to Herbert Read, a work of art can thus be a sense of liberation of our personality. Normally we are inhibited and repressed, but when we let ourselves be drawn into that special, to us personal, work of art, we can feel a sense of release, a sublimation.

Complex psychology but worth a moment to consider whilst having that conversation with those pictures that especially speak to us.

*

We cannot be part of that picture, but that picture can be a part of us.

*

Art does not provide our essentials for survival. Thinking about the American psychologist Abraham Maslow's 1943 paper *A Theory of Human Motivation* in the journal *Psychological Review*, we have an innate set of priority needs, starting with the physiological that is food and shelter.

This is followed by our safety to ensure we live without the fear of being eaten or killed. Once that is as secure as we can make it, we then need to feel love and have a sense of belonging.

Then follows our self-esteem and from there the seeking of knowledge and education.

Once all this is underway in our world we start to create and seek out the aesthetic.

So, we have a place to live and food in the fridge. We have security with locks on our door and police to protect us. We then seek companionship. We'll then need to understand our world and ourselves, so we go to school, evening classes, distance learning. From there we think about decorating our place and going out to cultural events, enjoying nature, forest bathing or being by the sea on in the mountains. Whatever appeals to us as individuals.

It is at this point that we seek what is known as self actualisation and this can take many forms. It's the opportunity now presented within our secure world for us to concentrate on our creativity. This could be making things, creative cooking, housekeeping, being a parent or grandparent, a loving spouse or partner and of course drawing and painting. It is the realisation of our potential.

How does the role of the gaze fit into this? If we are not fed, if we are under personal threat, if we have no sense of belonging and have low self-esteem it is most unlikely that we'd enjoy gallery visits unless of course we find that viewing art improves our mental well-being as it does with most of us. So, it is at the stage of self-esteem and a desire for cognitive development that our involvement with the arts starts to kick in.

Bottom line, we do not need art to survive. Many historical cultures did not have art until their civilization was safe and secure enough and indeed prosperous enough to allow artists to even exist and then to have the time and support to not have to tend the fields but to create art in whatever form that society wanted. Time could be devoted towards the aesthetic.

This runs contrary to Charles Darwin's theory of evolution and natural selection. We can only survive against the hostility of nature and other tribes by getting rid of inefficiency and waste. Art uses up time and effort and does not provide the lower essentials of Maslow's hierarchy of needs.

Moving up this hierarchy is contrary to Darwin. And that is the beauty of the human being's capacity physically and mentally to soar above other species and to evolve to the point of self-actualisation.

Therefore, when we are in that gallery looking up at that picture it may be worth considering how we have evolved to this point in time where artists can spend the time being creative and we can use their achievements for us to be able to appreciate the world of the aesthetic and indeed, journey beyond that point to become self-actualising beings ourselves.

The Subjective Notion of Beauty

From triangles, spirals and golden sections we move on to the subjective notion of beauty.

Beauty as the old adage goes, is in the eye of the beholder. It is subjective. As Sir Ernst Gombrich would state **"Art is not about perfection but about capturing the imperfect beauty of the world."**

With our picture what is meant by beauty? The representation of the landscape, still life or portrait? The impression of light and form or the line, colour and shapes of abstract art?

Beauty could also apply to the success the artist has achieved in conveying an ideal, of depicting history, the telling of a tale, the religious symbolism, the political statement.

Beauty by a stretch of the imagination could also apply to the artist's depiction of ugliness, distortion and uncomfortableness.

Beauty can be achieved by the artist's conveying emotions that strike a chord with us or conversely leaving us cold and disorientated or even anti.

Beauty is a unity of formal relations among our sense perceptions and is a most fluctuating phenomenon.

The Greeks idealised beauty in their statues such as the Apollo Belvedere and the Romans adopted the classical Greek icons of beauty. Unfortunately, with little evidence of pictures remaining with us from the ancient world, we make our judgements from the three-dimensional remains.

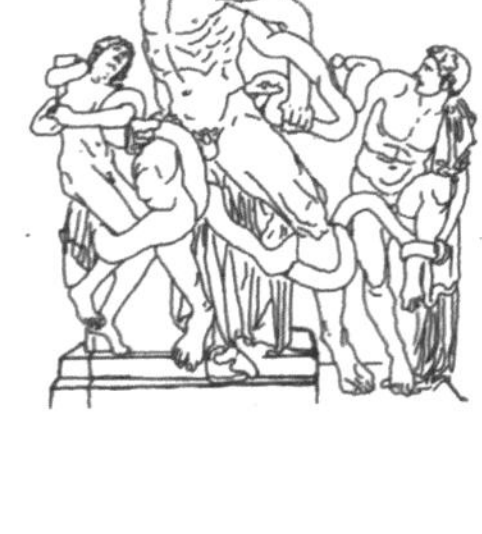

Byzantium introduced the divine and in medieval times the introduction of fear in the face of the mysterious and implacable world.

So, we have differing values of beauty introduced by different civilizations.

It was the Renaissance that evolved for us what we now consider the form of beauty. Colours, forms, composition, balance and harmony with the arrangements of all these things into a pleasurable vision before us. Fibonacci's symmetrical balance.

Figura serpentinata or serpentine figure. It was the discovery of the Laocoon in Rome in 1506 that inspired artists to treat their subjects to movement, to gentle and graceful twisting of pose and posture, contributing to the harmony of the picture and hence appealing to our visual sensibilities.

*

The notion of the numinous

You stand before a picture, it may be religious, it may be a landscape, it could even be a portrait, but whatever, it may have an unaccountable profound effect on your inner feelings, even beyond empathy and certainly sympathy.

Some works have an esoteric mysticism that we cannot explain. That is if we allow ourselves to be affected by what we see.

The work can best be described in respect of its effect on us as 'numinous fascinans' a definition defined by Rudolf Otto a German theologian at the beginning of the 20th Century.

It basically means acknowledging the presence of a divine, however you wish to describe such, by appealing to our visceral innermost emotions.

Most human beings have an irreducibly, non-rational experience of the numinous that is the interior presence of the transcendent or divine however you wish to define such. The 'numen' presents itself fundamentally as 'wholly other' having two distinct poles of 'feeling content':

Mysterium tremendum: a sense of something mysterious, overwhelming, and daunting which elicits from us a sense of diminution, humility, submission, and creatureliness.

Mysterium fascinans: a sense of something fascinating, desirable, good, caring, and comforting which invites us into its fullness, fulfils us, and in so doing produces a unique kind of spiritual joy or bliss.

Can a mere picture do this for us?

The role of the gaze.

The source of illumination and light

The artist's choice of their source of light can be either to simply illuminate the scene or to create and support their meaning or message. An artist's decision regarding the source of light is naturally a very powerful tool.

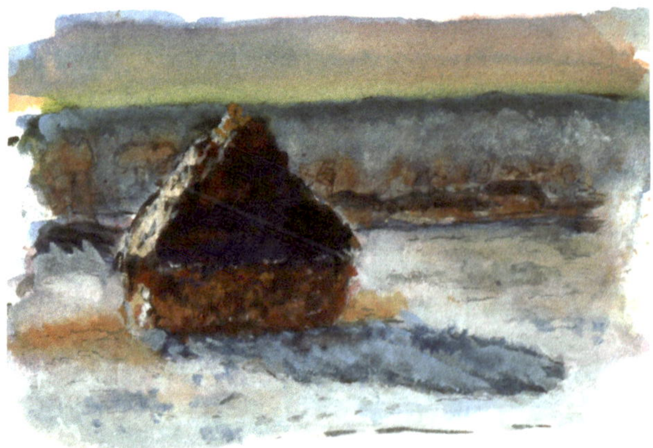

Monet's '*Haystacks*' reflect his primary subject matter being the changing light itself. The haystack is of secondary importance – merely a platform for the light to be displayed on. And as we've previously explored, it was from artists such as Monet and the Impressionists that the light itself became the purpose of the painting.

Moving back a few years to Manet one of the reasons *Olympia* was so interesting was the manner in which he lit his scene. Similarly, with *A Bar at the Folies-Bergère*. Look carefully to see if you can identify the source of the light.

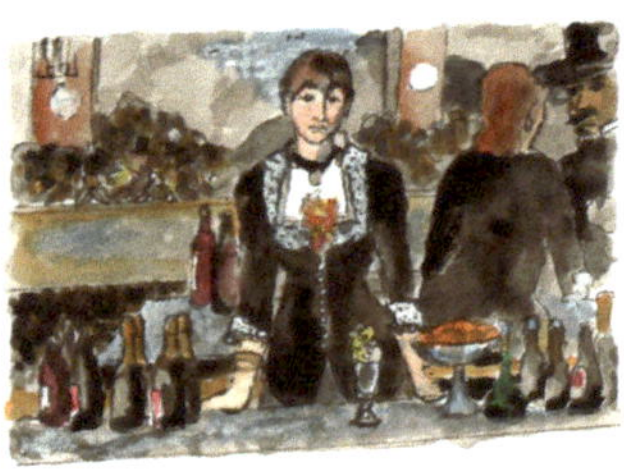

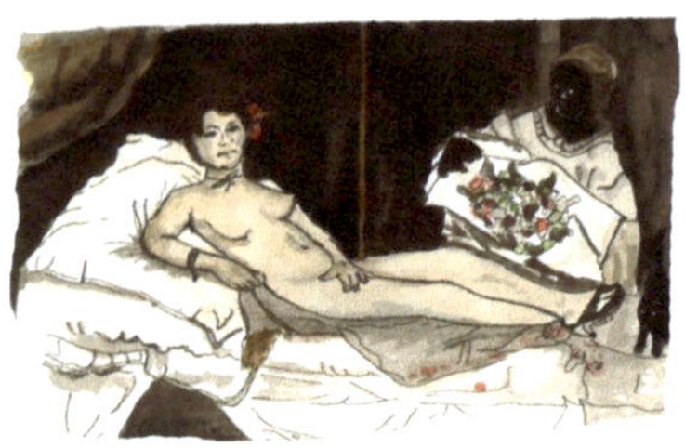

It is difficult, isn't it? That is because you the viewer could be considered the source of light. It is not obviously coming from above, below or a window or door, a bulb or a candle. If indeed you are the source of the light, how much does that involve you? And that was Manet's intention, to draw you in as part of the voyeuristic viewing of the naked woman Olympia and the vulnerability of the barmaid.

Thanks to the enigmatic Manet, we've a whole dimension of thought to consider.

Compare Manet's manipulation of light source with Michelangelo Merisi da Caravaggio's *Madonna of Loreto* painted in 1606.

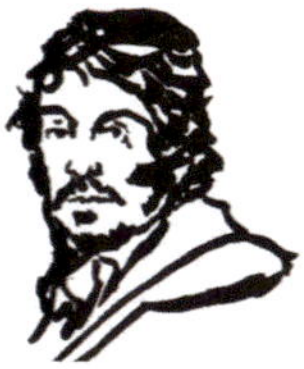

"Buon Giono. In most of my works you'll notice that I concentrated on the shadows, chiaroscuro, to emphasise my subject matter. Here look to see if you can see the source of the light. It's not coming from the doorway. It cannot be streetlight it's too bright. It's not coming directly from the Christ child or Mary as they are similarly illuminated. I'll leave it to you to decide where the light is coming from. Is it you?"

Michelangelo Merisi da Caravaggio 1571-1610

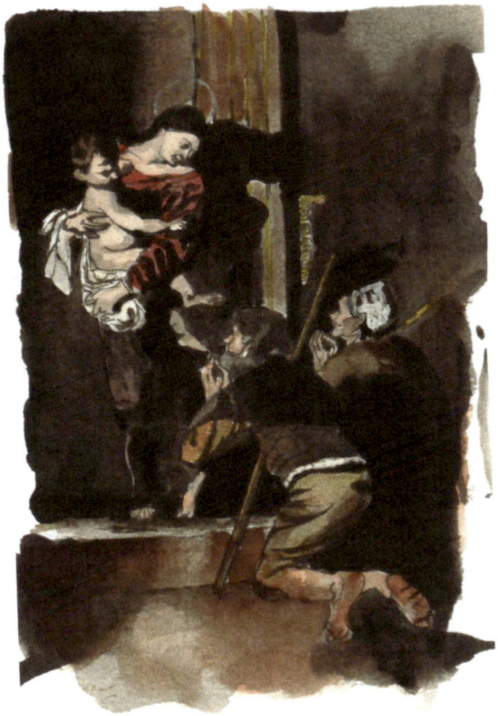

Is Caravaggio's light coming from you as with Manet's *Olympia*? Is its source divine? Perhaps there is a streetlamp – but in a 16th Century small town Italian backstreet? Caravaggio's use of illumination was deliberate: you are being invited into the picture as the holder of the lamp. Also look to see how the light radiates from the bottom of the picture drawing your view upwards and into the drama, especially as the intended display site of this picture was such that the step would have been at your head height.

Here's an interesting thought - were the Hollywood directors and producers influenced by Caravaggio's use of light? Compare 1930 and 1940s Hollywood classics such as *Casablanca* with Caravaggio's lighting of the *Madonna of Loreto*.

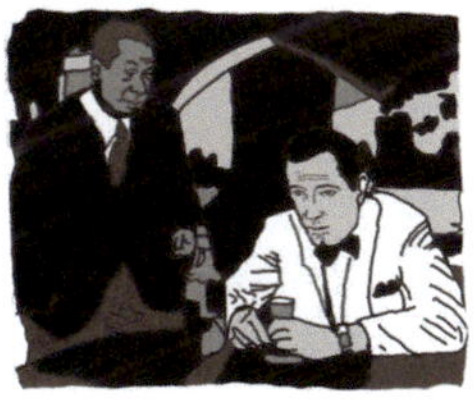

Caravaggio's shadows create volume as well as adding to the drama of the piece. This is only found in western art and not in Islamic, Asian, Persian or Indian art. Caravaggio's drama and lighting produced him as a brilliant genius in the story of the evolution of western pictures.

"Being one of the few well-known women painters of my time I painted my picture *Giuditta e la Fantesca* in 1625. I give here an extract to illustrate my use of light"

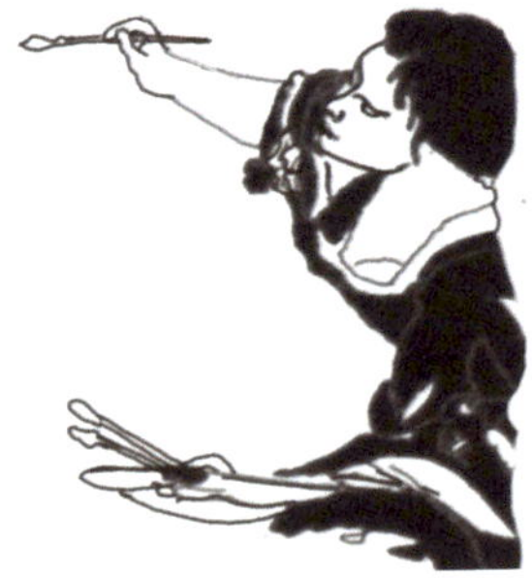

Artemisia Gentileschi
1593–c.1656

Here we can see the obvious source of the light – the candle – creating an atmosphere of drama and suspense.

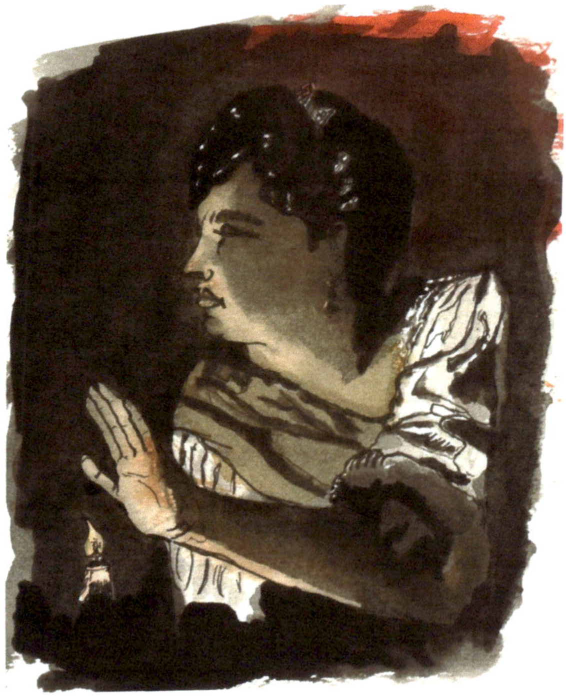

If you look carefully at most works, until the 19th century you will see that light sources had been identified merely to illuminate the scene before you. Natural lighting from the sun or artificial sources. Casting shadows so effectively as with Caravaggio.

"And what do you think the main subject matter is in my painting *The Sower*? The figure? The sun? The light?"

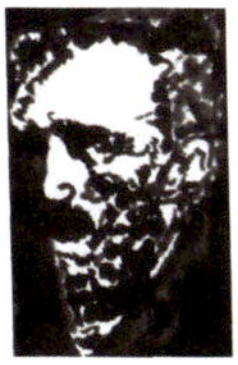

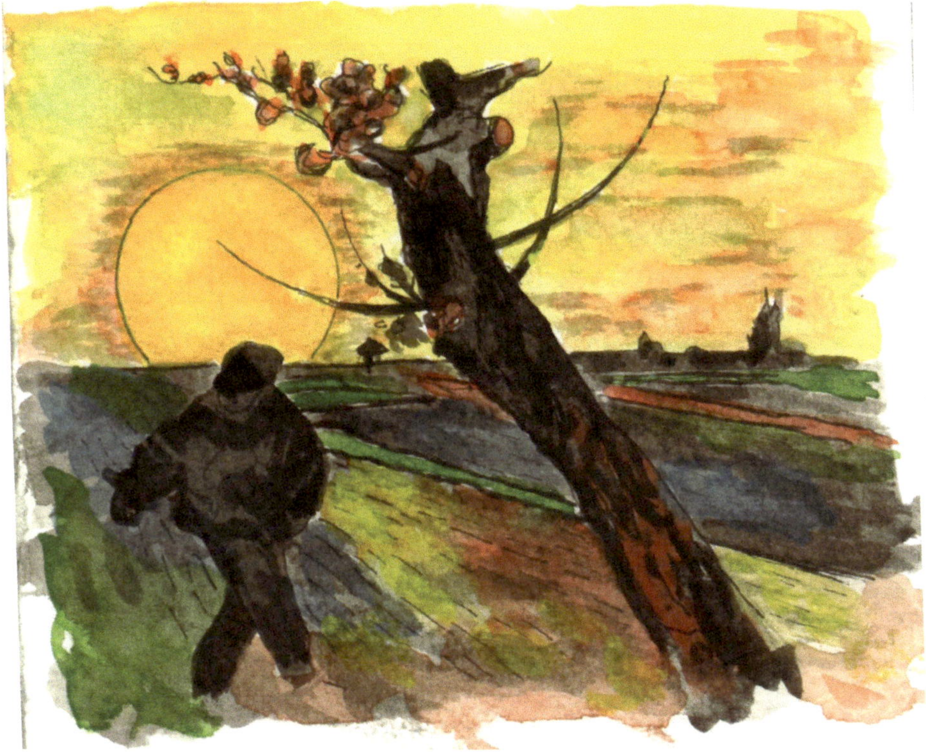

There are paintings where the light source is fundamentally important, but you can't see it, through to paintings where the light itself is the primary subject matter as we've seen with Impressionism.

Remember the light source and the way the artist has treated illumination and its source and used it in their armoury of tools.

The dynamism of colour

We know how important colour is and may even take it for granted. It adds to the prettiness of a picture, to the drama and to the overall effect.

We humans unlike some animals, can see all the variations in colour, light and hue.

Enjoy the way the artist has used their colours in the composition. There are schools of thought in respect of the relationship between colours, their vibration, the juxtaposition and opposition of colours. The colour spectrum was developed many years ago in this respect.

As an example of how Renaissance viewers would have interpreted colour in the works they were looking at, in 1435 Leon Battista Alberti, Italian humanist author, artist, architect, poet, priest, linguist, philosopher and cryptographer – the epitome of the Renaissance, in his 1435 book *Treatise of Painting,* codified colour: white – purity, red – charity, yellow/gold – dignity, with the elements being: red – fire, blue – air, green – water and grey – earth. Renaissance viewers would have understood this codification as they would have appreciated the importance and value of lapis-lazuli blue – usually reserved for the Madonna's cloak given its expense, as they would have appreciated symbolic meanings behind gestures and poses.

Compare with today's interpretations of emojis.

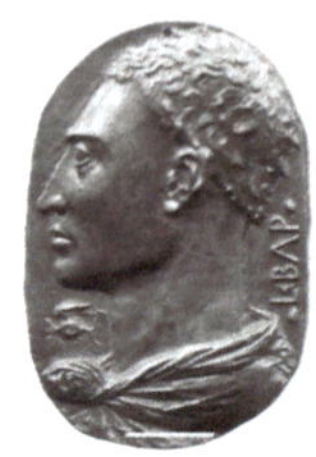

Leon Battista Alberti 1404 – 1472

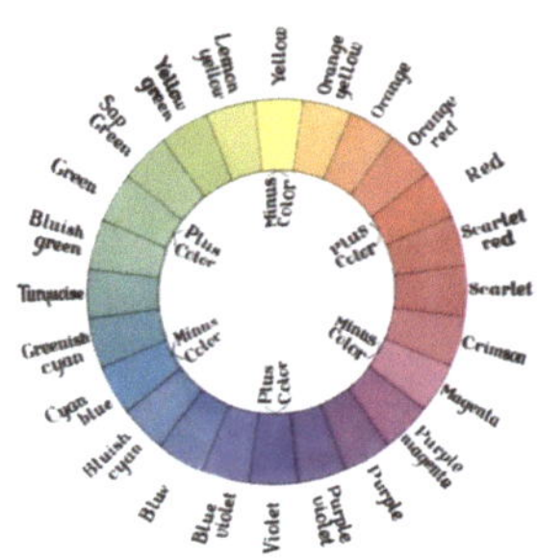

Look at Gainsborough's 1770 *The Blue Boy.*

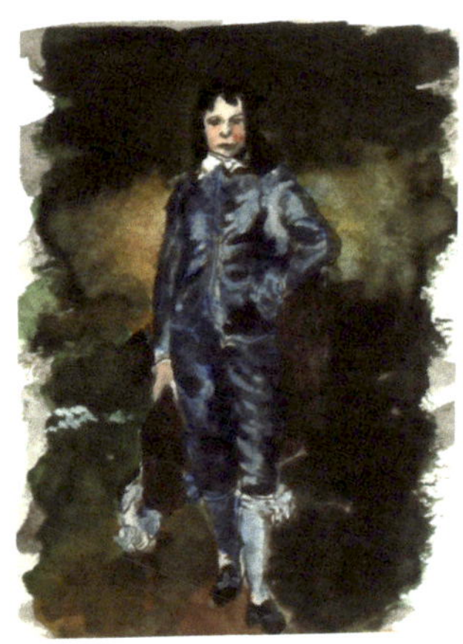

The figure itself is the primary subject matter and therefore given the constraints of the canvas, should in all reality be projected forwards but Gainsborough chose the clothing to be in blue thus visually pushing the figure into the background. Blue pushes back, red projects forward. That *is* the vibrancy of colour.

Whilst the colour blue is the topic, some research informs us that it is apparently the most popular colour to the human eye and orange the least popular.

Gainsborough painted his *The Blue Boy* in response to his rival Joshua Reynolds, who said:

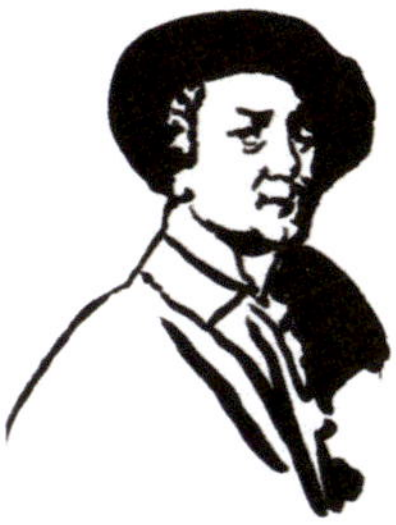

"... the masses of light in a picture be always of a warm, mellow colour, yellow, red, or a yellowish white, and that the blue, the grey, or the green colours be kept almost entirely out of these masses, and be used only to support or set off these warm colours; and for this purpose, a small proportion of cold colour will be sufficient. Let this conduct be reversed; let the light be cold, and the surrounding colour warm ... and it will be out of the power of art, to make a picture splendid and harmonious."

Sir Joshua Reynolds 1723 –1792

Gainsborough's emphasis on using blue was in complete contrast to Reynold's dictum.

JMW Turner was one of the greatest natural colourists the world of art has known. He was revolutionary against pure tonal harmony and with his genius use of colour, he was able to portray the power and majesty of nature.

Now look at Gustav Klimt's *The Birch Forest.*

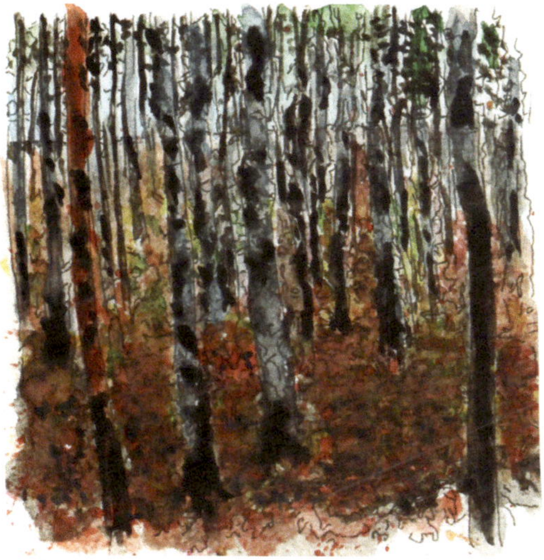

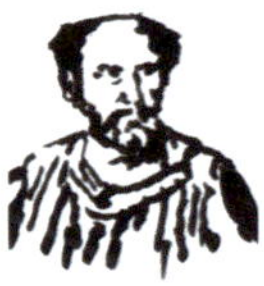

"Here I have painted my birch trees in grey and blue and my fallen leaves in the background in red and orange. The result is almost as though the birch tree trunks are pushed into the background and the leaves pulled forward in terms of colour, but the trunks are clearly to the fore and many of the leaves to the rear. Thus, creating flattened tree trunks, almost falling into secondary position against the leaves that should be receding into the rear."

Cézanne is attributed with colour application defining the form of a picture. This by its respective intensities that it creates the illusion of three-dimensional form. Form conveyed directly by colours irrespective of light and shadow.

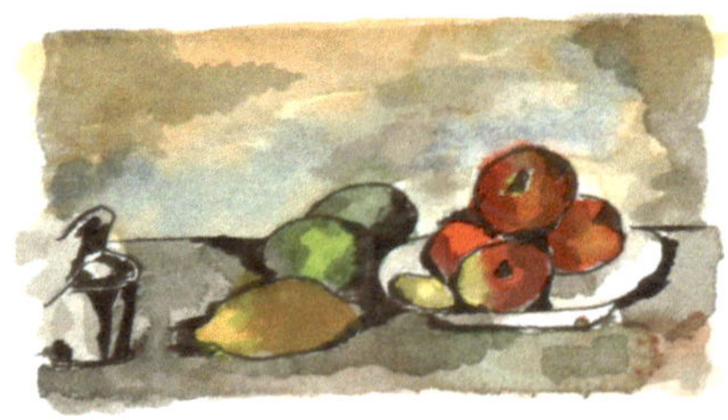

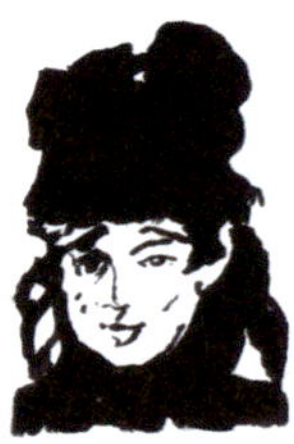

Berth Morisot

"It was Renoir, myself and the other Impressionists that many consider to be the main influences on the liberation of colour – colour used in its own right, for its own power."

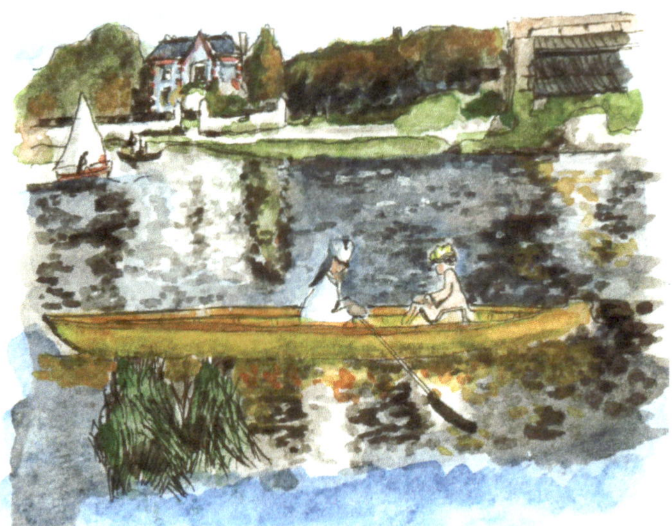

"With my 1879 Impressionist painting *The Seine at Asnières (The Skiff)* I've tried to make the yellow skiff vibrate against the river's almost artificial depth of violent blue."

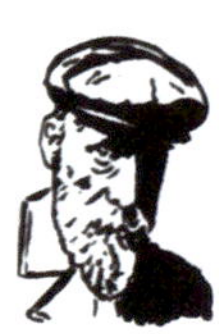

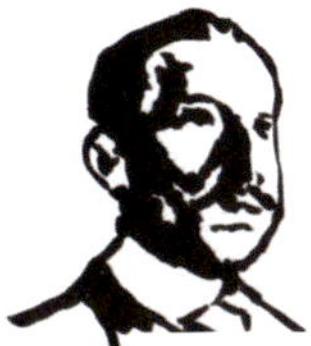

Andre Derain

"I was part of the group called The Fauves or The Wild Beasts. This title was attributed to us because of our wild use of colours. Unnatural maybe but to emphasise the exciting use of colour, its liveliness and vibration capability. Look at my *Collioure: le port de pêche* »

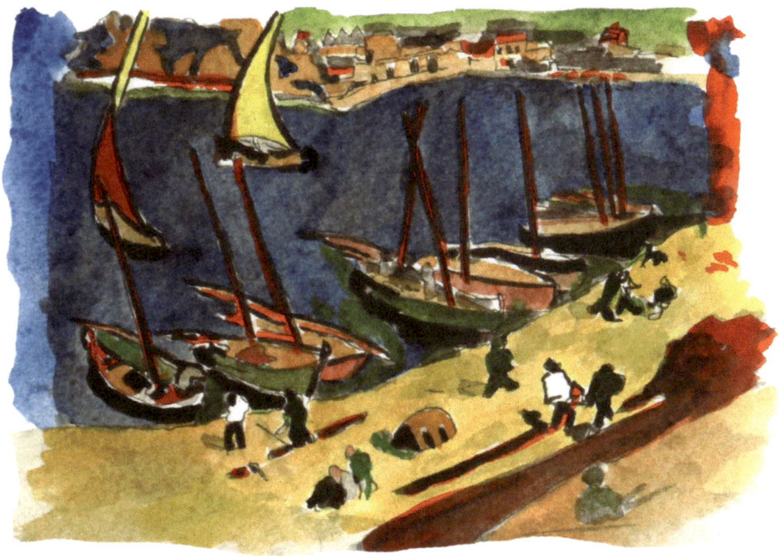

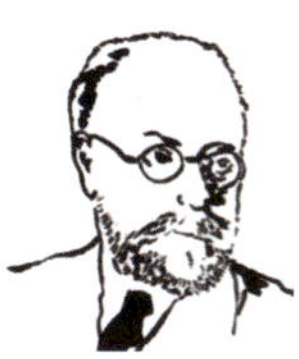

Henri Matisse

"Look at my work afresh. As I got older, I couldn't paint so I cut out shapes and placed them together to emphasise the relationship of colours."

The Snail 1953

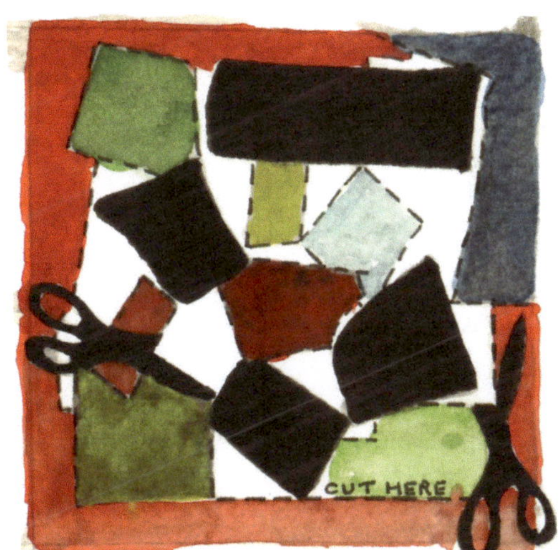

Colour, beautiful, picturesque of course, but also a powerful tool to really make a huge contribution to a picture's overall form and composition. Decorative versus verisimilitude. Colour appealing to our sensibilities.

Enjoy working out exactly what the colours are doing. Even consider how colour can symbolise emotions for instance red for passion, white for purity, black as darkness, purple as shown in religious hierarchy and of course Mary the Madonna's blue and Mary Magdaline's red.

John Ruskin deserves a last word on colour:

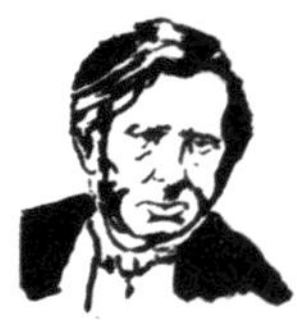

"All people, completely organized and justly tempered, enjoy colour; it is meant for the perpetual comfort and delight of the human heart; it is richly bestowed on the highest works of creation, and the eminent sign and seal of perfection in them; being associated with life in the human body, with light in the sky, with purity and hardness in the earth – death, night, and pollution of all kinds being colourless".

The viewing eye

The term 'period eye' was originated by the influential art historian Michael Baxandall in his book *Painting and Experience in Fifteenth Century Italy* published in 1972. Here the author invites us to look at works of art from the perspective of a contemporary viewer.

How would you have viewed the painting if you were there when it first appeared against the circumstances of the work's cultural influence: yours and its socio-political, historical and religious background?

Consider who was the painting painted for? What relationship may the artist have had with their patron or audience in general? What constraints or free will were they working under?

Let's start by looking at some iconic Renaissance pieces.

Raphael's *School of Athens* in the Vatican was designed and executed with a view to it being viewed by the Pope and the clergy of the time. How may they have viewed it and how might that differ from your viewing of it today?

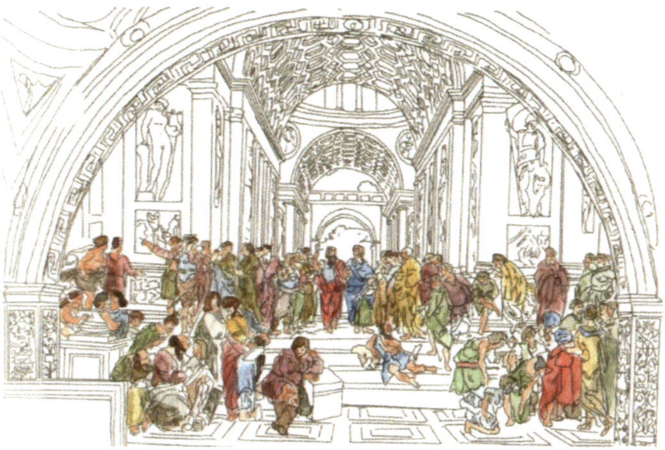

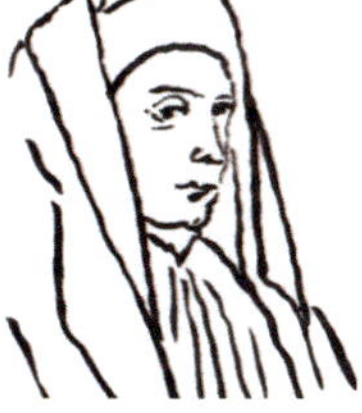

Giotto de Bondone

"I painted this work called The *Kiss of Judas* in 1305 as a panel for the The Scrovegni Chapel in Padua."

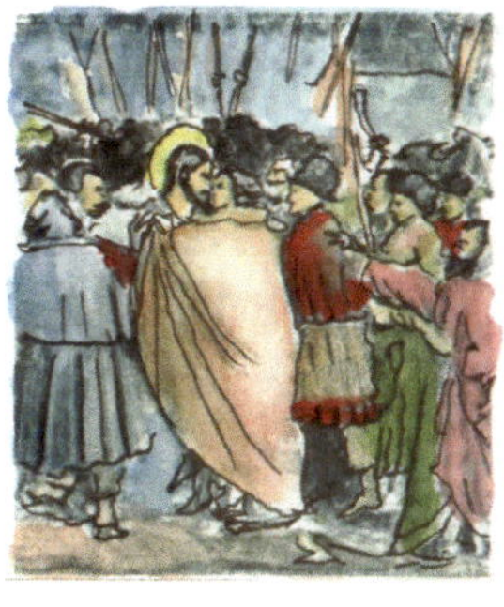

Giotto's work was completed for the Catholic Church. The Church wanted painters or craftsmen, to illustrate stories from the Bible. We have the early Catholic Church's approach to its flock: to illustrate, to control, to encourage. Salvation and redemption, whatever your point of view. Hellfire and damnation or heavenly bliss. Or both.

Leonardo's *The Last Supper* was also painted for the clergy as well as the commissioning nobility, the Duke of Milan.

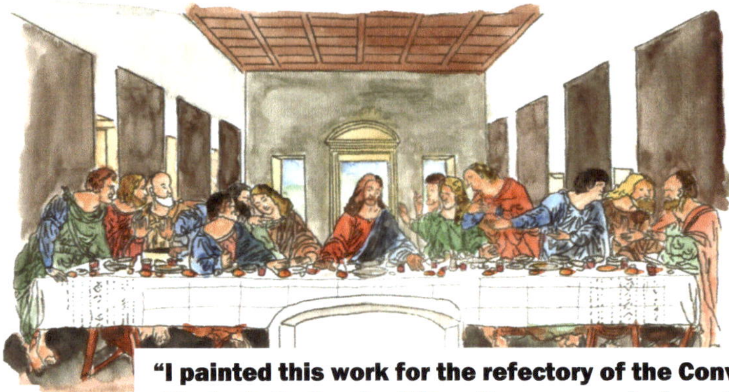

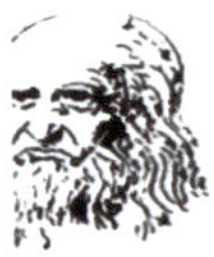

"I painted this work for the refectory of the Convent of Santa Maria delle Grazie, Milan. It was commissioned as part of a scheme of renovations to the church and its convent buildings by my patron Ludovico Sforza, Duke of Milan for the brothers of the convent to enjoy and to be visually inspired by the story."

Look at the movements and gestures of the disciples and Jesus Christ, the physiognomies, indicating each player's mental condition, attitude and even intention.

You as a 16th Century viewer would understand all the detail and the artist's intention. But can you say as a 21st Century viewer that you understand it in the same way as your 16th Century counterpart?

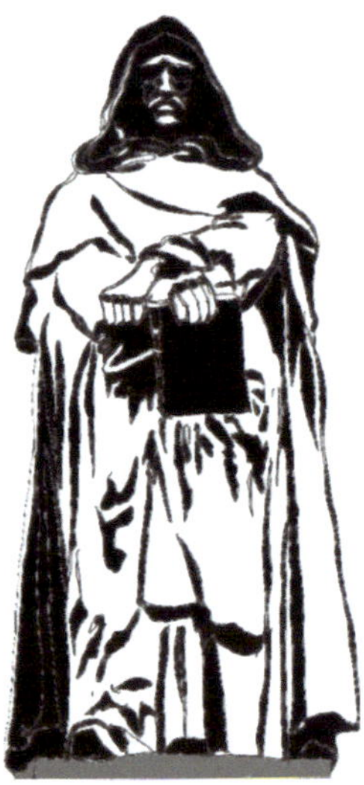

Artists in this period worked with gestures, nuances, poise and postures, knowing that their audience would recognise the messages. Symbols, icons and codes.

Preachers of the time would have toured Europe spreading the message from the Church. They were apparently skilled visual performers with a codified range of gesticulations. Giordano Bruno's travels for instance.

Giordano Bruno 1548 - 1600

"Here is one of the principal female figures in my 1482 work *Primavera* or *Allegory of Spring.* Consider her hand gestures. What do you make of them? Conducting the music? Inviting you into her realm? Peace and goodwill? I know my intention. My 1482 viewers would have their opinion. What is yours?"

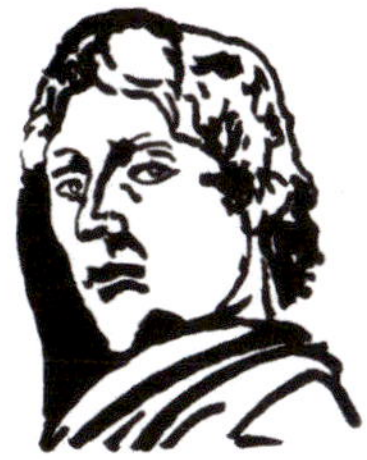

Sandro Botticelli c. 1445 –

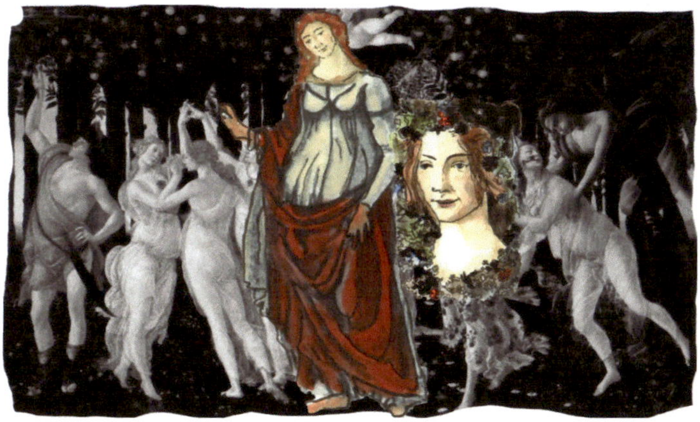

The Renaissance: the era of man being at the centre of things and in control of his destiny, the rise of humanism.

"I painted my Sistine Chapel ceiling for Pope Julius II and the papal conclaves between 1508 and 1512."

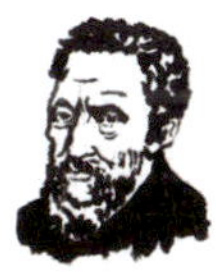

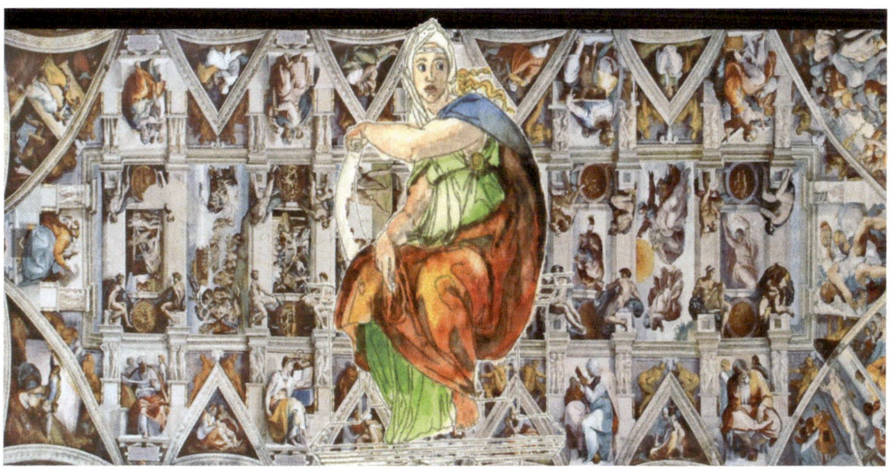

The *Sistine Ceiling* is religious in subject matter but look at how Michelangelo depicts human beings in all their glory. Unabashed nakedness. Proud and dignified. Adam almost on a par with God. Don't forget that Michelangelo was paid handsomely for this work by the church. He is therefore on a tight balancing act of meeting a Renaissance Pope's requirements, together with his own religious beliefs against the background of the increasing humanism of the times.

Look at the gestures, the nuances, the colours and their roles, the poise and postures, the interrelationships of the figures.

Artists relied on their viewers having the knowledge and interest to interpret and understand the depictions before them.

Artists also relied on their viewers' understanding of and respect for proportionality and architectural exactness, hence so many examples of buildings being precisely depicted with great emphasis on perspective and the vanishing points.

All understandable to 16th Century viewers, but would this all be the same to you?

Think yourself back to the 16th Century and ask yourself 'how would I have viewed this work within the socio-economic, religious and cultural world that I would have occupied?' And then: 'how does that differ from my standpoint today?'

Today as in the past, people's perceptual skills may mean that different viewers perceive paintings in different ways, but perhaps we'll never know for certain because we cannot swap our visual mechanisms.

Also, taste differs between people and between eras as we well know.

We all bring to our viewing a baggage of information, assumptions, cultural identities, relationships, and moods, attitudes – drawn from our individual and unique experiences, circumstances and disposition.

Apply this to different eras' period eyes and you have an incredibly complex mix.
Also remember the influence of photography and the Internet.

We are familiar with many works of art before we ever see them for real. Think from your viewing eye what it must have been like to see Michelangelo's *Sistine Ceiling* without any fore-knowledge, or Manet's *Olympia* with no pre-warning.

Think of the mediaeval congregation seeing the biblical depictions in marvellous colour and clarity of message. No wonder they were awe-struck or that Parisians in the 1860s were shocked. No wonder Michelangelo was considered divine.

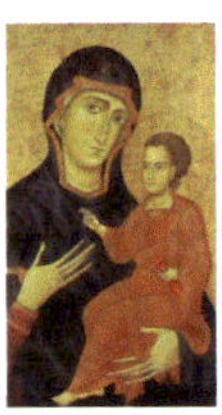
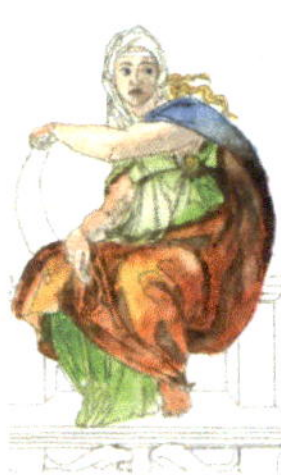
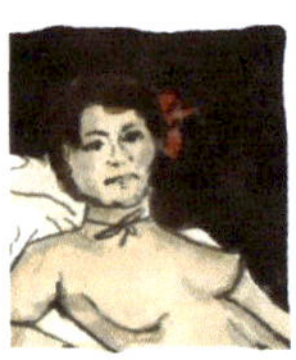
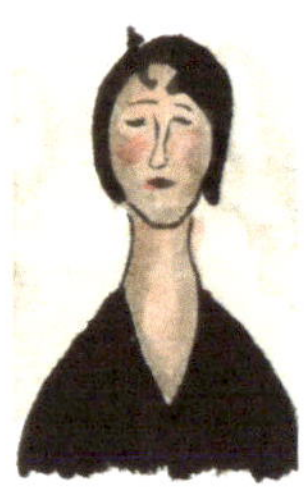
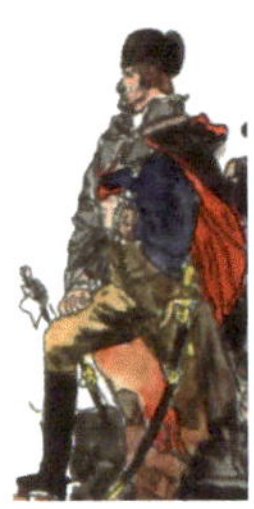

How would you have received these pictures in the 16th, 17th and 19th Centuries? How do you view them today? How would you in the 17th Century have looked upon the image of Charles I or Oliver Cromwell?

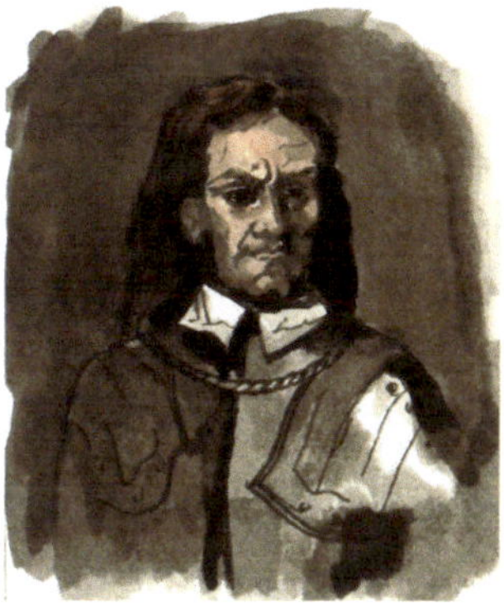

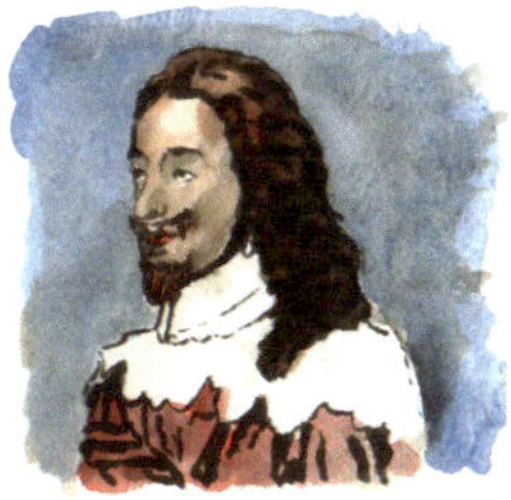

How would the French have looked upon The Duke of Wellington in 1815?

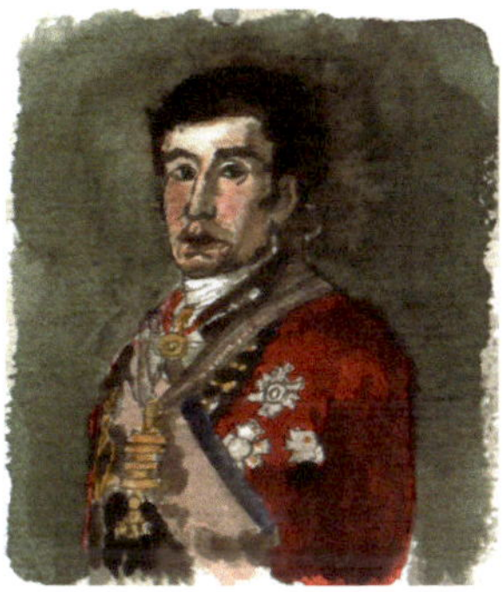

Francisco de Goya (1746-1828) *The Duke of Wellington* 1812-18)

What would you think if you in the 18th Century looked upon the picture of the landed gentry in *Mr and Mrs Andrews* knowing how they used their labour force and where they derived their fortune from. How do you feel today knowing that Frances Andrews married Robert at the age of 16?

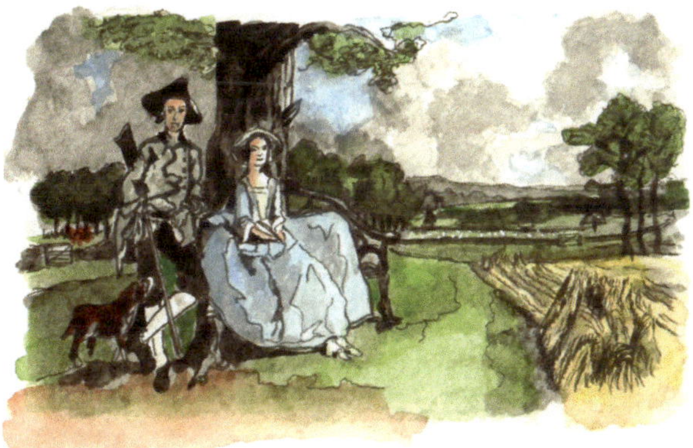

Values change. Perspectives change. The period eye is an intriguing exercise especially when it highlights how we view society and the people and systems that make it up.

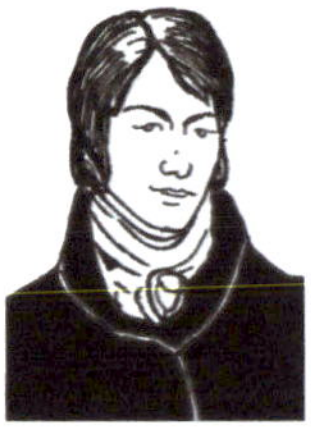

"I painted my *The Hay Wain* for my own enjoyment and also for display at the Royal Academy with a view to attracting a purchasing customer."

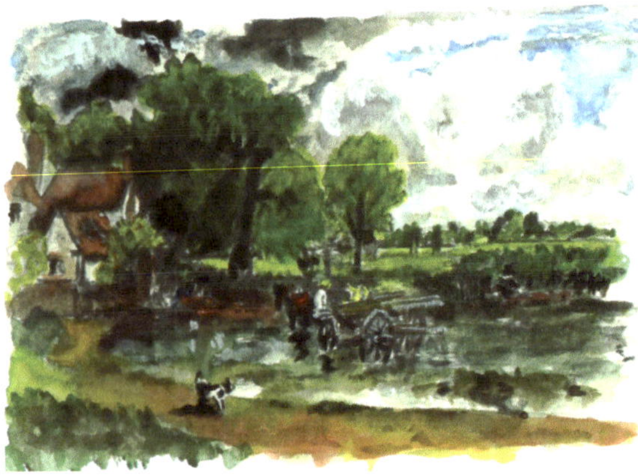

John Constable's 1821 *The Hay Wain* was designed and executed in the early 19th century when there was tremendous economic and cultural change. It was painted at the time of rural riots and the labouring classes rising up against landowners and poverty. This work is generally regarded as a pretty, rural idyllic depiction but when considering it further from the perspective of the early 19th century, it can be viewed as extremely unsettling.

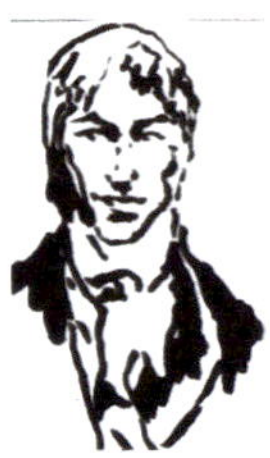

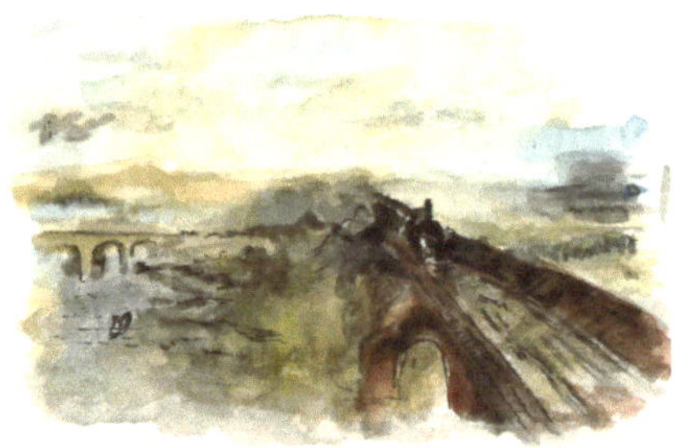

"I also painted my *Rain, Steam and Speed* for display and sale at the Royal Academy."

As we know, these artists were painting at a time following the onset of the Industrial Revolution and all its implications as they and presumably their audience perceived it having a positive or adverse effect on mankind and the environment.

The period eye's perspective against your perspective: does it differ do you think?

We've briefly looked at socio-cultural influences, but what of the effect of the commercial market? Let's just dip our toes into the subject.

At the end of the 19th century, the artist Paul Cézanne, who came from a wealthy family, was able to indulge his passion for painting without the need for patronage or other forms of funding. The influence on Cubism as we know can clearly be seen.

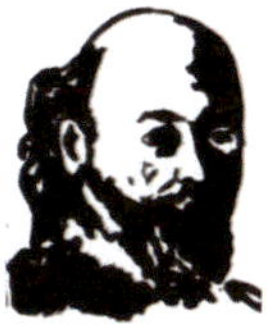

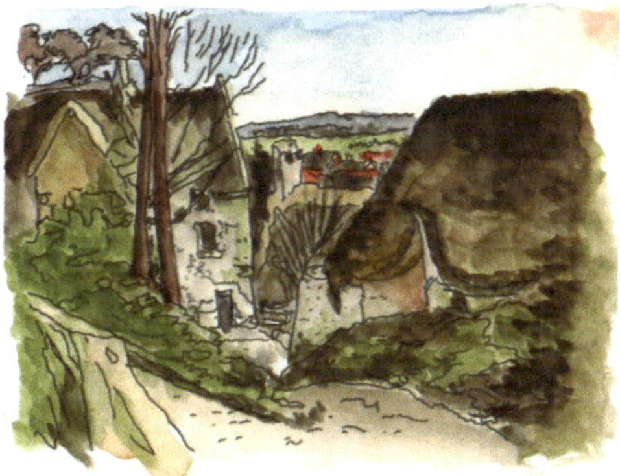

"I was able to use my economic freedom to experiment and develop my own style without the need to indulge a patron or meet market demands. If I had to meet commercial reality, would Modern Art have developed as it did? Would Modernism ever have evolved as it did? Would the demand have been created?"

In the early 20th century Pablo Picasso and George Braque's first Cubist works were initially painted as experimental avant-garde. Receiving incredible bourgeois consumer interest in Paris, further work was simply produced to maximise the "keeping up with the Joneses" demand for their work.

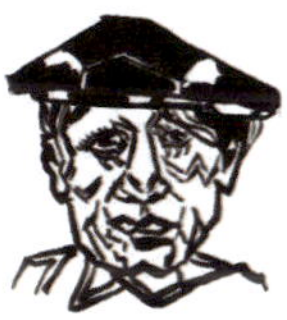

"I made a small fortune from Cubism"

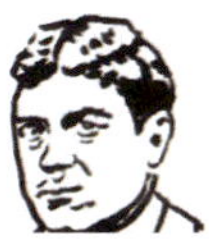

"As did I, Georges Braque and I worked closely with my friend Pablo to decorate the walls of the rich and affluent with our works."

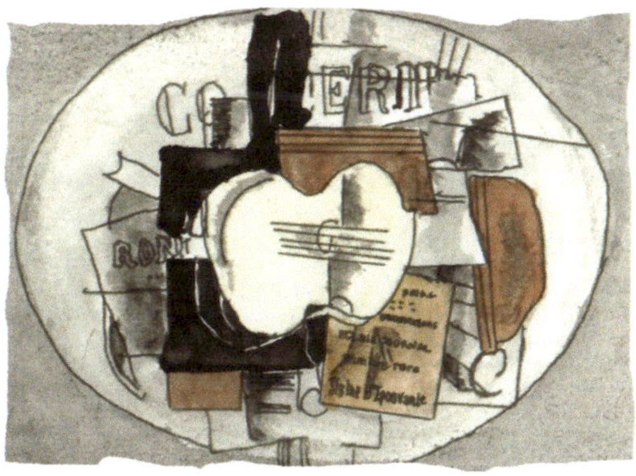

And in respect of the financial and social status background of the viewers, look at a painting such as Georges Seurat's 1884 *Bathers at Asnières*.

Seurat studied the problem of light and colour in a thoroughly scientific manner. Pointillism. Pixels.

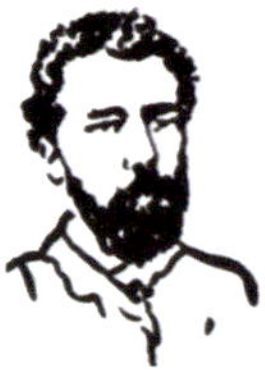

Georges Seurat

"Position yourself as an end of the 19th century French citizen either bourgeois or proletariat. In the painting do you see a life of leisure and enjoyment, or do you see a brief break from the demands of working? Look at the background. Look at the nature of the various subjects, their dress, their gaze, their relaxation or their anticipation of a return to their workplace? From your perspective as a late 19th-century perusing viewer, how would you interpret this painting? Perhaps with a more rigid class divide opinion than you would as a 21st century viewer? Or maybe you as a modern viewer would have more sympathy for the hard-pressed workers than your bourgeois 1884 counterpart?"

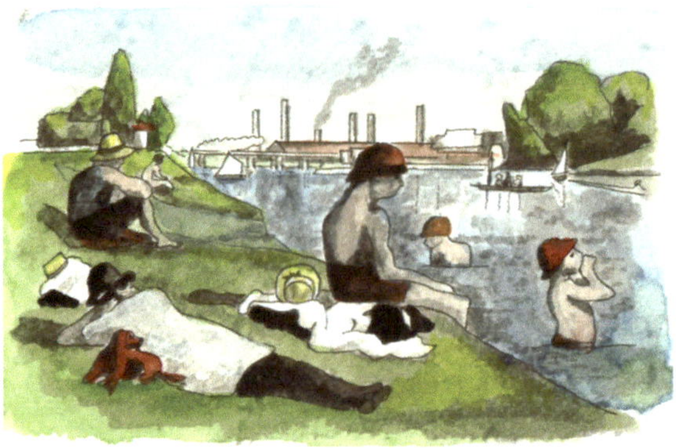

The St Ives group of painters included Ben Nicholson, Christopher Wood, Alfred Wallis and Patrick Heron. Also, the Newlyn School of Artists, that practiced across the Cornish peninsula.

Amongst these artists was Frank Bramley who with his 1887 *Eyes and No Eyes* resisted the contemporary appeal to depict the rural rustic and Cornish fisher-folk as nothing but angst and maritime life as harsh and unyielding. That is what the viewing public wanted to see from the safety and comfort of their cities, not people taking enjoyable respites.

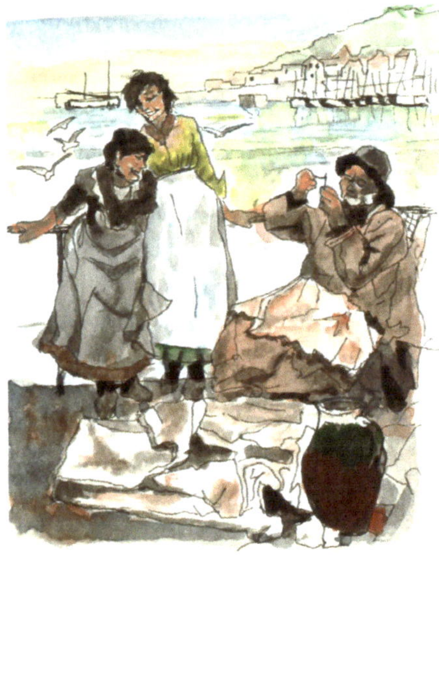

How do you view it from your own personal situation and circumstances? How would you have viewed it as a Cornish fisherman's wife in 1887?

Apply your period eye.

*

John Singer Sargent, an American artist working in London and Paris. Whilst in Paris after much cajoling eventually managed to paint a portrait of the high socialite, belle and outstanding beauty, Amelie Gautreau after much stalking and much declining on her behalf. This presumably with the consent of her husband Pierre Gautreau, a wealthy merchant.

Unfortunately, his first attempt showed her with one of her dress straps dangling off her shoulder. The strap apparently fell whilst sitting. Quickly, she attempted to readjust it, but Singer Sargent said, "No, mon Cherie. It is perfect as it is."

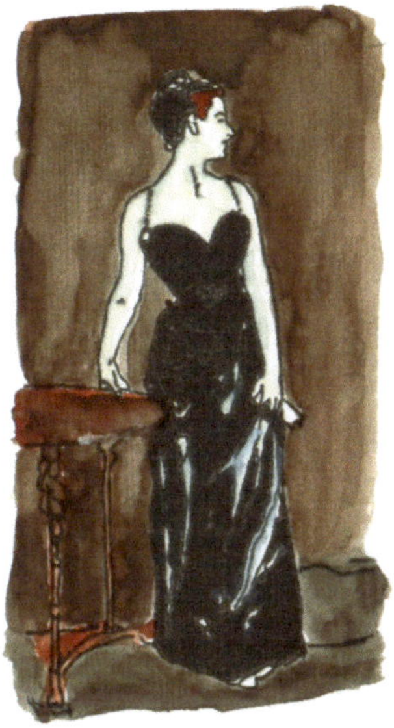

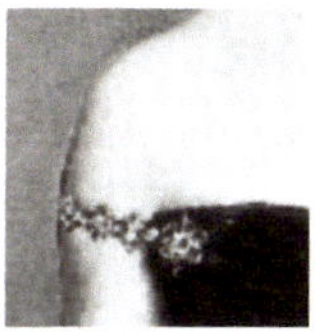

***Madam X* 1883**

Tragedy.

When exhibited in Paris it caused an outrageous scandal, men swore, women fainted. Thus, it ruined her precious reputation alleging that rather than a respected aristocratic socialite she was in fact a lady of loose morals. She had to withdraw from polite society.

Singer Sargent was not allowed to paint until after the exhibition and indeed for some time received no more commissions, after all, who would want their wife or daughter painted so erotically?

He did alter his subject, placing the offending strap back on her shoulder as we know the work today, but it was too late. The offending picture remained in the exhibition, Singer Sargent was not allowed to alter it there and then.

Fleeing to England from Paris, eventually his career picked up again, but Amélie never recovered.

How would we view the falling strap today?

*

In 1919 Paul Nash (1889-1946) painted *The Menin Road*. Before The Great War such depictions of the total destruction of the landscape and de-humanisation of man would have been totally alien and unfamiliar to viewers. With our eyes, we have become accustomed to such images.

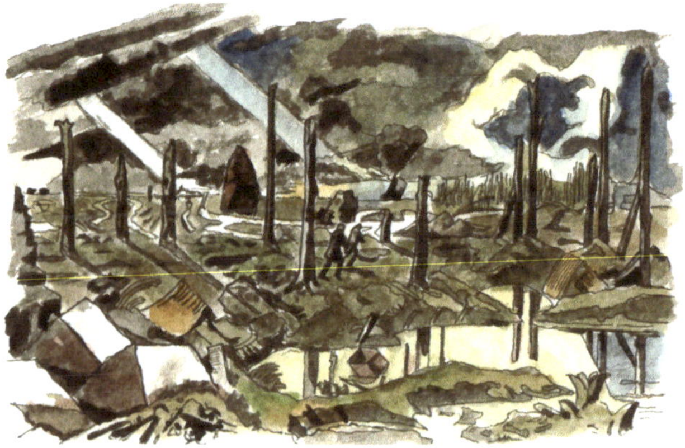

The influence of the mass media has made us familiar and maybe even sanitised to such images. In 1919 media was in its infancy and of course there was the matter of censorship.

What influence will access to the Internet now have? What influence has the freedom of the Press and its images had?

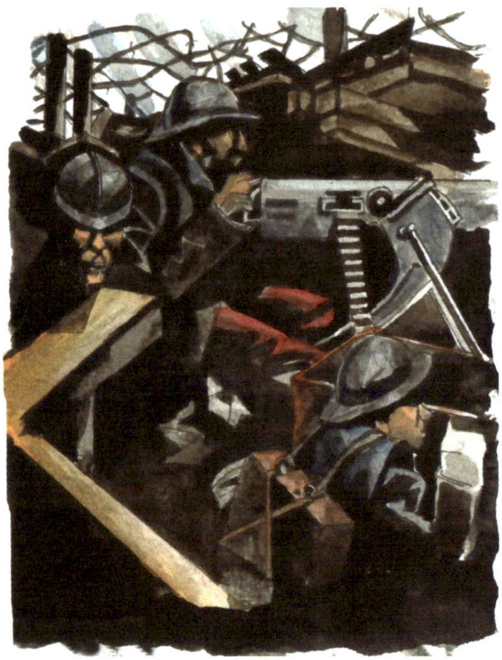

Similarly with Christopher Nevinson's 1915 *La Mitrailleuse*. Humanity depicted as never before as brutal machines. Again, we have become used to such images. In 1915 people were not. The 1915 viewing eyes of the time saw this image differently to how we see it today.

Contrast Nash's and Nevinson's considerably realistic and human approach to that of the Victorian British Empire Lady Butler's 1881 work *The Charge of the Greys*. The heroes charging to their death and glory during the 1815 Battle of Waterloo. How would a Victorian at the height of the British Empire look upon it? How do you view it today?

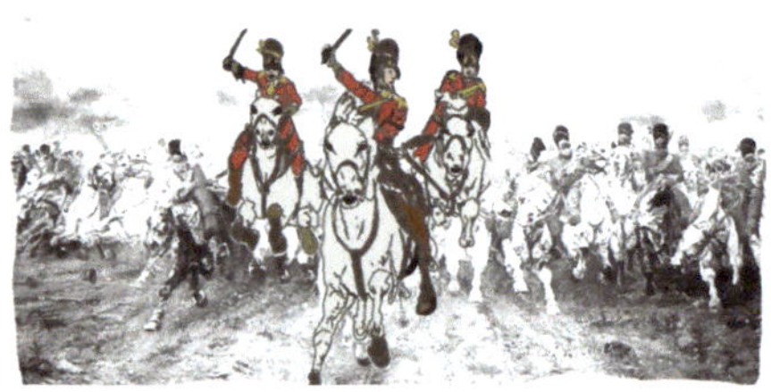

Painted after the Second World War, look at Jackson Pollock's *Number 1A* one of his famous drip paintings. The Abstract Expressionists worked in New York in the 1940/50s when America emerged as the dominant world force but yet confronted by the apparent threat of the Soviet Union and the onset of the Cold War.

The Abstract Expressionists were used as American propaganda and diplomatic hegemony, political, values and economic influence, to create the impression of American freedom of expression and liberty. Or so the rumour goes.

Seen through the period eye, Abstract Expressionism can be viewed as the epitome of the American dream especially in contrast to the western perception of Soviet threat to liberty.

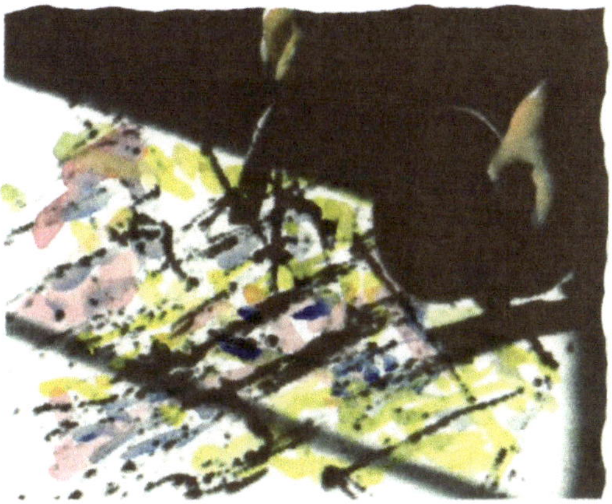

In the 21st-century we as viewers look at a painting and attempt an interpretation from our own cultural and socio-economic standpoint. We may be offended or uncomfortable with acres of naked flesh, and we may feel not at ease with realistic images of the crucifixion, with gallons of flowing blood, beheadings, slaughtering. We don't scare of images of Satan or Hell as did our mediaeval forefathers did.

We are 21st-century viewers, and it is our prerogative to view a painting from the perspective of our own values and socio-cultural situations.

However, to understand the painting in as much depth as we wish to, it can be very illuminating to transport ourselves back to the period within which the painting was completed and look at it from a vastly different viewpoint, the viewpoint of the period eye.

*****

Let's conclude by referring to an iconic image from a particular movement in art: American Western Art. Why this movement? It dramatically places into perspective two ends of a cultural and philosophical spectrum.

Frederick Remington 1861–1909 painted and sculpted many works depicting romanticised images of the American Wild West. He was responding to market demand.

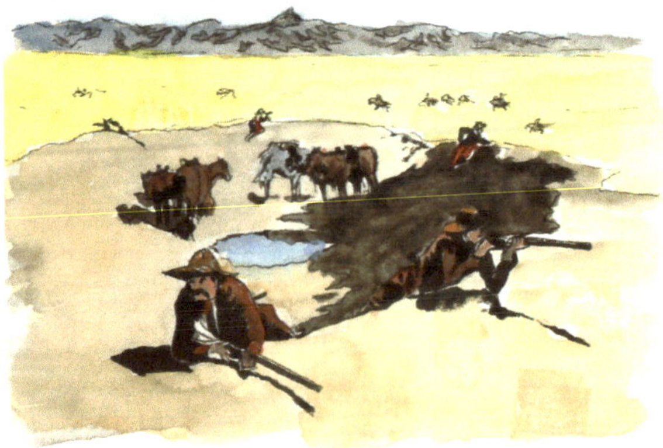

Take this example of *Fight for the Waterhole* 1903. Think of it in terms of your modern interpretation and understanding of the American Wild West and your knowledge, beliefs and values of the period depicted – the 16th to 19th Century drive westwards, the Pioneers, the Conquistadors, cowboys, settlers and the impact it had on the Native American Indians; the growth of a continent's economy and influence; living room and colonization, reservations and reduced social status.

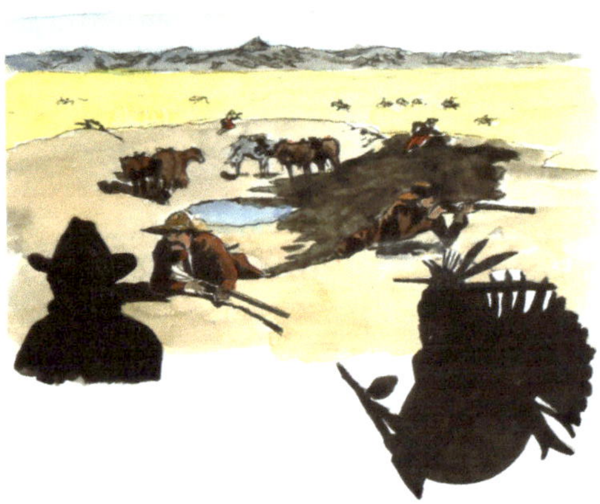

A monumental reflection. Your eye compared to that of Remington and his customers' viewing eyes.

Now think of the work from the perspective of your understanding of where a contemporary pioneer would come from and from where a displaced Native American Indian would come from.

One painting, one image, two completely different interpretations. Enjoy your own interpretation and story making and for a little more depth: think of how others may have seen it and what the person next to you is thinking.

Provenance

From considering the piece as a work of art, now simply think of the painting, irrespective of its subject matter, its composition or any other matter discussed in this book, as merely an object.

Simply paint applied to canvas supported by pieces of wood, whether it is a religious artefact a commercial object or an item of possession, a treasure, within public ownership or a municipal acquisition.

Think about John Constable's *'Hay Wain'*. Painted in 1821 it was originally hung at the Royal Academy exhibition where it failed to sell.

It was subsequently exhibited at the Paris Salon in 1824 where it was sold to a dealer called John Arrowsmith and brought back to the UK by another dealer DT White. It was then bought by an Isle of Wight resident, Mr Young. Mr Young's art dealer friend Henry Vaughan acquired the painting following Young's death and subsequently presented it to the National Gallery London in 1884, where it still hangs today.

How much is it worth today? Who knows? Only the open market would yield a price if bidders were set against bidders.

Is that the way it's become? A cultural value synonymous with the price paid by the wealthy.

Every month we hear of records being broken by works of art being sold on the open market.

The taste and predilections of the wealthy counting above all else? But compare today with the Medici, the Sforza, the Papacy and the royalty and aristocrats in 18th and 19th century Europe.

What's changed? Were they more artistically and culturally enlightened than today's super rich? Maybe, maybe not. What's the difference between Pope Julius II commissioning the Sistine by Michelangelo and an investment opportunity by a merchant banker? Answers on the back of an envelope please.

In 2011 Cezanne's *'Card Players'* sold for GB£147.7 million, in 2012 a Rothko sold for US$75 million and in 2013 a Leonardo sold for GB£44.5 million.

In 2014 a Manet sold for US$65 million, two works by Mark Rothko sold for US$40 and US$45 million and a Georgia O'Keeffe US$44 million.

A small Jasper Johns *'American Flag'*: US$ 36 million.

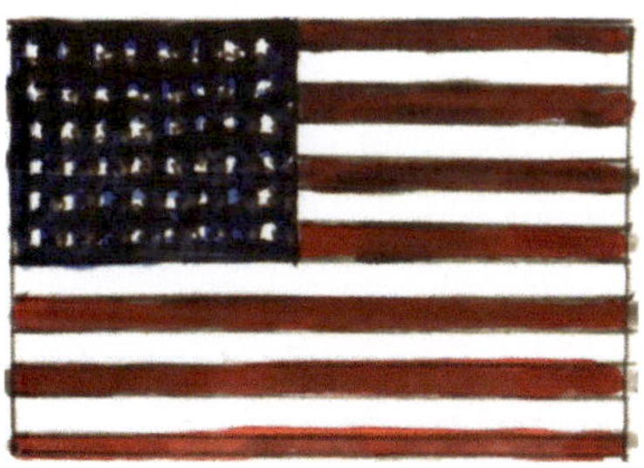

The 2014 autumn art market in New York saw US$2 billion in art sales: a record.

In 2014, Deloitte conducted a survey which showed that 76% of art professionals viewed art, at least in part, as an investment, rising from 53% two years previously. Leonardo's *Salvador* Mundi was exhibited in Hong Kong, London, San Francisco, and New York in 2017, and then sold at auction at Christie's in New York on 15 November 2017 for $450,312,500.

In 2015 a Gauguin sold for US$300 million.

At the Kawamura Memorial DIC Museum of Art near Sakura Japan are works by Matisse, Chagall, Ernst, Monet, Picasso and Renoir. Also a Jackson Pollock, Cy Twombly and Rembrandt. Seven panels by Mark Rothko with an auction price for one Rothko securing US$68.9mn. In the garden can be found a Henry Moore.

This was all a result of Japanese companies in the 1970s, 1980s and 1990s being so wealthy they could invest in fine art to adorn their museums and company walls. These companies were told they were worth billions and consequently they spent and spent hard. Perfectly legal but blurred at the edges. Across corporate Japan with the company Nomura as an example, visitors may sit underneath a Monet and a Chagall and at another company Marubeni, even a Botticelli. A further company has a Cezanne. Just to name a few.

In 1990 the sum spent on fine art in Japan was US$ 3.3bn.

Bankers and the wealthy are treating art as any other asset class, driving prices up and up following and affecting market forces rather than simple aesthetics.

These are just a few examples of how the art market can fetch fantastic prices and seem immune to the economic situations faced by most people.

In 1987 Japanese insurance magnate Yasuo Goto paid nearly UD$40 million for Vincent Van Gogh's '*Still Life: Vase with Fifteen Sunflowers*' at auction at Christie's London. A record setting purchase at the time.

Interesting to think that in his own lifetime, Vincent experienced great difficulty in selling his work, relying economically on his brother Theo. Vincent painted many versions of his sunflowers, each now with their own provenance.

On the 5th October 2018 at Sotheby's auction house, London, a framed picture of Banksy's *Girl with a Balloon* sold for GB£ 1,042,000 (at the time US$1,366,672). During the sales process the picture automatically shredded halfway down within its frame. To quote Sotheby's "it is the first artwork in history to have been created during an auction".

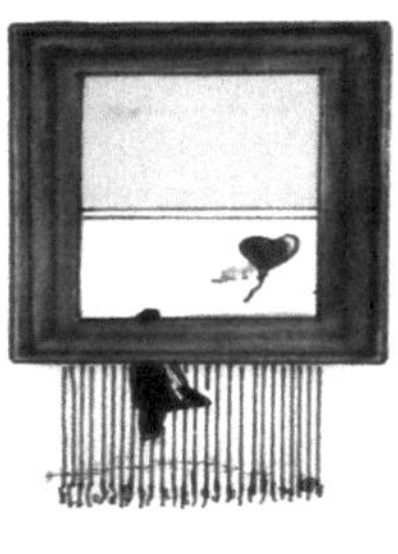

The buyer proceeded with their purchase.

On 14th October 2021, 3 years later almost to the day, it sold again at Sotheby's for GB£18,582,000 (at the time US$ 25,327,452) a mark up of GB£17,540,000 (at the time US$23,960,780).

Has the value of art become high-jacked by investors without taste? And if so: Who says they're without taste? Watch this space.

Display

An aside you may find interesting. Going back to the evolution of art: think about how the size of paintings has changed over the years. Then think about where it was possible for artists to display their works. Medieval castles? No, too damp and cold, but churches, yes. The growth of wealth amongst the aristocratic and merchant classes led to substantial improvements in accommodation and with all that new wall space.

Johannes Vermeer in the Dutch Golden Age painted works that could be hung on walls in local merchants' modest abodes. So not too big.

Galleries became prominent in later years, so artists were able to paint pictures for prominent display on large walls.

With the growth of civic buildings so the demand for appropriate paintings grew. Where would Jacques-Louis David have found himself without the French Revolution and Napoleon's Empire and the buildings created around the culture of the time?

"I don't think my *Napoleon Crossing the Alps* will fit into that hovel."

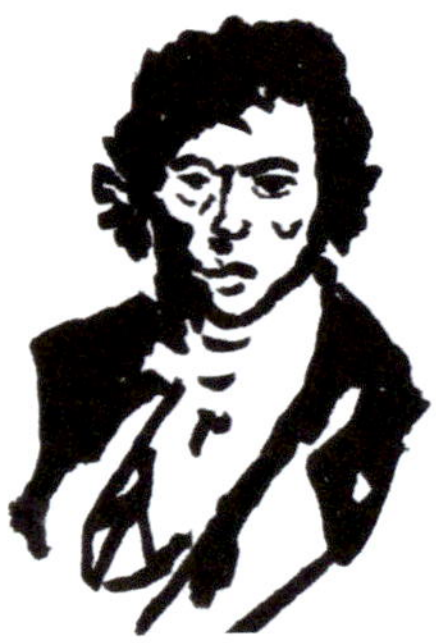

Jacques-Louis David

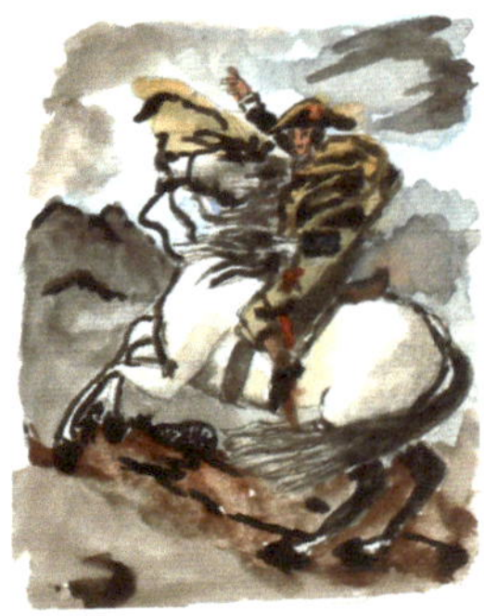

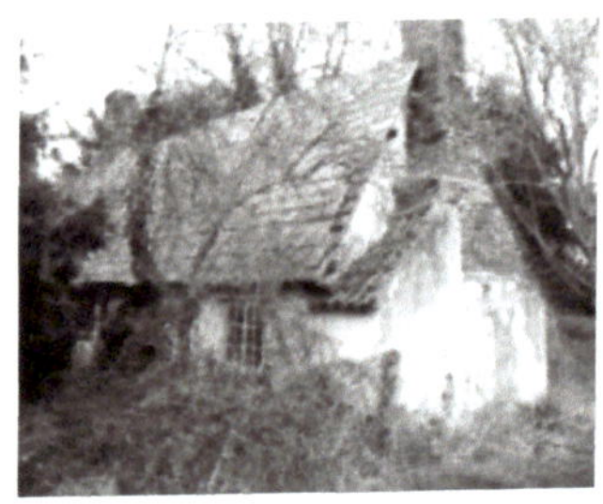

And indeed, where would Constable and Turner be without the Royal Academy and the growth of Academy viewings? The Salon des Refuses and the Impressionists, and now even Banksy without walls?

Consider this question of display, would the painting even have existed if there was nowhere suitable to display it? Without a wall, Leonardo would have had a problem. And he was only able to paint on such a massive scale because of the nature of the building within which the wall was constructed. Without the recent invention of paper, Leonardo and Michelangelo would have had to think about the medium to complete their sketches on. Without the invention of paint tubes, would plein-air painting have been so possible?

Hiroshige would have struggled without the discovery of Prussian blue paint colour and maybe Saint Thomas Aquinas would not have been so adamant that the Virgin Mary's robe should always be blue without the availability of the expensive Afghanistan, lapis lazuli.

When you are next in a gallery, look at the gallery layout. Is the painting you are looking at displayed as a component of a period movement or is it displayed alongside other

paintings by the same artist? Is it displayed in a setting with other similar subject matters, in other words as part of a theme?

Essentially, how does the painting in question relate to other paintings alongside it, above it, below it, on the wall opposite, in the gallery we have just come from or are about to move into?

What is the influence of the curator, the house owner, the organisation for example the National Trust, the American National Trust for Historical Preservation, and UNESCO even? What is the influence of the patron for example the Impressionists' collector Paul Durand-Ruel, Vincent van Gogh's brother Theo? And of course, there is you as a viewer and maybe a collector.

Paintings should not be displayed on any wall in an accidental random fashion. Thought should always be given to position and placing and the relationship with other works on display.

What thoughts from the curator or patron do you recognise? What display influence do you perceive?

Avant-garde to establishment acceptability

Finally, when does the avant-garde become part of the establishment? When do renegade or rebellious artists become the establishment?

'Establishment' refers to the recognition by officialdom and society at large. The formal and legal framework of the community's rules and regulations and accepted mutual values and traditions lending authority and legitimacy to whatever is being established.

Therefore, in respect of the world of art, it would be public and private galleries, catalogues raisonné, the body of formal critics, collectors, the media. Hence ranging from traditional galleries such as MoMA New York, Tate London, Saatchi, Guggenheim through to local institutions such as Saltaire in Yorkshire UK, Mass MoCA in New England and of course thousands of similar organisations across the world.

Impressionism was originally completely nonacceptable to the art establishment in the form of the Paris Salon but is now of course firmly part of the establishment. Similarly with Manet, and Picasso's Cubism.

In more recent times the YBA (Young British Artists) exhibiting in the London Royal Academy's 'Sensation' event were until that time renegade even in respect of post modernism but by being exhibited in the prestigious Royal Academy and given that institution's seal of approval, they became part of the establishment.

Greyson Perry, Jeff Koons, David Hockney, Salvador Dali: all avant-garde rebels against the art norm of the time but once accepted by the art world as such. The rest is history.

Without Peggy Guggenheim, Charles Saatchi, Roger Fry or curators at the Tate Modern, the Pompidou or MoMA New York, where would Tracey Emin, the Post-Impressionists and Abstract Expressionism be?

Greyson Perry is now Sir Grayson Perry, and Tracey Emin is now a Member of the Royal Academy and was made a Dame Commander of the Most Excellent Order of the British Empire (DBE) in the King Charles III's Birthday Honours in 2024. Banksy's works sell for millions.

Without you bidding at Sotheby's or Christies' what would be the value of art? To what extent has economics contributed to the fame, popularity and even vogue of certain artists?

The power of the curator, the collector, the media, the bourgeois. Conceptual art is now established.

Street Art is a great example. Originally graffiti tagging, the style evolved in communities across the world.

Street Art is now recognised as an art form in its own right to the extent that in many places authorities and businesses commission or at least condone the art practice.

Street Art is a movement, originally back-street, that has successfully spread across the globe in all cultures and in all situations. New York to Tokyo, Valparaiso to London, Berlin to Jerusalem to Cape Town. No art movement has ever before had such a global reach.

If that's not rebellious, revolutionary, outsider art becoming part of the establishment, what is?

Leonard Hilton McGurr aka Futura 2000, foremost street artist of New York City, now an established design brand name.

And never lose sight of the Banksy phenonium.

Conclusion

So, the next time you are in a gallery or at an exhibition, take stock.

You can now concentrate more on those works that particularly grasp your attention and rather than just ticking them off as seen, ponder at will and explore the rich depth behind the painting, to become intimate with the painting, to allow your emotions to become involved, to let the work reach out and the artist to communicate with you, to substantially add to your enjoyment.

Take your time. Perhaps spend particular time in front of a few, maybe even one piece and allow yourself space for indulgence rather than whizzing from one gallery to another.

Look at that picture before you. Chat to it and the artist. Be receptive and patient in discovering details and wholeness, background and context. Think about its construction and history.

Your sensations will be awakened, and words may not describe your feelings. You may experience something transcendent, secular or divine according to your personal philosophy.

It's your prerogative to ask your own questions and arrive at your own conclusions. To perceive endeavour, hopes, fears, joy, sadness, to better understand the human mind and heart.

Move on from that picture and the adventure re-starts back in the real world and you'll be taking something more with you that might even have changed you a little.

And when you are at that dinner party or simply enjoying a coffee at the gallery, you can indulge in the very rich tapestry of a fulfilling conversation about art, confident in the knowledge that you know what you are talking about. Congratulations.

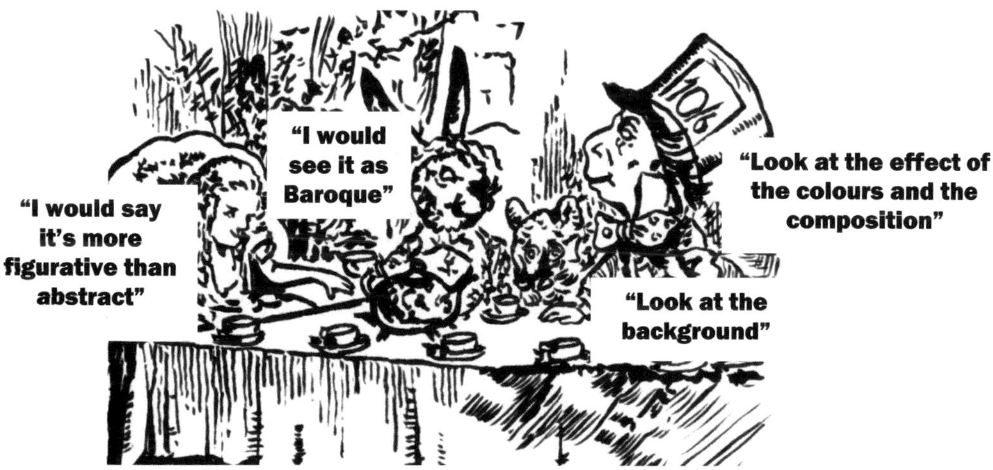

Simply enjoy...

Select Bibliography

Agnati, Tiziana. *Artemisia Gentileschi.* Giunti.

Anfam, David. *Abstract Expressionism.* Thames and Hudson. 1999

Barrell, John. *The Dark Side of the Landscape*. Cambridge University Press. 1980

Battistini, Matilde. (Trans. Sartarelli, Stephen). *Symbols and Allegories in Art*. The J. Paul Getty Museum. 2005

Baxandall, Michael. *Painting and Experience in Fifteenth Century Italy.* Oxford University Press. 1985

Baxandall, Michael. *The Limewood Sculptors of Renaissance Germany.* Yale University Press. 1980

Benton, Janetta Rebold. The History of Western Art. Thames and Hudson. 2022

Berger, John. *Ways of Seeing.* Penguin. 1972

Bradley, Fiona. *Movements in Modern Art – Surrealism.* Tate Gallery Publishing. 2005

Botton de Alain. *Art as Therapy.* Phaidon 2016

Brook Timothy. *Vermeer's Hat.* Profile Books 2009

Burckhardt Jacob. *The Civilization of The Renaissance.* Phaidon Press 1945

Button, Virginia. *St Ives Artists, A Companion.* Tate Publishing. 2009

Cars, des Laurence. *The Pre-Raphaelites.* Thames & Hudson 2013

Casazza, Ornella. *Masaccio and the Branacci Chapel.* Scala. 1990

Clark, Kenneth. *Civilisation.* John Murray. 2005

Couldrey, Vivienne. *The Art of Louis Comfort Tiffany*. Bloomsbury.1989

Cuzin, Jean-Pierre. *Louvre, Le. La peinture française*. Scala. 1982

D'Alleva, Anne. *Methods and Theories of art History*. Laurence King Publishing. 2005

Danto, Arthur, C. *What Art Is*. Yale University Press. 2013

Darwent Charles. *Surrealists in New York.* Thames & Hudson 2023.

Edsel Robert M. *Monuments Men.* Arrow Books 2010

Elkins, James. *Stories of Art.* Routledge. 2002

Fletcher Catherine. *The Beauty and the Terror.* Bodley Head 2020

Forrer, Matthi. H*iroshige, Prints and Drawings.* Royal Academy of Arts. 1997

Foucault, Michel. *Manet and the Object of Painting*. Tate Publishing. 2009

Frascina, Francis and Harrison, Charles (Ed). *Modern Art and Modernism – A Critical Anthology*. Harper & Row. 1986

Fuchs, R.H. *Dutch Painting*. Thames and Hudson. 1996

Gombrich, Sir Ernst Hans Josef. *The Story of Art*. Phaidon. 1984

Gombrich, Sir Ernst Hans Josef. *Gombrich on the Renaissance.* Vols 1 – 3. Phaidon. 1993

Gompertz, Will. See What You're Seeing. Penguin. 2024

Gough Michael. *The Origins of Christian Art*. Thames & Hudson 1973

Hagen Rose-Marie & Rainer. *Bruegel*. Taschen 1994

Hall, James. *Hall's Dictionary of Subjects and Symbols in Art*. John Murray. 1985

Harrison, Charles. *Modernism*. Tate Publishing. 1997

Haycock David Boyd. *Paul Nash*. Tate Publishing 2016

Hicks Carola. *Girl in a Green Gown*. Chatto & Windus 2011

Hoog Michel. *Cézanne The First Modern Painter*. Thames & Hudson 1994

Jackson, Kevin. *The Worlds of John Ruskin*. Pallas Athene and the Ruskin Foundation.

Jennings, Humphrey. *Pandemonium 1660-1886*. Icon. 2012

Johns Jonathan. *Earthly Delights*. Thames and Hudson 2023

Jones, Jonathan. *The Lost Battles*. Simon and Schuster. 2011

Jones, Jonathan. *The Loves of the Artists*. Simon and Schuster. 2014

Jones, Roger & Penny, Nicholas. *Raphael*. Book Club Associates. 1983

King, Ross. *Michelangelo and the Pope's Ceiling*. Pimlico. 2002

King, Ross. *Brunelleschi's Dome*. Pimlico. 2000

King, Ross. The Judgement of Paris. Chatto & Windus. 2006

King, Ross. *Leonardo and The Last Supper*. Bloomsbury. 2012

Kranzfelder, Ivo. George Grosz. Taschen. 1994

Laclotte, Michel. *Le Louvre. La Peinture étrangère*. Scala. 1987

Langdon, Helen. *Caravaggio: A life*. Chatto & Windus. 1998

Lewison, Jeremy. *Interpreting Pollock*. Tate Gallery Publishing. 1999

Lippard, Lucy R. *Pop Art*. Thames and Hudson. 1991

Little Helen. *David Hockney*. Tate Publishing 2017

Little, Stephen. *ISMS – Understanding Art*. Herbert Press.

MacCarthy, Fiona. *William Morris*. Faber and Faber.1994

Maclean Caroline. *Circles and Squares*. Bloomsbury 2020

Mullins Edwin. *Alfred Wallis Cornish Primitive Painter*. Unicorn Press 2014

Naylor, Gillian. *William Morris by Himself*. Little, Brown and Company. 1988

Néret, Gilles. *Gustav Klimt*. Taschen. 1993

Nochlin, Linda. *Courbet*. Thames and Hudson. 2007

Perry, Grayson. *Playing to the Gallery*. Particular Books. 2014

Pescio, Claudio. *Uffizi,The*. Bonechi. 1988

Phillips Sam. *...isms Understanding Modern Art*. Bloomsbury 2014

Plumb, J.H. *The Penguin Book of the Renaissance*. Penguin. 1961

Pollock, Griselda. *Vision and Difference*. Routledge. 1988

Preziosi, Donald. Ed. *The Art of Art History: A Critical Anthology*. Oxford University Press. 1998

Read Herbert. *Art and Society*. Faber & Faber 1936

Read Herbert. *The Meaning of Art*. Faber & Faber 1931

Renner, Rolf Günter. *Edward Hopper*. Taschen. 1993

Rowland, Ingrid D. *Giordano Bruno*. Farrar, Straus and Giroux. 2008

Schianchi, Lucia Fornari. *Correggio*. Scala/Riverside. 1994

Schmidt Peter. *Ghent Altarpiece. The* Ludion 2020

Shone Richard & Stonard John-Pau.l *Books That Shaped Art History*. Thames and Hudson 2017

School of Life. *Art Against Despair*. The School of Life 2022

Shearman, John. *Mannerism*. Pelican Books. 1984

Smee, Sebastian. *Paris in Ruins*. One World. 2024

Spalding, Frances. *British Art Since 1900*. Thames and Hudson. 2002

Sunderland, John. *Constable*. Phaidon. 1981

Tafuri, Manfredo. *Venice and the Renaissance*. MIT Press. 1995

The Art Book. Dorling Kindersley. 2017

Thompson, Jon. *How to Read a Modern Painting*. Thames and Hudson. 2008

Vasari, Giorgio. *Lives of the Artists*. Penguin Edition. 1985

Webster, Lesley. *Anglo-Saxon Art*. The British Museum Press. 2012

Wolf Norbert. *Friedrich*. Taschen 2003

Wolfflin, Heinrich. *Principles of Art History*. Dover Publications Inc. 1950

Wood, Christopher. *The Pre-Raphaelites*. Book Club Associates. 1981

Directories and Catalogues with no author or editor attributed

Branacci Chapel, The. Electra. 1998

Courtauld Gallery Masterpieces. Scala/Courtauld Gallery. 2007

D' Orsay. Scala. 2000

Hermitage Picture Gallery. Alfa Colour Art Publishers. 2010

Norman Rockwell, The Best Of. Courage Books.

Leonardo da Vinci, Painter at the Court of Milan. National Gallery, London. 2011

MoMA Highlights. MoMA. 2013

Museum of Fine Arts. MFA Houston. 2000

National Gallery Collection, London. National Gallery. 1987

Newlyn School Paintings, The Little Book of. Penlee House and Museum.

Paul Mellon's Legacy: A Passion for British Art. Yale University Press. 2007

About the author

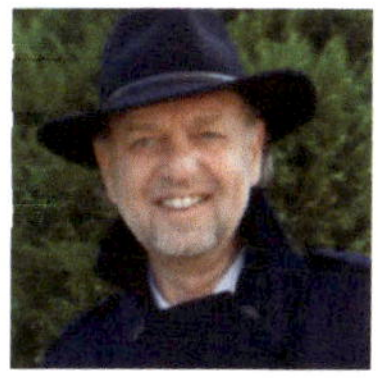

Al W Beckett is a writer, speaker and commentator on many aspects of arts, from his blog site www.art-tales.org through to this latest book 'The Conversation of Art'.

He is extensively qualified in art history and enjoys researching into the impact of art on the individual and society with particular reference to the Renaissance and modern times.

Al has helped to introduce 'Sip and Paint' evenings into the UK, where beginners to seasoned artists enjoy creating their own paintings influenced by iconic masterpieces, using their own freestyle or Al's guided tuition and sketches. Wine, music, fun and laughter, a deep appreciation of artworks and a proud picture to take home.

An artist himself, Al creates paintings, drawings, sculpture and crafting using traditional methods, as well as new age technology.